PLAUTUS

The Rope and
other plays

TRANSLATED BY
E. F. WATLING

PENGUIN BOOKS
BALTIMORE · MARYLAND

Penguin Books Ltd, Harmondsworth, Middlesex, England
Penguin Books Inc., 3300 Clipper Mill Road, Baltimore 11, Md, U.S.A.
Penguin Books Pty Ltd, Ringwood, Victoria, Australia

—

This translation first published 1964

—

—

The terms for performance of these plays
may be obtained from the League of
Dramatists, 84 Drayton Gardens, London
SW10, to whom any applications for
permission should be made

—

Made and printed in Great Britain
by Cox & Wyman Ltd,
London, Reading, and Fakenham
Set in Monotype Bembo

CONTENTS

INTRODUCTION

THE comedies of Plautus are the earliest complete works of Latin literature that we possess; and we possess them virtually in the form in which they were collected and edited a little more than a century after his death; the twenty plays, and a fragment of a twenty-first, are with little doubt those selected as genuine by the critic M. Terentius Varro out of a large body of imitative or contaminated work. Already in his lifetime and shortly afterwards the name of Plautus was a hallmark which his competitors were anxious to attach to any productions which could claim even a partial relationship to the master.

The volume and completeness of the extant work, and the brightness of the image which it presents of a single and original genius, make all the more remarkable, and regrettable, the scantiness of the available evidence – outside the works themselves – as to the personal life of the author, the sources and method of his work, and the theatrical conditions for which he worked. His name itself is a matter of doubt, but has been explained as follows. *Titus*, the son of a similarly named father, was born in the Umbrian town of Sarsina about 254 B.C. Coming at an early age to seek his livelihood in Rome, he was employed as a stage assistant to a company of players, and soon discovered a talent for acting. He had already acquired, after the Italian custom, a second name derived from a physical peculiarity: *Plautus*, the flat- or broad-footed man. His success in the playing of stock comic parts led to his being dubbed with the name of one of them – *Maccus*, the clown of popular farce. By some means or other he saved sufficient capital to leave the stage and go into business as a merchant shipper, but this venture rapidly collapsed and left him again out of work. He was unable or unwilling to resume his theatrical connexion – or if he did he filled in his time between engagements by working as a miller's labourer. In any case, what time he could spare from milling or acting he employed to good purpose in studying Greek drama, and from about his fortieth year he became increasingly successful and famous as an adaptor of Greek comedies for the Roman stage. When the time came for him to be acknowledged and rewarded by the privilege of Roman citizenship, it was necessary for Titus Flatfoot the Clown to assume a formal *praenomen, nomen*, and *cognomen*, and he became TITUS MACCIUS PLAUTUS. As there was in fact a *gens Maccia*, his adoption into this clan was convenient and appropriate. Whether his name was in fact *Maccus* or *Maccius* has always been uncertain (owing to the ambiguity of the genitive case *Macci* cited with the titles of his plays), and indeed for some centuries a misinterpretation of the literary evidence led to his being known as M. Accius Plautus.

This – and the date of his death, 184 B.C., according to Cicero – is all that the extant tradition can tell us; and clearly it amounts to little more than might have been guessed or invented about a figure notable in his own day but of whom no tangible record other than his written work was ever preserved. Meagre as it is, the tradition even raises doubts as to its own accuracy. Could the profession of acting, or stage-management, in the early years of his life, have been a young man's only gainful occupation, or one likely to lead to an early and affluent retirement? The theatre was nothing like an established full-time industry in Rome at that date; plays were commissioned for certain periodical festivals and acted on a single day or for a short series of days; as far as our evidence goes, it would seem that the licensed occasions for play-acting (*ludi scaenici*) before 200 B.C. probably did not amount to more than ten days in the year.

We have, of course, no idea in what circumstances Plautus left his native town. He may have been already in possession of some patrimony, or may even have been a slave – and thus (it has been suggested) introduced to Greek language and literature in the capacity of favoured pupil of some cultivated master. Stage actors were, in any case, in a sense slaves, if not always strictly in that category; subject at least, as long as they chose to put up with it, to the absolute control of their employer, and subject to dire penalties for incompetence or slackness in their craft ('the whip for anyone who has made a mistake, and a drink for those who haven't' is the prospect looked forward to by the actors speaking the epilogue in *Cistellaria*). It is difficult to resist seeing some connexion between this fact – the slavery of actors and Plautus's close association with their class – and the brilliantly vivacious portrayal of the slave characters in his comedies. He drew the accepted comic types – the old men gullible, irascible, or lecherous – the young men lovelorn and usually prodigal – the maidens virtuous, the matrons formidable, and the courtesans professionally seductive – on conventional lines, though not without individual subtleties. But his slaves are never mere conventional types or incidental adjuncts to the cast; they are the instigators and pivots of most of the comic intrigues, and each one of them, down to the smallest bit-player, springs to life with an individual and irresistible spontaneity. If we had to point to one particular feature of Plautine comedy that bears the clearest mark of indigenous and original invention, it would surely be the impudent, the indispensable, the endlessly resourceful, the badgered, bullied, and beaten, but ever coming-up-smiling Plautine slave.

But now we must approach the oddest fact about the

reputation of Plautus – that nobody knows for certain how much he originated and how much he translated from his Greek predecessors. The vast amount of research, and bewildering variety of conjecture, that have been expended on this problem, have proved virtually nothing but the impossibility of finding textual support for the strong general impression, which every reader receives, of an original and inventive hand at work in 'Plautus'. It is known that the plays were usually based on Greek models – that is, on examples of the Greek New Comedy of the late fourth century. We possess the names of some of the Greek authors, a large number of titles and quotations from their works, and five plays of Menander sufficiently complete to be readable. But nowhere is there any fragment of text by which the Latin of Plautus could be checked, as translation, against a Greek original. Even if a few isolated lines could be compared, we should still need to find a complete Greek comedy comparable to its Plautine successor, in order to form any idea of the Latin translator's way of working.

That the plays of Plautus actually were, at least in some cases, translated from the Greek, appears directly from internal evidence such as – to mention only one instance – the reference in the prologue of *Rudens* to Diphilus as the author of the play; and indirectly from the received literary tradition as attested, for example, by Cicero (*De Fin.*, 1:2:4) when he describes Roman comedy as '*fabellas Latinas ad verbum de Graecis expressas*' ('plays in Latin literally translated from the Greek'). But both these types of evidence need qualification. If a prologue mentions a Greek original, it does not guarantee that the original has been faithfully and completely reproduced; in some cases the contrary is indicated: in the prologue of *Casina* we find an acknowledgement of the Greek authorship (Diphilus again), and the Greek title, and a synopsis of the plot, with a reference to a young man who has been sent away from home by his father; then – 'but you mustn't expect to see this young man in the play we are giving you today; he won't be coming home; Plautus didn't want him, so he has broken down the bridge by which he would have returned'. In other words, he took leave, when it suited him, to make alterations in the construction of the play.

As to the general practice of imitation of Greek models, the reader to whom these facts are new may be wondering how it comes about that the only extant specimens of Roman comedy are merely second-hand versions of Greek comedy. Were there no native productions, and did the writers of comedy never seek their material in local and contemporary life? They did, but we have no examples of the kind. The extant plays belong to the class known as *fabulae palliatae*, that is, by definition, plays in Greek dress and therefore representing, at least superficially, Greek manners. Of other recognized types of drama the most clearly defined were: (1) *fabula Atellana* – rustic farce employing stock clownish characters such as the Maccus already mentioned; (2) *fabula praetextata* – serious dramas on legendary or historical themes or even contemporary public events; (3) *fabula togata* – light domestic comedy of Italian middle-class or village life. That the first of these categories should have left no written specimens of its kind is not surprising. Of the other two the names of some authors, some titles, and indirect allusions to their contents are all that remain to tantalize us with a sense of great loss. Even one or two specimens of these native comedies would have added much to our knowledge of the normal social life of the time.

What is pertinent to our present purpose is the knowledge that such varied forms of entertainment did exist. And it is not a very bold step to assume that in practice – theatrical practice being apt to make its own way regardless of academic theory – the formal boundaries could occasionally be over-stepped. The same writers, actors, and audiences were familiar with all these types of drama, and nothing could have pre-vented a certain amount of cross-infection from one to another. What we should expect, then, is exactly what the texts of the Plautine plays themselves suggest: an original type of play, based on the theme of a Greek model, using so much of its predecessor's plot and dialogue as might be needed to keep the action going, but digressing freely into elaboration of comic situations and verbal banter in the native popular vein.

It is easy enough to find the small incidental clues to Plautus's interpolations: when he uses the word *pergraecari*, 'to behave in Greek fashion' (that is, with reprehensible extravagance or affectation) – when he makes someone say 'if you're surprised at such behaviour, don't forget we are supposed to be in Athens, not in Rome' – when he uses Roman legal, military, or political terms in figurative or punning senses – it is obvious that he is not merely translating, even if some of his verbal tricks are happy approximations to similar effects in the original. (And perhaps this may be the place for the translator into English to admit that some of *his* word-play may be gratuitous invention, to compensate for the loss of such Latin puns as defy translation.) For the broader problem of Plautus's use of plot, the absence of any model for exact comparison handicaps all attempted solutions. But from such comparison as can be made, the same impression of free adaptation, and often of a change in the comic emphasis, emerges.

When, with the loss of political belligerence and intellectual freedom, Athens lost the robust virility of Aristophanic comedy, her dramatists discovered, in due course, the art of fiction – the charm of lightly amusing narratives in dramatic form, comfortably reassuring tales of misfortunes mended by kindly providence, quarrels amicably settled by justice and good neighbourliness, lost children restored to their parents, the course of true love threatened by adverse winds but finally guided into safe harbour. The comic traits of character incidentally emerging from such tales gradually built themselves up into the stock types of the New Comedy, and as the plots were cut to a pattern, so the characters, like the pieces on a chessboard, became standardized for use in an infinite variety – subject to the rules – of situations.

Such plots, and such characters, provided Plautus with all he needed as a foundation on which to build his own style of Graeco-Roman comedy. He was not, it would seem, primarily interested in the plot for its own sake. He was ready to 'break down bridges' and to take short cuts, to gain time for the exploitation of comic opportunities on the way. Where the New Comedy tended towards a romantic or sentimental treatment of courtship and marriage, Plautus is more likely to make satirical fun of the hazards of matrimony or to mock with gentle irony the extravagant raptures of the lover. A typical New Comedy theme (perhaps traceable to a ritual origin) is the recognition of a lost child through the discovery of 'tokens'; this appears in its Plautine dress in *Rudens* – where the affinities to Menander's *Arbitration* are obvious, though this is not the acknowledged source. But in Plautus's play, not only is the love story reduced to the smallest proportions (the lovers never meet on the stage, and the young man makes only brief appearances) but the discovery and recognition of the tokens is conducted in an atmosphere of hilarity rather than romance – thanks to the interventions of the slaves Gripus and Trachalio. Even the fortunate father is only permitted an occasional note of emotion and tends rather towards irony and opportunism; his most Menandrian speech of moral edification is neatly deflated by his irrepressible slave's retort ('I've heard actors in comedies spouting that sort of stuff . . .'). As for the rest of the play, it will need a ghost from the grave to convince us that the doleful bickering of Labrax and his confederate, the battle for possession of the luckless young women, the tussle of Gripus and Trachalio for the treasure trove, and the ribald retorts of Sceparnio are the work of a Latin translator bound to the letter of his Greek text.

In his portrayal of slaves – where, as has been suggested, the voice of Plautus seems to come across most unmistakably – this further characteristic may be noticed: he likes to bring two contrasted types into opposition – the uncouth, aggressive, and perhaps more honest, against the artful and sophisticated lightweight; and he uses this trick sometimes to enliven a comparatively unimportant incident. In *Mostellaria*, the plot requires a slave to attend and escort his master Callidamates from the drinking-party and so reveal to the returning owner what is going on in the house. Plautus (as I guess) provides *two* slaves, Pinacium the rough bullying type and Phaniscus an elegant and sycophantic youth; and so an extra comic point is gained when the old gentleman pointedly confines his attention to the latter, only to learn some most unwelcome news.

When all is said and done, however widely students may differ in their estimates of Plautus's originality, his place as a constructive artist is most securely based on the admiration, sometimes to the point of veneration, which he won from his contemporaries and immediate successors. There were dissenting voices – notably that of Horace, who thought 'our ancestors were far too indulgent to the humour and poetry of Plautus' – because for the Augustan purist the rules of style had become set in a very different mould and 'literature' had withdrawn to a safe and respectable distance from the vulgar sounds of the street and market-place. The reasons for this change from a vernacular to an academic mode of composition may also be the reasons why, after Plautus and his nearest successor Terence (already tending towards a more classic style), vernacular comedy received little new blood; drama became a literary art, and popular entertainment was provided by spectacles and physical contests.

The competition of popular attractions was of course a factor which had an influence on the Plautine theatre. 'Theatre' in the architectural sense is here an anachronism; the first permanent theatre in Rome was built in 55 B.C., a hundred years after a previous attempt to provide such a building had been suppressed. What sort of temporary equipment served the purposes of drama before then can only be a matter of conjecture. An ordinance providing seats (presumably movable and in the open air) for senators, in 194 B.C., suggests the picture of an open arena, with an acting area, raised or flat, some kind of background setting, and an indeterminate space for standing or promenading spectators as far as, or further than, the voice could carry. From passages of the prologues which obviously depart from the Greek text to interpolate remarks appropriate to the Roman performance, we can pick up some impressions of the rough and ready conditions of the show, the crowding and the noise, the need to capture attention by shock tactics, to compete with the acrobats and rope-dancers in the neighbouring enclosure. A faithful reproduction of a Greek New Comedy piece would scarcely have held its audience, without the broader comic or topical touches. It is rather surprising that so much intelligent wit did prevail, and that the baser elements were kept in a subordinate place. Plautus could supply the baser elements as well as anyone, but it should not be held against him that his most shameless farce *Casina* was not only revived but commended (in the prologue as rewritten for a revival) to the younger generation of playgoers as a masterpiece of the golden age of comedy known to their fathers.

In these conditions, the staging of Plautus's plays, in his own day, must have been of a simple kind – even though the plays lent themselves equally well, in later centuries, to increasingly elaborate productions, up to the degree represented by such a theatre as the Palladian Teatro Olimpico of Vicenza. Rules of practice applicable to Plautus's own time cannot be safely deduced from the evidence of later years; and, though much research has been applied to such matters as the construction of the house doors which are a feature of almost every Plautine scene, interpretation of the evidence has been too often, it seems to me, restricted by the conventions of realistic proscenium theatre – by the assumption that everything mentioned in the play must be literally visible on the stage. Now that our own theatre has rediscovered the principles of 'open' staging, appreciation of Plautine stagecraft should be less hampered by fallacious traditions. The Plautine stage was the reverse of realistic. Instead of an illusion of reality there is an open approach to the audience, a drawing-in of the audience to participation in the play. Long solo speeches, or brief asides, may be delivered confidentially to the audience and at the same time, if necessary, overheard and countered by asides from other speakers; illusion is discarded in such exchanges as: 'Speak quietly'; 'Why, are you afraid of waking them [*the audience*] up?'; and 'Here is the gold [*offering property money*]; of course it isn't really gold, it's only beans; they feed cattle on this in barbarian countries.' In relation to stage setting, the effect of the 'open' technique is that the dialogue supplies the setting. In the realistic theatre the dramatist, relying on practicable setting and properties, writes stage directions – '*he knocks at the door*', '*she comes down the stairs*'. Ancient dramatists, it seems, never wrote stage directions; but Plautus, for his theatre of the imagination, supplies plenty of 'built-in' directions – to the point of redundancy, we may sometimes feel; he is always telling us explicitly what is happening, what is about to happen, or even what has just happened – 'I am going to knock at this door'; 'The door is opening, and here comes my master'; 'Why are you trying to force open that door?' The inference from these, which are only the most elementary, examples of his method is surely *not* that such-and-such a setting of houses and doors (or rocks or sand-dunes) *must* have had visible and solid existence on the stage; on the contrary, the more explicit the 'spoken stage directions' the less need is there for visual realism; a blind audience could follow every move in a Plautine play.

In the same way, the fiction (frequent in Plautus) that two persons are so far away from each other as to be mutually inaudible, or even invisible, can just as well be *acted* on a stage twenty feet wide as on one sixty feet wide – which we are sometimes told *must* have been the minimum width of a Plautine stage (as if the actors could then be audible to the audience but not to each other!) The ability of Plautus to carry his hearers' imagination over a wide range of locality is well seen in *Rudens*; whatever distance we may assume to lie between the cottage, the temple, and the wild seashore, our imagination travels effortlessly from one to the other, and the same acting area represents now one now another part of the landscape. In *Mostellaria*, the lady's dressing-room, the drinking party, and possibly part of the scene at Simo's house, require a kind of imaginary *ekkyklema* (exposure of the interior), but probably no actual interior setting was attempted. There is, it is true, evidence that a kind of alcove setting was used in later theatres for such purposes as this; and a modern producer could think of several amusing solutions of the problem. It remains unlikely that Plautus's own arena stage employed any elaborate architecture.

After this, it is hardly necessary to add that the stage directions in this volume are my own; they are intended to assist the reader's visualization of the action, but not to solve all production problems, still less to imply any theory about the practice of the ancient stage. There is the question of intervals, for instance. The division of the play into acts, which has come down to us in the manuscripts, is an academic refinement imported into the texts by later hands and has little or no relevance to the structure of the play. I have omitted the act-numbering but indicated places where a pause is possible though not obligatory. I should mention also that, to avoid overloading the text with bracketed directions, I have dispensed with the rubric 'aside' (which would otherwise occur with tiresome frequency) except where the intention of the speaker might be in doubt.

With the aim of putting these plays into a form suitable for the modern English stage, I have allowed myself either expansion, for greater clearness, or compression, for dramatic speed; preferring, that is to say, the pace and idiom of our own speech to a cautious reproduction of Latin diction – but always without any omission or reconstruction of the sequence of the dialogue. (Those who read these versions beside the Latin text will find that they follow primarily the Oxford Text of Lindsay, with occasional variants derived from the Loeb or Budé editions.) And I have preferred, in general, prose to verse.

This last point could be the subject of longer debate than can be attempted here. The prosody of Plautus – a system of intricate metrical versatility – was perhaps his most original contribution to the Roman stage. But though we may, with difficulty, scan his verses, we are far from being able to visual-

ize (that is, to 'auralize') the way in which they were spoken
or sung on the stage. A considerable part of each play was
'sung' to a flute accompaniment; but the lyrical – that is the
more metrically varied – portions cannot be regarded as
analogous to the lyrics of a modern musical play, distinct in
style from the dialogue which carries forward the action.
Plautus does not appear to have used specific types of metre
characteristically for particular kinds of mood or situation.
The same natural and colloquial idiom runs through all the
varied metrical schemes – a natural idiom, though enlivened
by ingenious puns, alliterations, and assonances. Attempts to
translate the dialogue into an English metrical form are hampered by lack of any equivalent stage convention. The Gil-
bertian lyric is a particularly unsuitable model, having (as in
Gilbert) the disadvantage of making all the characters speak in
the same artificial idiom, or else use language in their songs
quite different from that of their spoken lines. Nevertheless, I
have made some use of a loose iambic rhythm, and other
metrical forms, to give relief to the longer solo passages; and
there seemed to be good excuse for a song or two in *Rudens*.
These vagaries may be regarded as experiments alongside the
general rule of prose.

   To the founder editor of this series, eighteen years after my
first experience of his kindly guidance in the early days of the
Penguin Classics, I am again indebted for generous encouragement and perceptive criticism. I have also profited much from
the advice and scholarship of Professor Eric Laughton and
Mrs Betty Radice, who have read and in many places improved
my versions. Such errors as remain are entirely my own.

1963   E.F.W.

The Ghost

(MOSTELLARIA)

INTRODUCTORY NOTE TO
THE GHOST

IF Shakespeare knew this play, and borrowed directly from it the names of the two slaves Tranio and Grumio* – for a quite different use – he did not find in it any further useful material; he wanted good plots, and plot, in the sense of a convincing motivation and progression of events, is not the prime merit of *Mostellaria*.

Event follows event, one complication leads to another, but from the first it is obvious that Tranio's ingenious deceptions can only lead up a blind alley to end in his exposure and capitulation and a weak conclusion of apologies and forgiveness. Nevertheless, the escapade while it lasts is highly entertaining, conducted in an agreeable tone of civilized fun-making, and with the minimum of physical violence or verbal abuse. Tranio, of course, is threatened with all the direst penalties; but nobody takes these very seriously, least of all the irrepressible joker himself.

Mostellaria means literally 'the ghost story'. The Greek poet Philemon wrote a ghost comedy; so also did at least two others, Menander and Theognetus. There is perhaps a trace of patchwork in Plautus's version, in the fact that the young lovers Philolaches and Philematium are lost from sight, though frequently mentioned, after the early episode in which they appear, an episode which may have been derived from another source than the 'ghost' and 'house for sale' scenes. The absence of any Prologue (in which a hint or open acknowledgement of indebtedness is often given) is unusual; could it mean that

*The Taming of the Shrew.

this was a more than usually original composition? If Tranio's quip (on page 83) about the comic poets was intended as a clue, it has been variously interpreted to indicate (a) that Philemon or Diphilus was the original author, or (b) that neither of them was and that the line was Plautus's own idea.

The play is constructed for continuous action, which makes the traditional act divisions even more otiose than usual. There are only two points at which the stage is necessarily empty, and never an unnatural lapse of time. I indicate a third point where a pause is possible – on page 51, where, if preferred, the moneylender can enter before Tranio has time to make an exit.

For the monetary sums, which play an important part in this comedy, Plautus naturally used the Greek units: talents, minas, and drachmas. I have usually expressed the sums in drachmas, as being most convenient for English reading; but, where the other terms occur, it is to be understood that 1 talent=60 minas; 1 mina=100 drachmas. The talent, however, was a unit of weight and might vary in monetary value; this may explain why Tranio in one place mentions 2 talents as the price of the house which is elsewhere valued at 80 minas, or 8,000 drachmas.

CHARACTERS

THEOPROPIDES	an Athenian merchant
PHILOLACHES	his son
TRANIO	
GRUMIO	slaves of Theopropides
PHILEMATIUM	a courtesan loved by Philolaches
SCAPHA	her attendant
CALLIDAMATES	a young friend of Philolaches
DELPHIUM	a girl companion of Callidamates
PHANISCUS	
PINACIUM	slaves of Callidamates
SIMO	a neighbour of Theopropides
MISARGYRIDES	a moneylender
SPHAERIO	slave of Theopropides

Other slaves of Simo and Theopropides

*

The scene is at Athens, in a street before the houses of
Theopropides and Simo. There is an altar at the
front of, or below, the stage

THE GHOST

[*Outside the house of Theopropides an elderly and bucolic slave named* GRUMIO *is hammering at the door.*]

GRUMIO: Hey there, Tranio! Come out of that kitchen, will you! . . . Come out, young whipper-snapper! . . . Up to some saucy tricks among the saucepans, I'll be bound. . . . Come out here, you master's ruin! By gum, I'll give you what you deserve if I get you out on the farm, may I die if I don't. What are you hiding in there for, you smelly scullion? Come out here, I tell you!

[*At last* TRANIO *appears – a young and rather elegant slave.*]

TRANIO: Now then, pig, what's all this clatter about? Out in the street too? Where do you think you are? This isn't the country, you know. Get away from this house, please. Go back to your farm. Go and hang yourself, if you like, only stay away from this door. . . . What are you waiting for? [*Starting to pummel him*] This?

GRUMIO: Hey, hey, steady on. What's that for?

TRANIO: For being alive.

GRUMIO: I can bear it. I only wish the old master would come home – if he ever does come home again, with you eating the life out of him while he's away.

TRANIO: That's a lie – and it doesn't make sense either, woodenhead. How can a person eat the life out of a person when that person's somewhere else?

GRUMIO: You think me a country bumpkin, I dare say – witty city chap that you are – pretty witty city chit. I expect you know you're going to be sent out to the mill yourself before long. Yes, any day now you'll be joining the outdoor staff –

the ironclads. Better make the most of your time now, my lad. Drink and be merry, waste your master's goods and make a ruin of your master's fine young son. Drink with your friends all day and night, Greek fashion. Buy your women and set them free. Live like lords, with hangers-on feeding their bellies at your expense. Was this what your master told you to do when he went away? Is this the way he expects to find his house looked after when he comes back? Is this what you call being a good servant, playing fast and loose with your master's property and corrupting your master's son? Corrupted he surely is, for what I know, the way he's going on. Not so long ago he was known for the steadiest and best-behaved young man in all Athens; now he's top of a very different class. And that's thanks to your example and teaching.

TRANIO: Is it any business of yours what I am or what I do, damn you? Haven't you got any cattle to look after in the country? If I like drinking and wenching, that's my affair; it's my skin I'm risking, not yours.

GRUMIO: Bold as brass, ain't he?

TRANIO: Jupiter and all the gods strike you dead! Phew, you stink – mud-begotten clod of goat and pig dung; you stink of dog and goat and garlic.

GRUMIO: What do you expect? We can't all stink of perfumes, like you. We can't all lie on the best couches or feed on the finicky fodder you get. All right – keep your pigeons and poultry and game and fish, and let me enjoy the fare that comes my way. You're the lucky one; I'm not. We must take as we find – as long as I can have what good I've got, and you the trouble you're gonig to get.

TRANIO: You're jealous, Grumio, if you ask me; jealous because I'm doing well and you're not. It's only natural.

It's natural for me to keep women and you to keep cows;
me to have a good life, you to have a mucky one.

GRUMIO: Gallows-meat, that's what you are, and what you
soon will be, if I know anything about it – hustled through
the streets under a yoke, with goads through your guts,
when the master comes home.

TRANIO: Who knows? It might be you sooner than me.

GRUMIO: It won't, because I've not deserved it, as you have,
and still do.

TRANIO: Cut it out, will you, if you don't want to be
exterminated on this spot.

GRUMIO [*changing the subject*]: Have you got any greenstuff
for me to take out to the cattle? If so, let's have it . . . if
you're not eating it. . . .

[TRANIO *disdains to answer this.*]

Oh go to hell then; go on the way you're going; drink, eat
your fancy Greek food, fill your bellies with slaughtered
flesh –

TRANIO: Shut your mouth and get back to the farm. I have
to go to Piraeus for some fish for supper. I'll get some fodder
sent over to the farm tomorrow. . . . What are you standing
staring at me now for, crossbones?

GRUMIO: That's what they'll be calling *you* before long, damn
me if they won't.

TRANIO: 'Before long' they can do what they like, provided
things can stay as they are for the present.

GRUMIO: Have it your own way. I know one thing – what's
coming to you always comes quicker than what you're
looking for.

TRANIO: Leave me alone, will you, and get back to the farm.
Remove yourself. I can't waste any more time on you.

[TRANIO *goes off along the street.*]

GRUMIO: Off he goes; and don't give tuppence for my

warnings. Oh gods, help me. Let the master come back
soon. It's three years now he's been away. Let him come
home before the house and farm and everything goes to
ruin. If he doesn't, there's only a few months to go before
we're finished. . . . I'll get back to the farm. . . . And
here comes the young master . . . such a fine young lad he
was once, and now – utterly gone to the bad. [*He goes
away.*]

> [*The young man* PHILOLACHES, *whose appearance agrees
> with what we have just heard about him, comes out of the
> house, and probably just out of bed. When he has collected
> himself sufficiently to be aware of the audience, he addresses
> them with an engagingly innocent candour.*]

PHILOLACHES:

After much pondering and contemplation
And serious cogitation . . . or shall I say
Heart-searching – if I have anything
That can be called a heart; after much thought,
I say, and inward rumination – MAN,
It seems to me, MAN, in whatever station
He happens to be born, is rather like . . .
Somewhat resembles . . . something which, I think,
If I can illustrate my meaning . . . well,
It's this: I think a man, born on this earth,
Is rather like A NEW BUILT HOUSE. Observe –
I'll show you what I mean. You won't have noticed
The similarity, but I'll convince you –
I hope – indeed I'm sure that you'll agree,
Once you have heard my arguments. I'm sure
You'll say I'm right. So listen, if you please,
While I explain; because I shouldn't like
To keep this to myself; I want you all
To share my great discovery.

A house:
Now when a nice new house is built,
Properly finished, squared to rule and line,
Everyone likes it; everyone says the builders
Have done a splendid job; everyone wants it,
Or wants one like it, and starts saving up
And counting every penny towards the cost.
But then, alas, in comes a thriftless man
To take possession – a careless, idle man,
With an idle family, a dirty man,
A lazy man. What happens? Why, the house
Begins to suffer from the same defects.
A good house badly kept – it often happens.
Come storm and tempest, tiles fall off, roofs leak.
The careless occupant does nothing. Rain
Comes washing down the walls, drips through the ceilings,
Rots rafters, ruins all the builders' work.
The building goes from bad to worse; it's not
The builders' fault, and yet it happens so,
More often than not. A little money spent
Could stop the damage, but they put it off,
Do nothing till the walls are falling down;
And then – and then, of course, there's nothing for it
But to rebuild it from the bottom.

So much for houses.
Now I must try to show you why a *man*
Is like a *house*. The parents, in the first place,
Are builders of children; they lay the foundations;
They raise the structure up, and guide its growth
On firm straight lines, to make all good and true,
A credit to themselves, an ornament
In the public eye. They spare no pains or cost –

They do not call it cost – to groom their offspring.
They teach them letters, language, civic law;
They spend their all in substance and in labour
To make their neighbours envy them and wish
That they had children like them.

In due course
The time for military service comes;
Off goes the boy, committed to the care
Of some respected relative. And this
Is where the builder loses sight of him.
A year of service is enough to show
What's going to happen to the building!

   Just look at me. I was a lad
   Of modest manners, blameless life,
     While they were building me.
   Left to my own devices – well,
   It didn't take me very long
   To undo all the builders' work
     And make the house a ruin!

   Idleness was the rainy weather
   That sapped my timbers; showers of sloth,
   Hailstorms of carelessness, attacked me,
   Shook my foundations of respect,
   Twisted my lines of rectitude,
     And rapidly unroofed me –
   Which damage I did nothing to repair.

   Then love – ah, love was the next wet season.
   It poured like anything! – into my heart,
   Into my soul. I was flooded out!

Good-bye to fortune, faith, good name,
Honour, and virtue. Wear and tear
  Just left me fit for nothing.

And now my beams are rotten through and through,
Beyond repair, as far as I can see.
Nothing can stop the whole house falling down;
A dead loss — nothing can be done about it.

It makes me very sad to think
Of what I was, and what I am.
  I was a model child.
I really was — top of the class
In games and exercises — discus,
Javelin, fencing, running, riding —
I loved them all, and my example
Of hardiness and self-control
Became a pattern to my comrades.
Even the best of them all said
  That I could teach them something.

And now . . . I'm good for nothing. . . .
That's the one thing
That I have taught myself.

[*Now the door of the house opens and a beautiful girl named* PHILEMATIUM *comes out with* SCAPHA, *an elderly female attendant.* PHILOLACHES *keeps out of sight.*]

PHILEMATIUM: That was a lovely cold bath, Scapha. I don't know when I've felt so clean.

SCAPHA: Everybody's happy, then; it was a good harvest this year.

PHILEMATIUM: What has this year's harvest got to do with my bath?

SCAPHA: No more than your bath has to do with this year's harvest.

PHILOLACHES [*observing them from a distance*]: The lovely Venus herself! Here's the very tornado that stripped me of my roof of modesty and brought Love and Desire, as I told you, cascading into my upper storey; and I can't keep them out, no matter what I do. I'm soaked to the heart; the house is doomed.

PHILEMATIUM: Tell me, Scapha dear, how do you think this dress suits me? I want to look my best for my darling protector Philolaches.

SCAPHA: I don't know why you bother to get yourself up in these pretty fashions; you're pretty enough as it is. Lovers aren't interested in a woman's dress, only what's inside it.

PHILOLACHES: Gods! The old bitch is sharp enough. She's got the right idea about what a lover wants.

PHILEMATIUM: Well?

SCAPHA: Well what?

PHILEMATIUM: How do I look?

SCAPHA: You look all right in anything, with your figure.

PHILOLACHES: Good for you, Scapha! For that I'll give you ... I'll give you something or other. I can't let you praise my beloved for nothing.

PHILEMATIUM: I don't just want you to agree with me, you know.

SCAPHA: You're a funny girl, you are. Would you rather be spoken badly of, without reason, than be complimented, with reason? I wouldn't; I'd rather be praised without reason than criticized with reason, or have anybody find fault with my appearance.

PHILEMATIUM: Well, I like the truth, and I'd rather be told the truth. I can't bear a liar.

T–P–B

SCAPHA: Very well, then; you're beautiful, upon my oath you are, as I hope you love me, and as I hope your young man loves you.

PHILOLACHES: What's that, you old sinner? What sort of an oath is that – as you hope I love her? Why not as you hope she loves me? I won't give you anything after all, so there; you've lost what I promised you.

SCAPHA: Upon my word, I wonder at a sensible, clever, and well-educated girl like you acting so foolishly as you are doing now.

PHILEMATIUM: Why? Tell me, please, what am I doing wrong?

SCAPHA: You're doing wrong in keeping yourself for that young man alone; taking him for your master and turning your back on all others. It's a wife's business, not yours, to be the slave of one love.

PHILOLACHES: Jupiter! Does she want to ruin me? Gods and goddesses do their worst to me if I don't make the old woman starve and thirst and freeze to death!

PHILEMATIUM: I should be sorry to think you were leading me astray with your advice, Scapha.

SCAPHA: All I say is you're a fool, and you show it, if you think that fellow's going to be your friend and benefactor for evermore. Mark my words: when love grows older, it grows colder; and then he'll leave you.

PHILEMATIUM: I don't expect he will.

SCAPHA: What you don't expect happens more often than what you do. Anyway, if words won't convince you that I'm right, look facts in the face – in my face. What was I, and what am I now? I was loved in my time, as you are. I gave myself to one man, and what did he do? As soon as time had changed the colour of this head, he was off – left me flat. It'll happen to you.

PHILOLACHES: My fingers are itching to scratch her eyes out
– the wicked old meddler.

PHILEMATIUM: I was the one girl he chose to be his own,
and he bought my freedom with his own money. I think
it's my duty to be faithful to him alone.

PHILOLACHES: Gods! What a lovely and pure girl she is!
By Hercules, it was the best thing I ever did; I'm happy to
be penniless for her sake.

SCAPHA: My goodness, you are a fool.

PHILEMATIUM: Why am I?

SCAPHA: For caring about whether he loves you or not.

PHILEMATIUM: Why shouldn't I care, for heaven's sake?

SCAPHA: You're a free woman now, aren't you? You've
got what you wanted. If he doesn't choose to go on loving
you, that's his look-out; he'll have wasted that much money
on you.

PHILOLACHES: Count me dead if I don't exterminate the
old bawd! She's trying to corrupt the girl with her beastly
advice.

PHILEMATIUM: I can never fully repay the debt I owe him;
don't advise me, Scapha, to put him off with less than I owe.

SCAPHA: Let me tell you this, my girl; go on your knees
to one man while you're in the prime of your beauty, and
you'll bitterly regret it when you're old.

PHILOLACHES: Oh that I were a quinsy, to choke the life out
of the poisonous old hag!

PHILEMATIUM: Surely I ought to be no less kind to him now,
when I've got what I wanted, than I was before I got it out
of him by coaxing and cajoling?

PHILOLACHES: Damn me if I don't free you again, my love –
and slaughter Scapha!

SCAPHA: All right, if you're satisfied that he's going to
support you for ever and be your faithful lover for life

everlasting, you'd better go to him and stick to him and marry him.

PHILEMATIUM: It's common, I know, for people to trade their good name for profit; if I can keep my good name, that's all the wealth I want.

PHILOLACHES: By the gods, I'll not see you in want or poverty as long as I live. I'd sooner sell my father, if it comes to that.

SCAPHA: What's to happen to all your other lovers?

PHILEMATIUM: I think they'll love me all the more when they see I know how to repay a benefactor.

PHILOLACHES: If only someone would come and tell me my father is dead, I'd disinherit myself and make her his legatee.

SCAPHA: It won't last long, anyway; not in that house. Eating and drinking day after day and night after night; they don't know the meaning of economy. It's just sheer gluttony.

PHILOLACHES: You'll be the first to find out how economical I can be, old woman. You're not having a bite or a sup with me for the next fortnight.

PHILEMATIUM: If you have anything good to say about him, you may say it. Any more slanders, and I'll have you whipped.

PHILOLACHES: That's the spirit! I couldn't have made a better bargain if I had sacrificed to Jupiter as much in solid silver as I gave for that girl's freedom. You can see she loves me heart and soul, can't you? Oh, aren't I a clever boy! I've bought myself an advocate who can plead my cause.

SCAPHA: I can see that Philolaches is worth more in your eyes than all the other men in the world added together. I don't want a beating on his account, so I'd better agree with you, if you're so certain he'll be yours for ever.

PHILEMATIUM: Get me my mirror and jewel case, Scapha;
　quickly. I must get dressed in time to meet my beloved
　when he arrives.

SCAPHA: Mirrors are for women who are dissatisfied with
　their looks and their age. What do you want with a mirror?
　You can show it more than it can show you.

PHILOLACHES: That's a pretty speech, Scapha; for that I'll
　give . . . I'll give Philematium something presently.

　　[SCAPHA *brings out of the house a mirror, jewels, and cos-*
　　metics. PHILEMATIUM *titivates herself.* PHILOLACHES *still*
　　remains aside, commenting and admiring.]

PHILEMATIUM: Is my hair attractive enough, do you think –
　every curl in its right place?

SCAPHA: You're always attractive enough, you don't need
　to worry about your hair.

PHILOLACHES: Did you ever see such a deceitful old creature?
　Just now she was all contradiction, now she's all agreement.

PHILEMATIUM: Give me the white lead.

SCAPHA: What do you want white lead for?

PHILEMATIUM: To improve my cheeks.

SCAPHA: You might as well try to improve ivory with ink.

PHILOLACHES: Ivory with ink! That's good. Bravo, well
　done, Scapha.

PHILEMATIUM: Give me the rouge then.

SCAPHA: Indeed I won't. Have some sense. Do you want to
　spoil a beautiful picture by over-painting? You don't need
　any make-up at all at your age, neither white lead nor Melian
　cream nor any of that stuff.

PHILEMATIUM: Take the mirror, then. [*She kisses the mirror*
　and hands it back to Scapha.]

PHILOLACHES: Ah me! She kissed the mirror! Oh for a
　stone to bash that mirror's brains out!

SCAPHA: You'd better wipe your hands on this towel.

PHILEMATIUM: Why on earth . . . ?

SCAPHA: As you've been holding the mirror, I'm afraid your hands may smell of silver. We don't want Philolaches to suspect you of handling money.

PHILOLACHES: She's the craftiest old bawd I've ever seen. Clever of her to think of that about the mirror. Naughty old bag!

PHILEMATIUM: Should I wear some scent, do you think?

SCAPHA: Don't touch it.

PHILEMATIUM: Why not?

SCAPHA: Goodness me, a woman's best smell is no smell. Those raddled old creatures who plaster themselves with perfume, toothless hags trying to hide their ugliness with make-up – what with scent and sweat together they smell like as if a cook's been mixing up too many different kinds of stew. You can't tell what they smell of, all you know is they smell horrible.

PHILOLACHES: She knows it all! She's been well taught. It's perfectly true, as most of you know if you've got an old lady at home who bought you with a dowry.

PHILEMATIUM: What do you think of this brooch and the cloak? Do they suit me?

SCAPHA: It's not my business to say whether they suit you or not.

PHILEMATIUM: Who else's business is it?

SCAPHA: Whose business? Why, Philolaches', of course. It's his business to know how to buy what will please you. Gold brooches and purple cloaks are the price a lover pays for his mistress's favours. But he doesn't want such things for himself, so there's no point in displaying to him something he doesn't want, is there? Purple cloaks are meant for concealing age; jewellery is to make an ugly woman more presentable. A beautiful woman will be more beautiful

naked than wrapped in purple. In any case, fine ornaments
are no use without good behaviour; fine ornament on bad
behaviour is worse than dirt. A fine figure is ornament
enough – more than enough – for any woman.

PHILOLACHES [*coming forward*]: I can't contain myself any
longer. . . . Well, what have you two been doing all this
time?

PHILEMATIUM: Making myself look nice to please you.

PHILOLACHES: You can't help looking nice. [*To Scapha*]
Go away, and take all this paraphernalia with you.
[SCAPHA *removes the toilet table. Other slaves will presently
bring out a couch, wine, and tables, creating a semblance of an
indoor scene.*]

PHILOLACHES: And now, Philematium my darling, I feel
a desire . . . to have a drink with you.

PHILEMATIUM: And I with you. All that you desire is all
that I desire, sweetheart.

PHILOLACHES: That's what I like to hear. That speech is
worth two thousand drachmas, and cheap at that.

PHILEMATIUM: Give me one thousand, darling. I don't
want to overcharge you.

PHILOLACHES: Give you a thousand? You're already one
thousand to the good. Well, work it out. I bought you for
three thousand.

PHILEMATIUM: Are you reproaching me now?

PHILOLACHES: Reproaching you? It's myself I ought to
reproach. But I never spent money in a better cause in my
life.

PHILEMATIUM: And I'm sure I was never better employed
than in loving you.

PHILOLACHES: Then the account balances, doesn't it? You
love me, I love you. We're both satisfied. May those
that wish us luck have the best of luck themselves; and

those that think ill of us, never have any such enviable fortune.

PHILEMATIUM: Come and sit down. [*To a slave*] Some water for our hands, boy. Bring the table over here. And the dice. [*To Philolaches*] Would you like some scent?

PHILOLACHES: What need of scent, when I am sitting next a nosegay? ... But look, isn't that my friend coming this way with his girl? It is; it's Callidamates and his girl. Here they come ... the troops are assembling, they're after a share of the spoils. Well, the more the merrier, my darling.

[*While the lovers settle to their drinking, the two visitors approach from the opposite side of the scene:* CALLIDAMATES, *a dissolute young man, already well primed, and his girl-friend* DELPHIUM *also a little tipsy. They are attended by a young slave,* PHANISCUS, *who will reappear later.*]

CALLIDAMATES [*singing vaguely*]:

> We're going to see Philolaches. ...
> We're going to ...

Where's that boy? [*To the slave*] Listen, you; I want you to come back for me later – but not too late. I shall be at this house here ... my friend Philol-ol-olaches' house ... have you got that? Those are your instr-structions.

[*The slave goes away.*]

> The place we were before
> Was such an awful bore,
>   The food was bad, the talk was worse,
> I bolted for the door.
>
> And now I think
> We'll get a drink
> With dear Philolaches. ...
>   For he's ... a jolly good fellow
>   And jolly good companee. ...

Do you think I'm a little bit inebri-ebriated?

DELPHIUM: Not more than usual.

CALLIDAMATES: Shall I kiss you? Shall you kiss me?

DELPHIUM: Yes, if you like.

CALLIDAMATES: You lovely thing. Take me, lead me. . . .

DELPHIUM [*supporting him*]: Ups-a-daisy! . . . don't fall down . . . lean on me.

CALLIDAMATES: Oh my darling, oh my darling . . . nurse me in your arms, my honey-love.

DELPHIUM: Hold up; you don't want to lie down in the street; can't you wait till we get to a couch?

CALLIDAMATES: Lay me down . . .

DELPHIUM [*dropping him*]: All right, I will.

CALLIDAMATES: . . . and let me lie . . . with all I hold . . . [*sinking and clinging to her*] within these arms. . . .

DELPHIUM: If you fall, I shall have to fall with you.

CALLIDAMATES: Then someone will have to come and pick us both up.

DELPHIUM: Oh dear, the lad's as tight as –

CALLIDAMATES: T-tight? You say I'm t-tight?

DELPHIUM: Come on, give me your hand; I'll look after you.

CALLIDAMATES: Here . . . hand . . .

DELPHIUM [*pulling him up*]: Now come with me.

CALLIDAMATES: Where are we going?

DELPHIUM: Don't you know?

CALLIDAMATES: Oh yes, I remember now . . . we're going home for a drink.

DELPHIUM: We're not; we're going in *there*.

CALLIDAMATES: So we are; I remember; in there. . . .

    [*They stagger towards Philolaches' house.*]

PHILOLACHES: Do you mind if I go and meet them, darling? He's one of my best friends. I'll be back soon.

PHILEMATIUM: 'Soon' is a long time.

[*The visitors arrive at the door.*]

CALLIDAMATES: Anyone at home?

PHILOLACHES: Yes, there is.

CALLIDAMATES: Philolaches! Greetings to my dearest friend on earth.

PHILOLACHES: The gods bless you, Callidamates. Come and sit down. . . . Where have you come from?

CALLIDAMATES [*pointing vaguely*]: From over . . . over-drinking.

PHILEMATIUM: Sit down, Delphium my dear. Give your friend a drink.

CALLIDAMATES: I think I'll just go to sleep. [*He does so.*]

PHILOLACHES: Does he ever do anything else?

DELPHIUM: If he's going to sleep, what am I going to do?

PHILEMATIUM: Leave him to sleep, my dear. Come on, pass the cup round. Hand it to Delphium first.

[*The party continues.*

Outside the house, TRANIO *returns from the harbour, in consternation.*]

TRANIO: It's all up. Jupiter Almighty is mustering all his forces and resources to put an end to me and my young master. We haven't a chance, Hope hasn't a leg to stand on, Salvation herself cannot save us if she would. My eyes have seen a mountainous monstrosity of mischief – at yonder harbour. The master has come home from his travels; Tranio is no more. Anybody here want to make some easy money? Anybody ready to be crucified in my place today? Where are all the punch-takers, chain-rattlers – or the chaps who are ready to rush the enemy's trenches for threepence? Anybody used to having his hide perforated with a dozen spears at once? I'm offering a talent to anyone prepared to jump on to a cross, provided he has his legs and arms double-nailed first; after that he can come and claim the

money, cash on the nail. But what am I wasting time here
for? I'd better get home double-quick. [*He goes towards the
house.*]

PHILOLACHES [*seeing him*]: Hullo, there's Tranio back from
the harbour. Now we shall get something to eat.
    [TRANIO *calls Philolaches out privately.*]

TRANIO: Philolaches!

PHILOLACHES [*joining him*]: What's up now?

TRANIO [*with a gesture of hopelessness*]: You and I –

PHILOLACHES: What about you and me?

TRANIO: We're dead men.

PHILOLACHES: Are we? Why?

TRANIO: Your father is back.

PHILOLACHES: No!

TRANIO: We're through. He's coming here. Your father.

PHILOLACHES: Where is he, for heaven's sake?

TRANIO: Here.

PHILOLACHES: Who told you? Who saw him?

TRANIO: I saw him myself.

PHILOLACHES: Oh my goodness! Where am I now?

TRANIO: I can answer that. You're sitting here drinking.

PHILOLACHES: You actually saw him?

TRANIO: I actually did.

PHILOLACHES: You're sure?

TRANIO: Of course I'm sure.

PHILOLACHES: It's the death of me if you're speaking the
truth.

TRANIO: What should I want to tell you a lie for?

PHILOLACHES: Whatever shall I do?

TRANIO: Tell them to get all this stuff out of the way. Who's
that fellow asleep?

PHILOLACHES: Callidamates. Wake him up, Delphium.

DELPHIUM: Callidamates! Callidamates! Wake up!

CALLIDAMATES: I am awake. Give me a drink.

DELPHIUM: Wake up. Philolaches' father has come home.

CALLIDAMATES: Long live Philol-olaches' father!

PHILOLACHES: He'll live all right. I'm dead! I'm dying!

CALLIDAMATES: You can't be both dead and dying.

PHILOLACHES: Do get up. My father's coming.

CALLIDAMATES: Is he? Tell him to go away again. I wonder what he's come back for. [*He goes to sleep again.*]

PHILOLACHES: Whatever shall I do? My father will arrive and find me drunk, the house full of guests and women. It's a nice time to be asking myself what to do, with my father at the door – as bad as digging a well when your throat's parched with thirst.

TRANIO: Look at him. He's dropped off to sleep again. Wake him up.

PHILOLACHES: Callidamates! Wake up, for heaven's sake. My father will be here in a minute.

CALLIDAMATES: Will he? [*Suddenly wide awake*] Your father, did you say? Give me my shoes! Come, arm me for the battle! I'll kill your father.

PHILOLACHES: Shut up, you idiot. You'll have us all killed.

DELPHIUM: Do be quiet, darling.

PHILOLACHES [*to slaves*]: Get hold of him. Take him away, quickly.

CALLIDAMATES: Pass me the p-pot, somebody, or I'll p-p – [*He is removed, protesting.*]

PHILOLACHES: Help! I'm dying!

TRANIO: No, you're not. I'll think of something to cure that feeling.

PHILOLACHES: I'm lost.

TRANIO: Never say die. I'll see you're all right. Look, what do you say if I fix it so that when your father arrives, he won't come in – what's more, he'll run for his life in the opposite direction? Only you others must get inside, and get all this stuff cleared away, as quick as you can.

PHILOLACHES: Where shall I be?

TRANIO: Wherever you prefer – with this one, or that one [*of the two girls*].

DELPHIUM: Hadn't we better go home?

TRANIO: Not at all, my dear. You go on with your drinking inside, just as if nothing had happened.

PHILOLACHES: Oh dear! It's all very well to be so comforting, but it makes me sweat to think of what you may be letting us in for.

TRANIO: Do you think you could just pull yourself together and do as I say?

PHILOLACHES: I think I can.

TRANIO: Then first of all, get inside, please, Philematium and Delphium.

DELPHIUM: We'll do anything you wish, Tranio.
    [*The girls go inside the house.*]

TRANIO: I hope they will, by Jupiter. Now listen carefully; this is what I want you to see to. In the first place, get all the doors locked. Don't let anyone make a sound inside the house.

PHILOLACHES: I'll do that.

TRANIO: As if there wasn't a living soul in the house.

PHILOLACHES: Right.

TRANIO: And nobody must answer the door when the old man knocks.

PHILOLACHES: Anything else?

TRANIO: Have the latch-key brought out here to me. I'll lock the door from the outside.

PHILOLACHES: Tranio, I commit all my life and hope into your hands. [*He goes inside.*]

TRANIO: We're all alike, aren't we? Master or servant, there's not a pin to choose between us for honesty – or dishonesty. Well, after all, a simple man, a chicken-hearted man, any man you like, however good or bad, can stoop to a dishonest action, on the spur of the moment; it's dead easy. But when it comes to planning and carrying out a nefarious scheme, a man needs to be a real expert to make sure that everything goes without a hitch – or he may find himself wishing he'd never been born. That's the way I intend to go about it, in this little caper we've set going; make sure everything goes smoothly and sweetly and doesn't lead to anything we might regret.

[*A slave,* SPHAERIO, *pops his head out of the door.*]

What the hell are you doing out here, Sphaerio?

[*He has, in fact, come to bring the key, which he shows to Tranio.*]

Oh yes, that's a good boy.

SPHAERIO: Master says he hopes you'll be sure and certain, whatever you do, to scare his father off from coming into the house.

TRANIO: You just tell your master I'll make sure his father doesn't even dare look at the house; he'll cover his head and run for his life. Give me that key and get inside and bolt the door. I'll lock it from this side.

[*The slave does as bid;* TRANIO *locks the door.*]

Now let him come. I'll put on a show for the old man here and now; there'll be no funeral games for him after he's dead. I'd better keep away from the door. . . . I'll watch from over here, and as soon as he arrives I'll give him something to think about. [*He retires to a corner.*]

[THEOPROPIDES *arrives from the harbour, with two slaves carrying his baggage.*]

THEOPROPIDES: Thanks be to Neptune for letting me out of his clutches to get home safe and dry – but only just.

Do you hear, Neptune? If you ever catch me putting a foot into water after this day, I give you leave to do to me whatever you hoped to do this time. I never want to set eyes on you again. It's the last time I entrust anything of mine to your keeping.

TRANIO: You made a big mistake there, Neptune – losing a good chance like that.

THEOPROPIDES: So here I am at home again after three years in Egypt. The family will be right glad to see me, I've no doubt.

TRANIO: They'd be right gladder to see someone bringing news of your death.

[THEOPROPIDES *goes up to the door, is surprised to find it locked.*]

THEOPROPIDES: What's the meaning of this? The door bolted and barred, in the daytime? I'll have to knock. . . . Is anybody there? . . . Will someone open this door?

[*He continues to hammer at the door;* TRANIO *approaches, as if just arrived from a distance.*]

TRANIO: Who can that be, outside our house?

THEOPROPIDES [*seeing him*]: It's Tranio. My servant Tranio!

TRANIO: Oh master, sir, Theopropides! Oh sir, I'm glad to see you, sir, safe home again. Are you as well as ever?

THEOPROPIDES: As well as ever, as you see.

TRANIO: Thank heaven for that.

THEOPROPIDES: But what's going on here? Have you all gone mad?

TRANIO: Why, sir?

THEOPROPIDES: What are you doing walking about the streets? There's not a living soul in attendance in the house, it seems; no one to open the door or answer my call. I've almost knocked the door to pieces.

TRANIO [*horror-struck*]: Oh, my goodness gracious! You've never touched the house?

THEOPROPIDES: Touched it? Why shouldn't I touch it? I've not only touched it, I've nearly broken the door down, I tell you.

TRANIO: You have touched it, then?

THEOPROPIDES: Of course I've touched it, and banged it.

TRANIO: Alack the day!

THEOPROPIDES: What on earth is the matter with you?

TRANIO: You couldn't have done anything worse.

THEOPROPIDES: What do you mean?

TRANIO: Words cannot tell you what a terrible, impious thing you have done.

THEOPROPIDES: What have I done?

TRANIO: Fly, sir, fly, I beseech you; avoid this house! Come away, come away, over here. [*He drags him as far away as possible.*] You're sure you touched the door?

THEOPROPIDES: How do you think I could knock at the door without touching it?

TRANIO: Alas, you have surely caused the death –

THEOPROPIDES: Whose death?

TRANIO: Of all your house.

THEOPROPIDES: May gods and goddesses cause your death for saying so.

TRANIO: I don't know how you're ever going to make peace for their souls and yours.

THEOPROPIDES: Why should I make peace? What on earth are you trying to tell me?

TRANIO [*seeing the slaves approaching the house*]: Stop! Tell those men to keep away.

THEOPROPIDES: Keep away, you two.

TRANIO: Don't lay a finger on the house. Touch the earth, all of you.

THEOPROPIDES: For the love of all the gods, tell me what this is about.

TRANIO: I'll tell you. Seven months ago we quitted the house and no one has set foot in it from that day to this.

THEOPROPIDES: What did you do that for?

TRANIO: Sh! Are you sure we're not overheard? Look round everywhere.

THEOPROPIDES [*having looked*]: Yes, we're quite alone.

TRANIO: Look again, to make sure.

THEOPROPIDES: No, there's no one about.

TRANIO: A horrible crime has been committed.

THEOPROPIDES: What crime? What are you talking about?

TRANIO: A crime. A horrible crime. An old and ancient crime.

THEOPROPIDES: An ancient crime?

TRANIO: So it seems, according to what we have found out.

THEOPROPIDES: Well, *what* crime, and who did it? Out with it.

TRANIO: A host took his guest by the throat and murdered him; the very man, I suppose, who sold you this house.

THEOPROPIDES: Murdered his guest?

TRANIO: And robbed his guest; and buried his guest; here in this very house.

THEOPROPIDES: How did you get on the track of this terrible occurrence?

TRANIO: I'll tell you. It was like this. One evening your son happened to be dining out. As soon as he got home, we all went to bed. We all went to sleep. There was a light burning which I had accidentally forgotten to put out. Suddenly he let out a terrible cry.

THEOPROPIDES: Who did? My son?

TRANIO: Don't interrupt, please. Just listen. He said the dead man had appeared to him in his sleep.

THEOPROPIDES: In his sleep? Really?

TRANIO: Yes, really. Listen. The dead man, so your son says, spoke to him as follows –

THEOPROPIDES: In his sleep?

TRANIO: He couldn't very well speak to him awake, could he, since he was killed sixty years ago? Really, sometimes you are so dense –

THEOPROPIDES: All right, all right, I won't say a word. Go on.

TRANIO: And this is what the dead man said, to your son, in his sleep: 'I am a stranger from over the seas; my name is Diapontius. But here I dwell; here is my appointed habitation. For Hades will not grant me leave to cross the waters of Acheron, since I was untimely slain. I trusted and was deceived. My host slew me in this house, and in this house he buried me, without rite or ceremony, secretly, in this very house, the villain; and he did it for my money. You must go hence, for this house is a house of abomination, a domicile of sin.' That is what the ghost said. As for the ghostly manifestations that have been going on here, it would take more than a year to describe them all.

[*A noise issues from the house.*]

THEOPROPIDES: Hark, what was that?

TRANIO: Oh my goodness, what was it?

THEOPROPIDES: Someone at the door!

TRANIO: The ghost walks!

THEOPROPIDES: My blood is frozen! The dead are coming to drag me to Acheron!

TRANIO [*aside*]: It'll be all up. Those idiots will blow the whole thing to pieces. And what'll happen to me if I'm found out, I shudder to think.

THEOPROPIDES: What are you muttering about?

TRANIO: Come away from the door, sir. Fly, sir, fly, I implore you.

THEOPROPIDES: Fly? Where to? Fly yourself.

TRANIO: I have nothing to fear. I have made my peace with the dead.

[*A voice within shouts*, 'Hey, Tranio!'
TRANIO *goes to the keyhole.*]

TRANIO: Call not my name, I beseech you. I haven't done anything. It was not I that knocked at the door.

THEOPROPIDES: What's happening, Tranio?

[TRANIO *hustles him away from the door.*]

Why are you keeping us out? Who were you speaking to?

TRANIO [*pretending relief*]: Oh, was it you calling my name? Oh, gods help me, I thought it was the dead man crying out because you had knocked at the door. But please, sir, don't stand here; do as I tell you.

THEOPROPIDES: Do what?

TRANIO: Fly; don't look back; cover your head.

THEOPROPIDES: Aren't you going to fly?

TRANIO: I've made my peace with the dead.

THEOPROPIDES: So you said. In that case, why are you so frightened?

TRANIO: Please don't trouble about me. I shall be all right. You just carry on, get away as fast as you can – and pray for help to Hercules.

THEOPROPIDES: Hercules, come to my aid! . . . [*He hurries off.*]

TRANIO: And mine . . . to get this old man properly twisted today. Look down, oh great immortal gods, upon my wonderful wickedness! [*He unlocks the door with his key and goes into the house.*]

*

[*Now along the street comes* MISARGYRIDES, *a money-lender and obviously a disagreeable character.*]

MISARGYRIDES: A more villainous year for moneylenders I've never seen in all my life. A shocking year it's been, as far as I'm concerned. I've spent whole days from dawn to dusk in the forum and haven't been able to lend a half-penny to a single soul.

[TRANIO *comes out of the house, with cheerful confidence, which rapidly ebbs when he catches sight of the moneylender. It will be some time, however, before they come face to face.*]

TRANIO: Who's this? Oh my goodness, this'll finish me for ever and all. This is the moneylender who lent Philolaches the cash to buy his girl. The cat will be properly out of the bag now, unless I can think of some way to prevent the old man finding out. I'll go and speak to him anyway. . . .

[*But before he can do so, he espies* THEOPROPIDES *approaching from the opposite side.*]

And here comes the master too . . . oh dear, what's brought him back so soon, I wonder? I hope he hasn't heard anything about this business. . . . Well, I'll have to go and speak to him first. Oh dearie me, I am in a funk; it's no fun having a guilty conscience like mine. However, come what may, I must carry on and try to cause more confusion – it's the only thing to do. [*He meets Theopropides.*] You're back soon, sir; where have you been?

THEOPROPIDES [*in dangerous temper*]: I've just met the man who sold me my house.

TRANIO: You didn't tell him anything about – what I told you?

THEOPROPIDES: Upon my word, I did. Every detail.

TRANIO [*aside*]: Oh! . . . my beautiful scheme blown to smithereens!

THEOPROPIDES: What are you muttering about?

TRANIO: Nothing. You really told him, did you?

THEOPROPIDES: I did indeed. I told him the whole story.

TRANIO: And does he admit the – what he did to his guest?

THEOPROPIDES: He flatly denies it.

TRANIO: Denies it? The scoundrel. Don't you mean he admits it?

THEOPROPIDES: No, I *don't* mean he admits it. If he had admitted it, I should have said so. Now what am I going to do?

TRANIO: What are you going to do? If you ask me, you'll have the man up before a judge – and for goodness' sake choose one who will believe my story – then you'll get him convicted as easy as a fox swallows apples.

MISARGYRIDES [aside]: I do believe that's Tranio, Philolaches' servant; they owe me money, and I can't get a penny of interest or principal out of them.

[TRANIO, *seeing him approach, edges away to head him off from Theopropides.*]

THEOPROPIDES: Where are you off to now?

TRANIO: Nowhere. . . . [*Aside*] If there was ever a more miserable devil, born under a more unlucky star . . . Now he'll come up to me while the master's here . . . oh misery me, I'm under fire from both sides. I'll have to speak to him first.

MISARGYRIDES: Good, he's coming this way. Perhaps he has got some money for me.

TRANIO: He looks very cheerful, drat him.

[*They meet.*]

Ah, Misargyrides, good day to you, sir.

MISARGYRIDES: Good day to you. I hope you're well. About that money –

TRANIO: Oh go away, you nasty creature. Every time I meet you, you stick your skewers into me.

MISARGYRIDES [*aside*]: I shan't get anything out of this fellow.

TRANIO [*aside*]: He's dead right.

MISARGYRIDES: Will you stop trifling with me, please?

TRANIO: Just tell me what you want, then.

MISARGYRIDES: Where is Philolaches?

TRANIO: Well now, as it happens, you couldn't have come at a more opportune time.

MISARGYRIDES: What do you mean?

TRANIO: Come this way, please [*trying to draw him towards Theopropides, who is still out of hearing*].

MISARGYRIDES [*resisting*]: Am I going to get my money?

TRANIO: You needn't raise your voice. I know you've got a beautiful one.

MISARGYRIDES: I'll raise it as much as I like. [*He refuses to move any further.*]

TRANIO [*trying a different tack*]: Just do something to oblige me, will you?

MISARGYRIDES: What am I to do for you?

TRANIO: Just go home, there's a good chap.

MISARGYRIDES: Go home?

TRANIO: Come back about noon.

MISARGYRIDES: Will you have any money for me then?

TRANIO: You shall have it. Now go away, please.

MISARGYRIDES [*furious*]: And why should I waste my time and energy running to and fro for you, I'd like to know? What if I stay here till noon?

TRANIO: Go away, I say. And by Hercules, I mean it. Go away!

MISARGYRIDES: I'll not stir from here till I get my interest.

TRANIO: Go away.

MISARGYRIDES: I want my interest. How much longer –

TRANIO: Hercules! If you don't –

MISARGYRIDES: I'll prosecute the man, damn me if I don't.

TRANIO: That's the spirit. Have a good shout and enjoy yourself.

MISARGYRIDES: I'll have my rights. You've been putting me off like this for long enough. If you want to get rid of me, give me my interest, then I'll go. My interest – and I won't say another word.

TRANIO: You can have the principal.

MISARGYRIDES: My interest! I want my interest first.

TRANIO: You obnoxious creature! If you've come here for a shouting match, shout as much as you like, he's not giving you anything; he doesn't owe you anything.

MISARGYRIDES: Not owe me – ?

TRANIO: You won't get a peppercorn. Are you afraid he'll skip off and go into exile to escape paying you the interest? After you've been offered the principal?

MISARGYRIDES: I don't want the principal. I want the interest first. The interest!

TRANIO: Oh shut up. You're not getting it; and you can do what you please; you're not the only moneylender in the world, I suppose.

MISARGYRIDES: My interest – I want my interest – give me my interest. Are you going to give me my interest, here and now?

TRANIO: Interest, interest, interest – it's the only word he knows. Be off with you. You're the most obnoxious vermin I ever saw.

MISARGYRIDES: You can't frighten me with that sort of language.

[THEOPROPIDES, *at some distance away, cannot help overhearing this altercation, and now intervenes.*]

THEOPROPIDES: You're having a mighty hot argument. I can feel it scorching me a mile off. What is this interest he's asking for?

TRANIO: Now then, here is Philolaches' father just come home from foreign parts. He'll oblige you, I'm sure. He'll give you your interest and your principal, so you needn't make yourself a nuisance to us any longer.

MISARGYRIDES: Well, I'll accept it, if he can give me anything.

THEOPROPIDES: What is going on, Tranio?

TRANIO: Sir?

THEOPROPIDES: Who is this man? What does he want? What is he saying about my son, and why is he pitching into you like this? What is this debt he is claiming?

TRANIO: Oh please, sir, give me the money and let me throw it in the dirty creature's face.

THEOPROPIDES: Let you –

TRANIO: Let me bash his face in with a bag of money.

MISARGYRIDES: I could easily do with a bag of money in the face.

THEOPROPIDES: What money are you talking about?

TRANIO: It's – well, it's a little debt Philolaches owes him.

THEOPROPIDES: How little?

TRANIO: About – four thousand drachmas. Don't say that's too much.

MISARGYRIDES: A mere nothing.

TRANIO: Listen to him. Isn't he the very pattern of the vilest race on earth – moneylenders?

THEOPROPIDES: I don't care who he is or where he comes from. What I want to know, and what I mean to find out, is, has my son really borrowed all that money at interest?

TRANIO: He owes four thousand four hundred drachmas actually. Say you'll give it him and let's get rid of the fellow.

THEOPROPIDES: Say I'll give it him indeed?

TRANIO: Just say you will.

THEOPROPIDES: *I* will?

TRANIO: *You* will. Just say it, please. Promise – oh do.

THEOPROPIDES: And what has become of the money? Just tell me that.

TRANIO: Oh, it's there all right.

THEOPROPIDES: Then if it's there, you can pay it.

TRANIO: That is to say – the fact is, your son has been buying a house.

THEOPROPIDES: Buying a house?

TRANIO: Yes – a house.

THEOPROPIDES [*unexpectedly delighted*]: Well, well; that's splendid! Philolaches is going into business after all. He's a chip off the old block, then. A house, you said?

TRANIO: I said a house. And do you know what sort of a house it is?

THEOPROPIDES: How the devil should I know?

TRANIO: Phew!

THEOPROPIDES: What do you mean, phew?

TRANIO: Words fail me.

THEOPROPIDES: Why? What is it like?

TRANIO: Windows wide as . . . It's a perfect suntrap.

THEOPROPIDES: Capital. Well done. How much did he give for it?

TRANIO [*counting, pointing finger at himself and the old man*]: One, two – two talents – but he had to put down a deposit of four thousand drachmas; so he borrowed the money and we paid the deposit. Do you see now? As soon as your house became . . . like I said, he bought himself another next day.

THEOPROPIDES: Very wise of him, by Hercules.

MISARGYRIDES: Excuse me, it's nearly noon.

TRANIO: Do pay him, sir, or this vomit will poison us. Four thousand four hundred we owe him, principal and interest.

MISARGYRIDES: Exactly. I ask no more.

TRANIO: I'd like to see you ask a penny more, by Herc'les!

THEOPROPIDES [*to Misargyrides*]: I'll deal with you, my lad.

MISARGYRIDES: Shall I have it from you, sir?

THEOPROPIDES: Ask me for it tomorrow.

MISARGYRIDES: Tomorrow – very good – tomorrow will do. I'll go, then. [*He goes.*]

TRANIO: And the curse of all the gods and goddesses go with him! [*Aside*] He very nearly knocked the bottom out of my scheme. Moneylenders – there's not a more despicable or more dishonest race of creatures on this earth.

THEOPROPIDES: Well then, whereabouts is this house that my son has bought?

TRANIO [*sunk again*]: Oh my life, I'm done for now!

THEOPROPIDES: Can you answer my question, please?

TRANIO: Oh yes, sir . . . yes . . . I'm just trying to remember the owner's name.

THEOPROPIDES: Well try and remember quickly.

TRANIO [*aside*]: Well I don't know . . . I might as well say it's this one in the next block, mightn't I? They say the best lie is a thumping lie. That's it – I'll say what the gods put into my mouth.

THEOPROPIDES: Have you remembered yet?

TRANIO: I wish he'd drop dead. . . . Yes, sir, of course I remember now . . . this house next door is the one your son has bought.

THEOPROPIDES: Really? No joking?

TRANIO [*aside*]: It'll be no joke if you don't give us the money – a good joke if you do.

THEOPROPIDES: He might have chosen a better position.

TRANIO: No, really, sir, it's an excellent position.

THEOPROPIDES: Upon my word, I'd like to have a look at the house. Knock at the door, Tranio, and fetch someone out.

TRANIO [*aside*]: This is the end. I'm on the rocks again. Whatever am I going to say?

THEOPROPIDES: Well, what are you waiting for?

TRANIO [*aside*]: Hang me if I know what to do. He's got
me this time.

THEOPROPIDES: Hurry up and fetch someone out, and ask
him to show me round.

TRANIO: Oh but sir, you can't do that. There are ladies here.
We'll have to see whether they have any objection.

THEOPROPIDES: Yes, yes; you're quite right. Go and find
out. Ask them. I'll wait outside here till you come back.
[*He walks away to the other end of the street.*]

TRANIO: Now all the gods and goddesses damn you to everlasting perdition, grand-dad. You upset my plans at every
end and turn, curse you.

    [*The door of the house opens:* TRANIO *sees who is coming
and keeps out of sight.*]

Well, here's a bit of luck. It's the master of the house himself, old Simo. I'll keep out of the way, and see if I can give
myself a bit of good advice; then I'll speak to him, when
I've decided what to do.

    [SIMO, *the owner of the house, is evidently a long-suffering
man, but placid, and just now in an equable mood after a
good lunch.*]

SIMO: That was the best meal I've had in this house this year.
I don't know when I've enjoyed my food so much. My wife
has just given me a capital lunch, and told me to go and have
a sleep. Huh! I don't think! There's more to it than that. It
isn't just by accident that she gives me a better lunch than
usual. She wants to get me into bed, that's what the old
lady wants. I don't think I care for bed just after lunch; no,
thank you; so I've slipped out quietly. I know she's waiting
for me, in a high old temper.

TRANIO: So there's trouble in store for the old man before the day's out. He's in for a bad dinner and a rough night.

SIMO: The more I think of it, the more sure I am: to have an old wife and a rich one is to say good-bye to slumber. It's a positive torture to go to bed. That's why I have now decided to take a walk into town rather than have a nap at home. I don't know how it is with you; I know how it is with me all right – or rather all wrong – and it'll get worse.

TRANIO [aside]: It will. You'll find you've stepped out into more trouble, old chap. And it will be no use blaming the gods; you have only yourself to blame. Well, I suppose I'd better go and speak to him. ... [A bright idea suddenly strikes him.] Why, that's it! I've got it! I've thought of a way to get round the old man; I'll fix it so that he helps to get me out of my fix. I'll speak to him now. ... The gods bless you, Simo.

SIMO: Bless you, Tranio.

TRANIO: I hope you are well.

SIMO: Pretty well, thanks. What are you doing here?

TRANIO: Talking to a charming old gentleman.

SIMO: Very good of you to say so.

TRANIO: Not at all.

SIMO: Oh yes it is. But I'm sorry I can't say I'm talking to a very good slave.

THEOPROPIDES [a long way away]: Tranio! Where are you? Come back here, you rascal.

TRANIO: Coming, sir.

SIMO [detaining him]: Wait a minute. ... How much longer is this going on?

TRANIO: Is what going on?

SIMO: What's going on in your master's house.

TRANIO: Why, what is going on?

SIMO: You know what I'm talking about. Of course you do.

You have to do what your young master tells you, I
suppose. But don't forget, life is short, my boy.

TRANIO: I don't understand. . . . Oh, I think I do . . . you
mean the way we're . . . going on . . . in there?

SIMO: Yes, I do. You're having a mighty pleasant time of it
now, aren't you? Quite the gentleman, eh? Wine and good
living to your heart's content.

TRANIO [*affecting frankness and contrition*]: Well, it *was* like
that, Simo. Things aren't so pretty now, though.

SIMO: Oh, how's that?

TRANIO: We're done for, Simo.

SIMO: Rubbish. You've had it all your own way up to now.

TRANIO: I don't deny we have been doing as you say. We
have had it all our own way. But the wind is blowing from
the other quarter now, Simo.

SIMO: Oho! What sort of wind?

TRANIO: A most dangerous wind.

SIMO: But your ship is safely tied up, isn't she?

TRANIO: Oh! [*breaking into tears*] . . .

SIMO: What's the matter, my good fellow?

TRANIO: I'm going to die! . . .

SIMO: Why, what – ?

TRANIO: We're going to be boarded, rammed, and sunk!

SIMO: I'm sorry to hear it, Tranio. What has been happening?

TRANIO: I'll tell you. The master has come home from abroad.

SIMO: Oh dear, that's bad. That means imprisonment for
you, and the cross to follow.

TRANIO: At your knees I implore you, don't give me away!

SIMO: Never fear; he shall not learn anything from me.

TRANIO: Oh bless you, master.

SIMO: Not that I'd care to have you for a servant, all the same.

TRANIO: Now let me tell you why my master has sent me
to you.

SIMO: In the first place, tell me this: how much does the old man know about your goings-on?

TRANIO: Nothing at all.

SIMO: He hasn't had a row with his son?

TRANIO: No, everything's fine; not a cloud in the sky. But he wants me to ask you, as a very great favour, to let him see over this house of yours.

SIMO: It's not for sale.

TRANIO: I know that. But the old man is planning to build on some women's quarters to his own house, and a bathroom, and a garden-walk, and a portico.

SIMO: What on earth is he dreaming of?

TRANIO: Well, it's like this. He's very anxious to get his son married, so that's why he wants to build new women's rooms. He says some architect or other has recommended your house as being fantastically well constructed; so he wants to copy it; if you have no objection. He's particularly anxious to follow your plan, because he has heard you have perfect shade in summer every hour of the day though the sun may be blazing in the vault of heaven.

SIMO: As a matter of fact, wherever else the shade may be, this is the one place where the sun's always blazing from morning till evening; it's like a dun at the door – can't get rid of it. There's not an atom of shade here, unless it's in the cellar.

TRANIO: I see; nothing shady about this house, then.

SIMO: Spare your jokes. I'm telling you the facts.

TRANIO: Anyway, he wants to look at it.

SIMO: He's welcome to look at it. And if there's anything that takes his fancy, he has my permission to copy it.

TRANIO: Shall I go and fetch him?

SIMO: By all means.

[*He remains near his house.* TRANIO *congratulates himself.*]

TRANIO: Alexander the Great and Agathocles, so I've heard tell, were the two top champion wonder-workers of the world. Why shouldn't I be the third – aren't I a famous and wonderful worker? The asses are saddled – this old ass, and that old ass. I'm in a new and profitable line of business; most mule-drivers saddle mules, but I'm saddling human mules; they're tough enough to carry anything, too! ... Now for this one; I'll go and speak to him. [*He crosses to Theopropides.*] ... Theopropides, sir!

THEOPROPIDES [*waking from a doze*]: Now who wants me?

TRANIO: Your ever-faithful slave, master.

THEOPROPIDES: Where have you been all this time?

TRANIO: Where you sent me; and I've got all you wanted.

THEOPROPIDES: Why the devil have you been so long about it?

TRANIO: The old gentleman was engaged; I had to wait for him.

THEOPROPIDES: Trust you to take your time over it.

TRANIO: Well I like that! I'd have you know, a man can't blow and suck at the same time. I can't be in two places at once, can I?

THEOPROPIDES: Well, what have you found out?

TRANIO: You may go in and inspect the house to your heart's content.

THEOPROPIDES: Good. Let's go, then [*waiting to be conducted*].

TRANIO [*trying to keep behind him*]: I'm not stopping you, am I?

THEOPROPIDES: You go first.

TRANIO: Look, the gentleman is waiting to receive you himself at the door. But I am afraid he's bitterly regretting having sold it.

THEOPROPIDES: Oh, why?

TRANIO: He wants me to persuade Philolaches to let him have it back.

THEOPROPIDES: Not likely! Every man must reap his own field. If it turned out a bad bargain, *we* shouldn't be able to get *him* to take it back, should we? A man must take home what he can get; there's no room for sentiment in business.

TRANIO: Well, don't stand here talking. Come on.

THEOPROPIDES: Right. Lead the way.

TRANIO: There is the gentleman.

    [*They meet Simo.*]

    Sir, I've brought you the gentleman I mentioned.

SIMO: I'm very glad to see you, Theopropides.

THEOPROPIDES: The gods be good to you, sir.

SIMO: I understand you want to see over my house?

THEOPROPIDES: If it's not inconvenient to you.

SIMO: It's perfectly convenient. Come in and have a look round.

THEOPROPIDES: Perhaps the ladies –

SIMO: There's no lady you need take any notice of. Go anywhere you like, just as if the house belonged to you.

THEOPROPIDES: As if – ?

TRANIO [*quietly*]: He's not very well, sir. Better not remind him you've bought it. You can see how ill he looks.

THEOPROPIDES: Yes, I do.

TRANIO: Don't act as if you'd got the better of him, or seem too pleased with the house. Don't say a word about having bought it.

THEOPROPIDES: I understand; very sensible of you, and very thoughtful. Well, then –

SIMO: Come in, please, and look at whatever you want to see, at your leisure.

THEOPROPIDES: It's very kind of you indeed.

SIMO: Not at all.

[*They move into the house, pausing to inspect the portal.*]

TRANIO: Look at this vestibule, sir; and the loggia. What do you think of them?

THEOPROPIDES: Very fine indeed; magnificent.

TRANIO: And those doorposts; see how thick and firm they are.

THEOPROPIDES: I don't think I've ever seen finer posts.

SIMO: My goodness, they ought to be. I had paid enough for them.

TRANIO: You hear, sir? He says 'I *had* paid' – poor man, he's almost weeping.

THEOPROPIDES: How much did you – had you – paid for them?

SIMO: Three hundred drachmas for the pair, plus the carriage.

THEOPROPIDES [*examining them*]: Wait a minute, though. Upon my word, I'm not sure that they are as sound as I thought.

TRANIO: Why, sir?

THEOPROPIDES: They're eaten away with woodworm at the bottom, both of them.

TRANIO: They were probably cut down at a bad season; that's all that's wrong with them; a coat of pitch will soon put that right. This is good Greek work, not that of some pap-eating barbarian jerry-builder. See how well the doors fit.

THEOPROPIDES: Yes, I see.

TRANIO: How neatly they go to bye-bye [*flapping the doors to and fro*].

THEOPROPIDES: Go to bye-bye?

TRANIO: Shut-eye – close their eyelids. [*He demonstrates the smooth closing of the doors.*] Are you satisfied?

T–P. – C

THEOPROPIDES: The more I see of it, the more I like it.

TRANIO: Do you like that painting of the crow teasing two vultures?

THEOPROPIDES: Where? I don't see any painting.

TRANIO: Don't you? I do. A crow standing between two vultures [*as he is standing between the two old men*] and plucking at them alternately. . . . Look in this direction, towards me, then you'll see the crow at any rate. Got it?

THEOPROPIDES: Hanged if I can see any crow there.

TRANIO: Well, look in your direction, then; if you can't see the crow perhaps you can see the vultures.

THEOPROPIDES: Damn it, I tell you I can't see any picture of a bird at all.

TRANIO: Sorry, don't bother. It's not your fault. Your eyesight is failing with age, I expect.

THEOPROPIDES: Everything I *can* see looks to me very satisfactory.

SIMO: It would be worth your while to see the rest of the house.

THEOPROPIDES: Yes indeed, I'm sure it would.

SIMO [*calling to a slave*]: Boy there, take this gentleman over the house; show him everything. . . . I'd take you round myself, only I have business in town.

THEOPROPIDES: No, no; send the boy away; I don't want an escort. I prefer to find my own way. I'd rather make my own mistakes than be led by the nose.

SIMO: I thought perhaps a guide to the house –

THEOPROPIDES: No, no, I'll go on my own. I don't need anyone to take me in.

SIMO: Go ahead, then.

THEOPROPIDES: I will.

TRANIO: Just a minute, sir. I'd better see if the dog –

THEOPROPIDES: Oh yes, do.

TRANIO: Dog, go away! Go away, dog! Brr! Get away to hell, will you, dog! Still there, are you? Brr! Go away!

SIMO: She won't hurt you. They're always quiet when they're in pup. You can go in without fear. I'll get off to town, then.

THEOPROPIDES: Yes, do. Have a pleasant walk.

[SIMO *departs.*]

Tranio, get them to remove that dog from the door, even if she is harmless.

TRANIO: Oh but look how peacefully she's lying. You don't want to make a fuss, do you, or be taken for a coward?

THEOPROPIDES: Very well. Follow me. [*He goes in.*]

TRANIO: I will . . . and not let you out of my sight from now on. [*He follows.*]

*

[*From along the street comes the slave* PHANISCUS *who has been told to fetch his master Callidamates home from the drinking party. He is an elegant and sophisticated youth. He finds his way to the house, listens for sounds from within, then pauses to address the audience.*]

PHANISCUS: The way to be a useful slave is to be afraid of trouble even when you've done no wrong. The ones who are not afraid of anything even when they *have* deserved trouble, are going the right way to *get* trouble. They may train for the cross-country – do a bunk – and when they get caught, what have they done? They've simply doubled their trouble – which is more than they can ever do with their money. They make a little trouble grow into a big one. The way I go about it is to see that if anyone gets into trouble it isn't me. I like to keep my skin the way it's always been – whole, and not beaten more than I care for. As long as I keep a watch on myself like that, I'll always have a roof over my head; trouble can rain on other people, not on me. You know, slaves get the masters they deserve. Good slaves, good masters; bad slaves, bad masters. In our house now, they're a shocking lot, wasteful with their money, and getting beaten every day. When the steward tells one of them to go and attend on the master, it's 'Oh, to hell; I'm not going; what's the hurry? I know, you've got a date yourself; out for a bit of grass on your own, old mule.' That sort of talk. Well, I'm not like that; I do my duty and do myself good as well. So that's why I'm here. I'm the only one of the lot who would come and see the master home. When he finds out about it tomorrow, he'll give those scoundrels a taste of oxflesh. Well, after all, I value their skins less than my own. I'd rather they were leathered sooner than I were roped.

[*Now one of his colleagues*, PINACIUM, *a rough fellow, follows him up and tries to stop him from knocking at the door; presumably he wants to claim the credit for himself.*]

PINACIUM: Hey, Phaniscus, wait! Stop there! Hey, wait, will you?

PHANISCUS: You let me alone.

PINACIUM: Saucy monkey! Stop there, you nasty parasite.

PHANISCUS: What do you mean, parasite?

PINACIUM: I mean you'd go anywhere for a bit of food.

PHANISCUS: And what's it got to do with you? My tastes are my own business.

PINACIUM: Bold as brass, ain't you, just because you're the master's darling.

PHANISCUS: Bah! you make my eyes sore.

PINACIUM: Do I? How?

PHANISCUS: With all that gas of yours.

PINACIUM: Ah, shut up, you – you cheating – false-coiner. . . .

PHANISCUS: You want me to call you names, don't you? But I'm not going to. My master knows me.

PINACIUM: Very likely. He ought to know his own favourite cushion.

PHANISCUS: You wouldn't talk like that if you were sober.

PINACIUM: I'm not taking orders from you, if you won't listen to me. Come on now, young rascal, we've got to go and meet the master.

PHANISCUS: Well, don't give me any more of your lip.

PINACIUM: I won't. I'll knock at the door. . . . Anyone in? Hey, is anyone there, to save me the trouble of smashing the door down? [*He goes on knocking.*] Open the door, somebody! . . . Not a soul about. Just what you'd expect from that pack of scoundrels. I'll have to watch my step or one of them may come out and set on me.

[*While he continues trying to solve the mystery of the empty house,* THEOPROPIDES *and* TRANIO *come out from next door.*]

TRANIO: Well, what do you think of the bargain?

THEOPROPIDES: I'm entirely satisfied with it.

TRANIO: You don't think he gave too much for it?

THEOPROPIDES: It's a gift, if ever I saw one.

TRANIO: You like it?

THEOPROPIDES: Like it? I'm delighted with it.

TRANIO: You like the women's rooms; and the portico?

THEOPROPIDES: It's a perfectly marvellous portico. I doubt if the city owns a bigger one.

TRANIO: It doesn't. Philolaches and I have measured all the porticos in the city.

THEOPROPIDES: Have you?

TRANIO: This is the longest of them all.

THEOPROPIDES: Ye gods, we've got a wonderful bargain.

If that man were to offer me six solid silver talents down for it, I wouldn't take it.

TRANIO [*aside*]: I'd see you didn't, by Hercules, even if you wanted to.

THEOPROPIDES: Yes, we made a good investment there.

TRANIO: It was a bold stroke, and you can say it was due to my advice and persuasion. I made him borrow the money for the deposit.

THEOPROPIDES: You certainly saved the ship. Let me see, eight thousand drachmas was Simo's price, wasn't it?

TRANIO: Not a penny more.

THEOPROPIDES: I'll see he gets it today.

TRANIO: I should – in case he cries off for any reason. Or better still, you could let me have it, and I'd let him have it.

THEOPROPIDES: Let you have it? No jiggery-pokery, mind you.

TRANIO: Well, sir; do you think I'd deceive you, even as a joke, by any word or act of mine?

THEOPROPIDES: Do you think I can afford not to be careful what I trust you with?

TRANIO: Sir, in all the years I've been with you, have you ever known me try to cheat you?

THEOPROPIDES: I've taken jolly good care you didn't, thanks to the gods and my own good sense. As long as I keep my eye on you, I know I'm all right.

TRANIO: I agree.

THEOPROPIDES: Now then, get off to the farm and tell my son I've arrived.

TRANIO: I will, sir.

THEOPROPIDES: And bring him back to town with you, as quickly as possible.

TRANIO: Very good, sir. ... [*Aside*] Now all I've got to do is to nip back by the garden door and rejoin my fellow-

jokers. I'll tell them that all's well and that I've got *him*
away from *here*.

[*He goes off, as if to the country, not looking at the house,
where the two slaves are still puzzling over the locked door.*]

PHANISCUS: Well, it's funny. There's not a sound of company, as there usually is. I can't hear a flute-player or anybody at all.

THEOPROPIDES: What's going on there? What do those
fellows want at my house? What are they looking through
the keyhole for?

PHANISCUS: I shall just go on knocking. Hey there, open
this door! Tranio! Open this door!

THEOPROPIDES: What do they think they're playing at?

PHANISCUS: Are you there? Open! We've come to fetch
our master, Callidamates.

THEOPROPIDES: Hey, you boys, what are you doing there?
What are you banging this house down for?

PINACIUM: What's it got to do with you, old'un?

THEOPROPIDES: Got to do with me?

PINACIUM: You're not a new police-inspector, are you –
sent to watch, listen, spy, and meddle with other folks'
business?

THEOPROPIDES: You've come to the wrong house.

PINACIUM: Eh? Has Philolaches just sold it, then? [*To his
fellow*] The old geezer's having us on.

THEOPROPIDES: I'm perfectly right. What do you want
here, anyway?

PHANISCUS [*very politely*]: I'll tell you, sir. Our master is in
there, drinking.

THEOPROPIDES: Your master? In there, drinking?

PHANISCUS: That is what I said, sir.

THEOPROPIDES: Well, you're a very charming boy, but –

PINACIUM [*brusquely*]: We've come to fetch 'im 'ome.

THEOPROPIDES: Fetch whom?

PINACIUM: Our master. How many times do you want telling?

THEOPROPIDES [*ignoring the rude fellow, to Phaniscus*]: My dear boy, nobody lives here. You seem to be an honest lad, at any rate.

PHANISCUS: Doesn't the young gentleman Philolaches live here?

THEOPROPIDES: He used to live here; but he moved some time ago.

PHANISCUS [*to Pinacium*]: The old man must be crazy. [*To Theopropides*] You're under a misapprehension, father; I'm positive he lives here, unless he left today or yesterday.

THEOPROPIDES: Oh no. Nobody has lived here for the last six months.

PINACIUM: You're dreaming.

THEOPROPIDES: I'm dreaming?

PINACIUM: You are.

THEOPROPIDES: Just keep quiet, please, and let me talk to this boy. No one lives here, my boy.

PHANISCUS: Well, he does. Yesterday and the day before that, and the day before that, four days, five days, six days, ever since his father went abroad, he's never stopped holding drinking parties for as much as three days together.

THEOPROPIDES: What *do* you mean?

PHANISCUS: Never so much as three days gone by, I tell you, but he's been eating and drinking, having women in the house, going it like Greeks – flute-girls, musicians brought in –

THEOPROPIDES: Who has been doing this?

PHANISCUS: Philolaches.

THEOPROPIDES: Which Philolaches are you talking about?

PHANISCUS: His father's name is Theopropides, I believe.

THEOPROPIDES: Gods above, it's the death of me if he's speaking the truth. I must ask him some more questions. ... You say that this Philolaches, whoever he is, is in the habit of drinking in that house, with your master?

PHANISCUS: That's right.

THEOPROPIDES: You're more stupid than you look, my boy. You must have been to some tavern and drunk rather more than was sufficient for you.

PHANISCUS: What!

THEOPROPIDES: Of course, that's it. You've come to the wrong house.

PHANISCUS: I know where I had to come to, and I know the place perfectly well. This is the house of Philolaches, Theopropides' son. And I know that after his father had gone abroad, on business, he brought a singing girl here, and paid for her freedom.

THEOPROPIDES: Philolaches did?

PHANISCUS: He did – a girl named Philematium.

THEOPROPIDES: How much – ?

PHANISCUS: Thirty.

THEOPROPIDES: Talents?

PHANISCUS: God in heaven, no! Minas.

THEOPROPIDES: And he set her free?

PHANISCUS: He set her free all right, for thirty minas.

THEOPROPIDES: Thirty minas – three thousand drachmas – for a girl, sold to Philolaches!

PHANISCUS: That's right.

THEOPROPIDES: And he freed her?

PHANISCUS: That's right.

THEOPROPIDES: And ever since his father went abroad he has been drinking continually with your master?

PHANISCUS: That's right.

THEOPROPIDES: And then he bought this house next door?

PHANISCUS: That's wrong.

THEOPROPIDES: But he gave the owner a deposit of four thousand for it?

PHANISCUS: Wrong again.

THEOPROPIDES: Damnation! I'm ruined!

PHANISCUS: I should say it's that young man that's ruining his father.

THEOPROPIDES: You speak like a true oracle.

PHANISCUS: I'm sorry. I wish it wasn't true. You're a friend of the man's father, perhaps?

THEOPROPIDES: His poor father! It's his death knell you've sounded.

PHANISCUS: After all, three thousand, that's nothing to what he has been spending in luxury and extravagance.

THEOPROPIDES: He has brought his poor father to the grave.

PHANISCUS: There's one servant there, I can tell you, who's the biggest criminal of them all – Tranio; he's the Hercules of money-spenders. But I'm truly sorry for the father; when he gets to know the truth, his poor old heart will burn up in red-hot cinders.

THEOPROPIDES: It will, if it's the truth you're telling me.

PHANISCUS: What reason should I have to lie to you?

PINACIUM [at the door again]: Hey there! Is anyone going to open this door?

PHANISCUS: What's the good of banging at the door when there's no one in? He'll have gone off on the booze somewhere else. Let's go –

THEOPROPIDES: Wait, boy –

PHANISCUS: – and look for him some other place; come on.

THEOPROPIDES: Must you go, boy?

PHANISCUS: You've got your freedom to cover your back; I've got nothing but to look after my master's business and fear his anger.

[*The two slaves depart.*]

THEOPROPIDES: Oh, this is the end of me! There's nothing more to be said. All this tale they tell me makes me feel as if I'd not been to Egypt at all but wandered into some strange outlandish place where I'm utterly lost. But I'll learn the truth now; here comes the man from whom my son bought the house.

[SIMO *comes back from his walk.*]

Ah, Simo; what are you doing now?

SIMO: I'm coming home from town.

THEOPROPIDES: Did you see anything interesting in town?

SIMO: Ay, I did.

THEOPROPIDES: Oh, what?

SIMO: I saw a funeral.

[THEOPROPIDES *groans.*]

SIMO: Yes, that was one interesting thing I saw; a funeral . . . a dead man's funeral . . . they said he'd only just died too.

THEOPROPIDES [*perceiving that he is being mocked*]: Plagues on your head!

SIMO: Have you nothing better to do than ask me what's the news from town?

THEOPROPIDES: I've just arrived home from abroad today, you see.

SIMO: Oh; well, it's no use expecting me to ask you to supper, because I have an engagement –

THEOPROPIDES: I'm not expecting anything of the sort.

SIMO: Tomorrow, though, if I've no other invitations, I'll have supper with you.

THEOPROPIDES: I'm not expecting that either. If you're not too busy at this moment, kindly give me your attention.

SIMO: With the greatest pleasure.

THEOPROPIDES: I understand you have received four thousand drachmas from my son Philolaches?

SIMO: I've never received a penny from him, to my knowledge.

THEOPROPIDES: From his servant Tranio, then.

SIMO: Still less.

THEOPROPIDES: As a deposit.

SIMO: Are you dreaming?

THEOPROPIDES: I am not. You must be, if you think you can pretend this never happened.

SIMO: What are you talking about?

THEOPROPIDES: I'm talking about the deal my son did with you while I was away.

SIMO: Your son did a deal with me while you were away? What about? When?

THEOPROPIDES: It seems I owe you eight thousand altogether.

SIMO: You certainly don't. But give it me, by all means, if you do. Fair's fair, and don't try to get out of it.

THEOPROPIDES: I have no intention of trying to get out of it. I shall pay you; the balance outstanding, that is. Don't attempt to deny that you've had four thousand already.

SIMO: For goodness' sake, look at me, and tell me this: what do you think you owe me four thousand drachmas for?

THEOPROPIDES: I owe it you as the balance of payment for the purchase of your house by my son.

SIMO: Your son bought a house from me? He never did. According to what Tranio told me, you wanted your son to get married and so you were thinking of enlarging *your* house.

THEOPROPIDES: I was? Going to enlarge my house?

SIMO: That's what he said.

THEOPROPIDES: Help! I'm dying! I'm speechless! Oh my dear friend, they're killing me!

SIMO: Is this some of Tranio's mischief?

THEOPROPIDES: It's all his mischief! He's tricked and misled me in the most shameful manner.

SIMO: You don't say so?

THEOPROPIDES: I do say so. He's done nothing but bamboozle me the whole day. For goodness' sake give me your help and attention.

SIMO: What can I do?

THEOPROPIDES: Come along to my house, I beseech you; come with me.

SIMO: Very well.

THEOPROPIDES: And lend me some of your slaves and whips.

SIMO: Come in and take your pick.

THEOPROPIDES: And at the same time I'll tell you of all the wicked tricks that man has played on me. . . .

[*They go into Simo's house.*]

*

[*A few moments later,* TRANIO *emerges from the door of the 'empty' house.*]

TRANIO: A man that's not able to show a brave heart in a tight place is not worth two pins. How much two pins are worth, I really couldn't say. Anyway, after the master had sent me off to the country to find his son, I popped back quietly by the back lane into our garden – the garden door opens into the back lane, you understand – then I opened the house and evacuated all our troops, male and female. Having got the whole battalion safe out of blockade, I convened a conference of my companions in complicity; whereupon they immediately ejected me from the party! Well, I said to myself, if I'm going to be sold in my own shop, the best thing I can do is to do what most other people do when they find themselves in a dangerous and complicated situation – make everything a bit more complicated and never give things a chance to settle down! ... [*On second thoughts*] And yet I don't know ... as far as I can see, there's no hope of keeping the master in the dark indefinitely; and there's no one I can take into my confidence or shift the blame on to. Perhaps I had better take a chance and face up to the master and try to make my peace with him – and the sooner the better. .˙. Hullo, someone coming out of next door. ... It's the master himself. I must hear what he's talking about first.

[THEOPROPIDES *is just coming out with some of Simo's strongest slaves in attendance.*]

THEOPROPIDES: Now then, you men wait here just inside the door, and as soon as I call you, out you come. Clap the handcuffs on the villain promptly. I'll waylay my joker outside the door, and then I'll give him something to laugh about, upon my life I will!

TRANIO: So the cat *is* out of the bag. Now it's up to you, Tranio.

THEOPROPIDES [*wily*]: I'm going to handle him carefully and artfully when he comes. I'm not going to show him the hook straight away; I shall pay out the line a little first. I'll pretend I know nothing of the truth yet.

TRANIO: The wicked old sinner! Crafty as any man in Athens, ain't he? No one's going to get round him – oh no; he's as tough as a stone. Well, here goes. ... [*He approaches the master.*]

THEOPROPIDES: Now I'm ready for him. ...

TRANIO: Were you looking for me, sir? I'm here at your service.

THEOPROPIDES: Ah, Tranio! Good! Did you manage all right?

TRANIO: Yes, sir; the family are back home from the country. Philolaches should be here very shortly.

THEOPROPIDES: You've got back just in the nick of time. I'm afraid our neighbour here is a thorough scoundrel.

TRANIO: Really sir? Why?

THEOPROPIDES: He says he knows nothing about you –

TRANIO: Nothing – ?

THEOPROPIDES: And denies that you ever gave him money.

TRANIO: Go on! You're joking. I bet he doesn't deny it.

THEOPROPIDES: What do you think – ?

TRANIO: I don't think, I know – I know you're pulling my leg now. He can't possibly deny it.

THEOPROPIDES: Gods above! I tell you he does deny it. And denies that he ever sold the house to Philolaches.

TRANIO: Hah! And I suppose he denies having taken a deposit for it?

THEOPROPIDES: He has undertaken to swear on oath, if I wish, that he never sold the house and never received any money for it.

TRANIO: We can bring witnesses.

THEOPROPIDES: That's what I told him.

TRANIO: What does he say?

THEOPROPIDES: He offers to let me interrogate his slaves under torture.

TRANIO: Don't you believe it; he never will.

THEOPROPIDES: Oh yes, he will.

TRANIO: I'll go and have it out with him.

THEOPROPIDES: No, wait. Perhaps I had better try the slaves first.

TRANIO: No perhaps about it. Just let me get at one of them.

THEOPROPIDES: Shall I have them brought out here?

TRANIO: The sooner the better. Or let me sue him for possession of the house.

THEOPROPIDES: No, I'll have the slaves questioned first.

TRANIO: You do that. I'll go and sit by this altar meanwhile.

[*He places himself, for sanctuary, at the altar in front of the stage.*]

THEOPROPIDES: What are you doing that for?

TRANIO: Ah, you don't know these people. If they're handed over for torture, they might try to take sanctuary here. I'll keep guard for you here, to make sure nothing goes wrong with the interrogation. [*He sits at the altar.*]

THEOPROPIDES: Get up, you silly fellow.

TRANIO: Oh no.

THEOPROPIDES: I forbid you to sit at the altar.

TRANIO: Why shouldn't I?

THEOPROPIDES [*conspiratorially*]: Don't you see? That's the one thing I want – that they should try to take sanctuary there? Obviously, it will make it all the easier for me to prove my case about the money, when I bring it into court.

TRANIO: You'd better do one thing at a time. Why give yourself extra trouble? Getting a case through the courts is no easy matter.

THEOPROPIDES: Come here a minute, anyway. I want your advice on one point.

TRANIO: I'll advise you from here. I can think better sitting down. And advice is all the better when it comes from holy ground.

THEOPROPIDES: Oh get up, and stop playing about. Look at me.

TRANIO: I'm looking.

THEOPROPIDES: You can see me, can you?

TRANIO: I can see you. If there were anyone between us, he'd die of starvation.

THEOPROPIDES: What do you mean?

TRANIO: Because he wouldn't get any change out of either of us. We're both as hard as nails.

THEOPROPIDES [*changing his tone*]: Tranio, this is the end!

TRANIO: What – what's the matter, sir?

THEOPROPIDES: You've fooled me –

TRANIO: How, sir?

THEOPROPIDES: You've fooled me properly, haven't you? You've wiped my nose –

TRANIO: And done it properly, I hope. You're not still dribbling, are you?

THEOPROPIDES: You've wiped all the brains out of my skull! I know! I have uncovered all your rascality to the very roots, ay, to the bottomless depths.

TRANIO: Me? I haven't done –

THEOPROPIDES: It's the fire and faggots for you now, carrion!

TRANIO: I wouldn't advise that; I taste better boiled than roast.

THEOPROPIDES: I'll make an example of you, may I die if I don't.

TRANIO: Do I set such a good example, that you want to –

THEOPROPIDES: Tell me this: what sort of a son did I leave behind me when I went away?

TRANIO: The usual sort, with feet, hands, fingers, ears, eyes, lips. . . .

THEOPROPIDES: That's not what I'm asking.

TRANIO: It's what I'm answering . . . But stay! Who comes here? Your son's friend, Callidamates. We can continue our argument with a witness – if you have any more to say.

[CALLIDAMATES *arrives, now fresh and alert; he has a word with the audience first.*]

CALLIDAMATES: I've had a good sleep and woken up sober. Philolaches has told me how his father has come home from abroad, and how his slave welcomed him with a little practical joking. Now he says he's afraid to come and meet his father. So he has appointed me as his best friend to be his spokesman and try to make his peace with the old man. Here he is too. . . . Theopropides, I hope you're well. I'm delighted to see you safe home from your travels. You must come and have supper with me tonight, do.

THEOPROPIDES: I thank you, no; but may the gods bless you, Callidamates.

CALLIDAMATES: You won't come? Oh, I am sorry.

TRANIO: Go on, say you will. If you don't want to, I'll go instead of you.

THEOPROPIDES: More of your jokes, rope's-end?

TRANIO: Can't I say I'd like to go to supper in your place?

THEOPROPIDES: You're not going to supper anywhere. I'll see you're taken off to a cross; that's all you deserve.

CALLIDAMATES [to Theopropides]: Never mind him, sir; you come and have supper with me.

TRANIO: Go on, say you will; why don't you?

CALLIDAMATES [to Tranio]: And what are you doing at that altar?

TRANIO: Someone who has just arrived set on me in his ignorance and frightened me. [To Theopropides] Now sir, will you tell him what I'm supposed to have done; we've got an umpire now, so let's have the debate.

THEOPROPIDES: Very well. I say you have led my son astray.

TRANIO: And this is what I say. I agree he has done wrong; I agree he bought a girl while you were away; I agree he borrowed money; and I can tell you he spent every penny of it. Has he done anything that isn't done in all the best families?

THEOPROPIDES: You're an astute advocate, my word you are. I shall have to be careful.

CALLIDAMATES: Well, it is for me to give judgement.

THEOPROPIDES: Yes, give us your verdict.

CALLIDAMATES [to Tranio]: Up you get, and let me sit in your place.

TRANIO: There's a catch in it, I expect. Can you promise that I have nothing to fear and that if you take my place you'll do the fearing in my place?

THEOPROPIDES: I'm already treating you a good deal more lightly than your impudence deserves.

TRANIO: A good thing too; I'm very glad you are; I like to see a greybeard showing the sense fitting for his age.

THEOPROPIDES: What I *am* to do with you, I don't know.

TRANIO: Tell you what – if you happen to know the comic writers, Diphilus or Philemon, you might give them the story of how your slave put it across you; you'd be giving them the finest plot of cross-purposes ever seen on the stage.

CALLIDAMATES: Just keep quiet a minute, will you. It's my turn to speak. Listen.

THEOPROPIDES: Say on, sir.

CALLIDAMATES: You know I am your son's best friend. He came to me for help, because he was ashamed to meet you, after the things he has done, which he knows you know he has done. Now I want to ask you, to entreat you, to pardon his youth and folly. He is your son; you must know that boys will be boys. Whatever he has done, I have been his abettor. I am to blame. The money he owes, principal and interest, the money he spent on his girl – I will pay it back; I'll find it out of my own pocket; you needn't lose a penny.

THEOPROPIDES: He couldn't have had a better advocate than you. Well, I won't be hard on him; I won't be angry. In fact, he can go on, now I'm here, as he did when I was away, with his girls, his drinking, and whatever he likes. As long as he is sorry for having wasted all that money, I'm satisfied.

CALLIDAMATES: Oh, he's very sorry.

TRANIO: So he's forgiven. What about me?

THEOPROPIDES: You, clod, you're to be hung and flogged.

TRANIO: Even if I say I'm sorry?

THEOPROPIDES: I'll see you dead first, as I live.

CALLIDAMATES: No, sir; pardon one and pardon all. Forgive Tranio his misdeeds, for my sake.

THEOPROPIDES: I'd rather grant you anything than let him escape a criminal's punishment for his criminal offences.

CALLIDAMATES: No; release him, please.

THEOPROPIDES [*as* TRANIO *makes unrepentant signs of joy*]: Look at the scoundrel – impudent to the last!

CALLIDAMATES: Stop it, Tranio, if you've any sense.

THEOPROPIDES: If you would stop asking me this favour, I'd soon stop his nonsense with a cudgel.

TRANIO: Don't trouble, sir.

CALLIDAMATES: Come, let me persuade you.

THEOPROPIDES: I don't want to hear any more.

CALLIDAMATES: For the gods' sake, I beg you.

THEOPROPIDES: I don't want to hear you, I say.

CALLIDAMATES: You cannot resist. Forgive him – just this once – please, as a favour to me.

TRANIO: You needn't worry, sir; I'm sure to do something wrong tomorrow; then you can punish me for both crimes at once.

CALLIDAMATES: Won't you say yes, sir?

THEOPROPIDES [*after a struggle*]: Ah, go on with you, then. Go away. You're pardoned. Go away – and this is the man you have to thank. . . .

   [*To the audience*]

           Spectators, there our story ends.
           Give us your hands, and be our friends.

                    EXEUNT

The Rope

(RUDENS)

INTRODUCTORY NOTE TO
THE ROPE

THERE is little evidence on which to assign any definite dates
to the plays of Plautus, and only an approximate chronological
order can be deduced from the comparison of their several
styles and subjects. The last line of the prologue of *Rudens* has
been supposed to date the play to a critical period in the
second Punic War, say about 211 B.C., but it need hardly have
any such precise reference. What is more evident is that this
play represents the height of the author's experience and
accomplishment, in the shaping and integration of plot, full-
ness of character-drawing, and diverting vivacity of dialogue.
Its difference in setting and atmosphere from all the 'street-
scene' plays, if not merely due to a lucky find among the
scripts of the Greek originator, must be credited to Plautus's
desire to experiment with a larger canvas and more varied
incidents. The play of Diphilus was apparently called *The
Handbag*; Plautus's habit of re-naming his adaptations is
perhaps an additional pointer to his free treatment of the
original; the *rope* is not so important a property in the play as
the *trunk*, or *portmanteau*, but its use as a title aptly focuses
attention on the crucial tug-of-war scene, as well as carrying
a smack of fishy and briny atmosphere. (The alternative
theory that '*rudens*' means 'howler', i.e. 'the storm', is hardly
supported by the known use of the word.)

The occasional use of verse in this translation is only a faint
reflection of the lyrical variety of the Latin. Readers who
would like to compare it with a fully 'operatic' version will
find one in F. A. Wright's translation (Broadway Transla-
tions, Routledge).

CHARACTERS

ARCTURUS	as Prologue
DAEMONES	an elderly Athenian, living in a cottage on the coast near Cyrene
SCEPARNIO	his slave, a burly ruffian who treats his master as an equal
GRIPUS	another slave, chiefly employed in fishing
PALAESTRA	daughter of Daemones, but long ago stolen by pirates and sold to a procurer
AMPELISCA	friend of Palaestra and in similar misfortune
PLESIDIPPUS	a young man of Cyrene, Athenian by birth
TRACHALIO	an ingenious rogue, slave of Plesidippus
LABRAX	a procurer
CHARMIDES	his friend
PTOLEMOCRATIA	an old woman, priestess and caretaker of a seaside shrine of Venus

Fishermen
Friends of Plesidippus
Other slaves of Daemones

*

The scene is the rocky coast near Cyrene, and comprises rough ground above the shore, the cottage of Daemones and a shrine of Venus. There is also an altar of Venus at the front of the stage

THE ROPE

[*In the hour before dawn, after a tempestuous night,* ARCTURUS *appears, as Prologue.*]

ARCTURUS:

In the great commonwealth of gods in heaven
I dwell, a fellow citizen of him
Who rules all men, all earth, all sea below.
You see me as I am, a bright white star,
Rising at my appointed time, in heaven,
And upon earth. Arcturus is my name.
By night, a god, a bright star in the sky –
By day, a mortal, walking among men,
As other constellations do, descending
To your world. For the lord of gods and men,
Great Jupiter, appoints us as his spies,
One here, one there, in various different places,
To watch how men behave, observe their acts,
Their characters, keep records of their piety
And virtue, so that he, through Fortune's hand,
May suitably reward this man or that.
Say a man brings false witness to obtain
False judgement, or denies a debt of honour,
We note his name and send it up to Jove.
From day to day, from hour to hour, Jove knows
Who's heading for trouble: a perjurer, perhaps,
Perverting justice, a deceitful claimant,
Will find his case re-tried by Jupiter
And, if found guilty, suffer penalties
Far greater than the gain he falsely won.

Such criminals, we know, persuade themselves
That by sufficient gifts and sacrifices
They can placate the wrath of Jove. They cannot;
They spend their labour and their wealth in vain.
No perjurer's prayer touches the ear of Jove.
To the repentant sinner's supplication
The court of heaven may be merciful;
There is no mercy for the hard of heart.
Therefore I charge all men of good intent,
Of blameless life and faithful piety:
Continue in your honest ways, be steadfast,
And earn the blessing that your deeds deserve.

Now to my purpose – and our *Argument*:
We are in Cyrene (since our author, Diphilus,
Will have it so). And here lives one Daemones,
In a country cottage by the sea – an exile
Here, in the evening of his life, from Athens.
He did no wrong; it was no fault of his
That drove him from his homeland; on the contrary
His difficulties were due to his good nature;
He lost a fortune by his generosity.
He also lost a little daughter; she
Was bought from a pirate by a wicked man,
A trafficker in women, who brought her here
To use her. So, one day, a young Athenian
(A fellow countryman of this Daemones)
Happened to see her coming out of school –
The music school – and fell in love with her.
He made an application to her owner,
With a view to purchase; the price was thirty minas.
He paid a deposit, the contract was signed and sealed.
However, the pimp, true to his trade, defaulted,

Repudiated his oath and all he had promised.
He had a friend, a bird of his own feather,
A rascally old Sicilian, banished for treason
From Agrigentum. This man, singing the praises
Of the Grecian girl, and the other attractive women
In the pimp's employ, persuaded him to move
To Sicily, where – he said – the pleasure-market
Was profitable and fortunes could be made
From brothel-keeping. And the pimp agreed.
They chartered a private ship, put all their goods
On board by night, the pimp having told the youth
(To whom he'd sold the girl) he was only going
As far as the temple of Venus (this one here)
To pay his vows – and even invited him
To meet him there for lunch. Then off he went
With all his girls on board. The young man heard
From other people that the bird had flown,
And down to the port he comes, to see the ship
Heading for open sea. I came to the rescue.
Seeing this innocent maiden being abducted,
I decided to help her, and destroy the pimp.
So what did I do? I raised a mighty storm
To trouble the waters. Am not I Arcturus? –
Most formidable of all the constellations,
Stormy at my ascent, and at my setting
More stormy still. The ship was smashed to pieces,
The pimp and his accomplice cast aground
On a reef of rock. The girl, and a companion,
Take to the lifeboat, frightened for their lives.
But they are safe . . . a wave has swung them off
The dangerous rock and carried them to shore
Close by the cottage where the kind old man,
The exile, lives. He's suffered too; the wind

Has blown off all his slates . . . and yes . . . here comes
The old man's slave, Sceparnio. . . . Next you will see
The young man coming along, the youth who bought
The girl from the pimp. . . .

　　　　　　　　Now I must go. . . .
　　　　　　　　Good-bye,
Keep well, and let your enemies tremble.

[*He disappears, as the play has already begun with the
entrance of* SCEPARNIO, *who comes from the cottage carrying a spade and surveying the damage of the night's storm.*]

SCEPARNIO: Ye everlasting gods! Neptune surely sent us
a fine old hurricane last night. Pretty well stripped the roof
off. Talk about storms! I haven't seen one like this since
that one in Euripides' play, *Alcmena*. Not a tile left on that
roof. Makes it lighter anyway, with all those extra windows!

[*He moves a little further off, looking for a place to dig for
clay.*

PLESIDIPPUS *comes along, with three friends.*]

PLESIDIPPUS: Well, I'm sorry, friends. I've taken you from
your business all for nothing, and never caught that pimp-
ing rascal at the harbour after all. Still, I thought it worth
trying, or I shouldn't have kept you all this time. I'm going
to have a look at this shrine of Venus, where he said he was
going to say his prayers.

SCEPARNIO: I'd better get digging up some of this god-
damned clay.

PLESIDIPPUS: Who's that?

[DAEMONES *comes out of the cottage.*]

DAEMONES: Hey there, Sceparnio!

SCEPARNIO: Who wants me?

DAEMONES: Your owner. Who did you think it would be?

SCEPARNIO: Your slave, am I?

DAEMONES: Well, I paid good money for you. We shall

need lots of clay; dig right down. As far as I can see, we shall have to do the whole roof over. It's about as much use as a sieve at present.

PLESIDIPPUS: Good morning, father; good morning to you both.

DAEMONES: Good morning to you.

SCEPARNIO: Father you call him? What are you, his son – or daughter?

PLESIDIPPUS: I'm certainly not his daughter, damn you.

SCEPARNIO: He's certainly not your father, sonny.

DAEMONES: I had a little daughter once, sir, but I lost her. I never had a son.

PLESIDIPPUS: The gods will give you one.

SCEPARNIO: They'll give you something, I hope – coming here bothering busy people with your chatter.

PLESIDIPPUS [to Daemones]: Do you live in this place?

SCEPARNIO: What's that to you? Having a look round, are you, to see if it's worth cracking?

PLESIDIPPUS: Your slave must be very valuable to you, sir, or else have independent means, to be so free of his tongue to a gentleman in his master's presence.

SCEPARNIO: Your friend must have very bad manners and think a lot of himself, to come creating a nuisance at another man's house where he has no business.

DAEMONES: That's enough, Sceparnio. . . . What can I do for you, young man?

PLESIDIPPUS: You might do something for that man of yours, who is so anxious to do all the talking when his master is present. I should like some information, sir, if it would not be troubling you too much.

DAEMONES: I am busy, but what is it?

SCEPARNIO: You could be busy going down to the swamp and cut some reeds for thatching, while it's fine.

DAEMONES: Shut up, Sceparnio. What is it, sir?

PLESIDIPPUS: Do you happen to have seen an old fellow, grey curly hair, wicked slimy-looking rascal –

DAEMONES: Often enough. Rogues of that sort have brought me where I am now.

PLESIDIPPUS: I mean, have you seen one hereabouts, bringing two girls to the shrine of Venus, making as if to pay an offering here – yesterday or today?

DAEMONES: No, I'm sure I haven't, my boy; no one has been there with offerings for some time now. If there had been anyone I should have seen them, I don't doubt. They are always coming to my place for water, or a light, or knives, pots, and frying-pans, one thing or another. They seem to think I've set up house for Venus and not for myself. However, there hasn't been anyone for several days lately.

PLESIDIPPUS: Oh dear, then there's no hope for me.

DAEMONES: There's nothing for you to fear here, I'll answer for that.

SCEPARNIO: If you were expecting a meal up yonder, you'd much better send word you'll be home for dinner.

DAEMONES: Is that it? You've been asked here to a meal and your host hasn't turned up?

PLESIDIPPUS: Something like that.

SCEPARNIO: There's nothing to stop you going home again hungry. It's Ceres you ought to be chasing, not Venus. Venus for love, Ceres for food.

PLESIDIPPUS: Cheeky devil.

DAEMONES [*looking towards the sea*]: Good gods, Sceparnio, what's that? Some men in the water near the shore.

SCEPARNIO: Guests coming to someone's farewell party, I expect.

DAEMONES: What do you mean?

SCEPARNIO: They look as if they've had a good wash over-
night.

DAEMONES: They've been shipwrecked.

SCEPARNIO: That's right. And we've been housewrecked.

DAEMONES [*still watching the sea*]: They're making a good
fight for it, though, poor devils; swimming to land as best
they can.

PLESIDIPPUS: Where? Where are they?

DAEMONES: There, to the right, quite close to shore now.

PLESIDIPPUS: Oh yes. Come on, boys! If that's the bastard
I'm looking for – Good-bye, sir – Take care of yourselves –
[*He and his friends dash unceremoniously off.*]

SCEPARNIO: We will, don't worry. [*Now taking more interest
in the swimmers*] Holy gods! What do I see? [*Looking in a
slightly different direction than before.*]

DAEMONES: What do you see?

SCEPARNIO: Two lasses, in a boat, all on their own; having a
rough time too, poor kids. ... Hey! ... Wow! that was
good. A wave just swept the boat away from the rocks
towards the beach. No pilot could have done it better. ...
By gow, I don't think I ever saw a bigger sea. If they can
get through those breakers they're all right. ... Now then,
this is the tricky part. ... One's overboard! ... It's not
deep, though ... she'll make it. Did you see her fall overboard? ... Good girl, she's up, on her feet ... she's coming
... all's well. What's the other one doing? ... She's jumped
ashore ... looks a bit scared ... fell on her knees in the
water. She's all right, though; she's out, on dry land. ...
Hey, what's she going that way for, damn it? Oh dear,
she'll get lost that way.

DAEMONES [*no longer interested*]: What if she does?

SCEPARNIO [*still watching*]: She won't have far to walk if she
falls off that rock she's making for.

DAEMONES: If you're expecting them to give you dinner, you can stay and look after them. If not, I should be glad of your services.

SCEPARNIO: Quite right, sir.

DAEMONES: Come along, then.

SCEPARNIO: I'm coming.

[*They go into the cottage.*

   PALAESTRA *appears, clambering over the rocks, wet and exhausted. She sinks down to rest and recover her spirits.*]

PALAESTRA:

   The tales you hear of other folk's misfortunes
   Are nothing to what you suffer. What have I done
   That the gods should treat me thus? Cast me ashore
   Like this in an unknown country? Oh poor me,
   Is this what I was born for? What a reward
   For my good life! Have I ever been undutiful
   To gods or parents? If so, then I deserve it,
   And I can bear it. Have I not been as careful
   As anyone could be, never to offend them?
   Then what a cruel, wicked, and unjust
   Thing you have done to me, gods. If this is the way
   You treat the innocent, how will the guilty learn?
      If I knew of any wrong I or my parents
   Had ever done, I would not pity myself.
   It is my master, the wicked things he has done,
   That have brought this misery upon my head.
   His ship and all that he owned are sunk in the waves.
   I am all that he has left. The other girl
   Is gone, lost; and I am all alone.
   If only she were safe, it would be some comfort.
   Now there's no hope, no help, no one to turn to. . . .
      All alone . . . in this lonely desolate place. . . .
   Rocks, and the sea . . . no one will ever find me.

T – P – D

I've nothing, but these clothes; no food, no shelter,
No hope . . . oh, what have I got to live for?
Where shall I go? I've never seen this place,
Never set foot on it before. There's no one
To show me where to find a road or path.
I don't know where to go . . . this way, or that way? . . .
      I see no sign of cultivation here. . . .
I don't know where I am . . . I'm cold . . . I'm frightened.
Oh father and mother, if you only knew
Where your poor daughter is, and what she suffers.
If this is I, your daughter born in freedom,
I might as well have been a slave; such sorrow,
Nothing but sorrow, have I brought you. . . .
      [*She lies silent and despairing.*
      From another direction AMPELISCA *appears, in similar*
      distress, but in rather better spirits.]

AMPELISCA: I want to die. Really I might as well sit down
   and die. What have I got to live for? I'm frightened to
   death in this terrible place. Every hope I had is gone. I've
   been everywhere round about, into every nook and cranny
   to find my friend, searching and shouting for her. I can't
   find her anywhere, and I don't know where else to look.
   I haven't seen a person I could ask where to go and where to
   look for her. It's like a desert, I've never seen a place so
   deserted. Well, if she's still alive, I'll not stop looking for
   her as long as I am.

PALAESTRA: Was that a voice?

AMPELISCA: Surely I heard someone.

PALAESTRA: Help me, good hope! Give me some comfort.

AMPELISCA: A woman's voice, surely.

PALAESTRA: It was. A woman. Is it Ampelisca?

AMPELISCA: Is it Palaestra?

PALAESTRA: I'll call; she may hear me. Ampelisca!

AMPELISCA: Who's there?

PALAESTRA: I, Palaestra.

AMPELISCA: Where are you?

PALAESTRA: In terrible trouble.

AMPELISCA: So am I, just as badly. I'm trying to find you.

PALAESTRA: So am I.

AMPELISCA: Let's follow our voices. Where are you?

PALAESTRA: I'm here. Come this way.

AMPELISCA: I'm trying to.

  [*Round the edge of a rock, at last they meet!*]

PALAESTRA: Catch my hand.

AMPELISCA: Here you are.

PALAESTRA: Ampelisca! Are you really alive?

AMPELISCA: Palaestra! Oh now I can touch you I really want to live again. I can hardly believe it. Oh hug me, my darling. Oh now I am happy again.

PALAESTRA: Just what I want to say. Come on, we must get away from here.

AMPELISCA: But where to, for goodness' sake?

PALAESTRA: We'll follow the beach.

AMPELISCA: Wherever you like. If we can walk in these wet clothes.

PALAESTRA: We must do the best we can.

  [*They move across the scene.*]

  Whatever is that?

AMPELISCA: What?

PALAESTRA: Look, that shrine there. On your right.

AMPELISCA: It looks like some holy place.

PALAESTRA: There must be people not far away, with a pretty place like that. God, whoever you are, help two helpless women and bring us out of our misery!

[*The priestess* PTOLEMOCRATIA *appears at the door of the temple.*]

PTOLEMOCRATIA [*mumbling a customary greeting*]: Do I hear suppliants at my Lady's door? Here they will find a goddess kind and gracious, before whom they need feel no fear.

PALAESTRA: Our reverence to you, holy mother.

PTOLEMOCRATIA: You are welcome. [*Becoming more human*] But, dear girls, wherever do you come from, your clothes so wet and ragged?

PALAESTRA: We've come from the beach close by, but that is a long way from where our journey started.

PTOLEMOCRATIA: You have travelled the blue roads on wooden horses?

PALAESTRA: Ay, yes.

PTOLEMOCRATIA: This is no state in which to approach the shrine, you know. Where are your white garments and thank-offerings?

PALAESTRA: Where indeed would we find offerings to bring you, two castaways just washed up on your shore? For mercy's sake, at your knees, we beseech you – we don't know where we are or what will become of us – give us shelter and protect us and take pity on us – we are homeless and helpless – we have nothing in the world but what you see.

PTOLEMOCRATIA: Give me your hands. Stand up, both of you. You will find no one more compassionate than me. But I've little enough of my own; a bare living, and that spent in the service of Venus.

AMPELISCA: Venus? Is this her temple?

PTOLEMOCRATIA: It is. And I have the honour to be her priestess. I'll do what I can for you, with the little I have. Come this way.

PALAESTRA: It is kind of you to receive us so, holy mother.
PTOLEMOCRATIA: One cannot do less.
  [*She takes them into the temple.*]

*

  [*A group of fishermen come up from the sea, singing snatches
  of song and interjecting remarks.*]
FISHERMEN:
            A poor man's life is a sad man's life
                If little he earns
                By the little he learns
            Yet he learns to be content . . .

  – Well, we don't look like millionaires, do we?

            A fisherman's tackle is all his trade
                His living he gets
                With his rods and his nets
            So it's down to the sea in the morning, boys . . .

  – That's right. No city life for us, no gymnasium clubs or
  sports grounds to exercise *our* muscles –

            Cockles and mussels and whelks and snails
                Scallops and urchins and
                Squids and skates
            We fish for our food in the sea, boys . . .

  – By hook or by . . . hand –

            If we don't get a haul or catch nothing at all
                We get a good dip
                In the briny-o
            Then home to no supper and bed, boys . . .

– It'll be no supper tonight, lad, with this sea running; unless a cockle or two –

– Well, let's go and pay our respects to Venus, and ask her to do her best for us.

[*As they move towards the temple,* TRACHALIO, *the slave of Plesidippus, comes along from the town.*]

TRACHALIO: I don't know where my master has got to. I've kept a look-out for him everywhere. When he left the house he said he was going to the harbour, and told me to meet him at the shrine here. ... Oh, there's somebody ... perhaps they can tell me ... I'll go and ask them. Hey, pirates, musselmen, hookbaiters, starvation-dieters! How are you doing? Perishing?

FISHERMAN: Of hunger and thirst, thank ye. What do you expect fishermen to do?

TRACHALIO: Have you seen a young fellow along this way – strong ruddy energetic-looking chap, and three others with him, toffs with cloaks and swords and all that?

FISHERMAN: Haven't seen anyone of that sort round here.

TRACHALIO: Or a pot-bellied old Silenus, bald head, beefy, bushy eyebrows, scowling, twister, god-forsaken criminal, master of all vice and villainy – and two pretty little females with him?

FISHERMAN: With all those accomplishments and qualifications he ought to be on his way to a gallows, not Venus's temple.

TRACHALIO: But have you seen him?

FISHERMAN: Not seen anybody, mate. So long.

[*They go.*]

TRACHALIO: So long to you. ... I thought so; I knew it; the master's been done in the eye; the old ponce has done a bunk; gone aboard and taken the girls with him. I foresaw it. I'm a foreseer. And the beggar invited master to meet

him here for a meal, the dirty double-crosser. Well, the
only thing to do is to wait here till he comes. I might ask
the priestess, though, if I see her. She may know something.
Yes, I'll ask her. She'll tell me.

[AMPELISCA *comes out of the temple, carrying an empty
pitcher*.]

AMPELISCA [*at the door, speaking back to someone within*]: Yes,
I will . . . knock at the door of that cottage over there and
ask for some water. . . . I understand. . . .

TRACHALIO: Surely I heard a voice?

AMPELISCA: Somebody here! . . . Who is it?

TRACHALIO: Is it Ampelisca, coming out of the shrine?

AMPELISCA: Is it Trachalio, Plesidippus's man?

TRACHALIO: It is.

AMPELISCA: It is! Trachalio!

TRACHALIO: Ampelisca! What are you doing here?

AMPELISCA: Not enjoying myself as much as a young girl
should.

TRACHALIO: Don't say that; you'll bring bad luck.

AMPELISCA: Nothing wrong with telling the truth, is there?
Where is your master Plesidippus?

TRACHALIO: Ha, where? In there [*the shrine*], I presume.

AMPELISCA: He certainly is not. No one has been here.

TRACHALIO: He hasn't come, then?

AMPELISCA: That is the truth, Trachalio.

TRACHALIO: Though I say it! How soon will dinner be
ready?

AMPELISCA: What dinner, for heaven's sake?

TRACHALIO: You're holding a celebration here, aren't
you?

AMPELISCA: Are you dreaming?

TRACHALIO: I know your owner, Labrax, asked my master
to meet him here for a meal.

AMPELISCA: I wouldn't be at all surprised. Double-crossing gods and men is just in that old pimp's line.

TRACHALIO: Then you're not offering a sacrament here, you and my master?

AMPELISCA: True again. You're as good as a soothsayer, Trachalio.

TRACHALIO: What are you doing, then?

AMPELISCA: It was this priestess here that took pity on us when we were in terrible trouble and danger; nearly dying we were, me and Palaestra.

TRACHALIO: Palaestra is here? My master's girl?

AMPELISCA: That's right.

TRACHALIO: Well, well, that's wonderful news, Ampelisca. Tell us all about this danger you were in.

AMPELISCA: Oh Trachalio, our ship was wrecked, last night.

TRACHALIO: Ship? What ship? What are you talking about?

AMPELISCA: Well, goodness, didn't you know how the old wretch tried to smuggle us off to Sicily, and put all his belongings on a ship? Now he's lost the lot.

TRACHALIO: Congratulations, Neptune! You win the jackpot. Nice work; just what the lying old sinner deserved. Where is he now, then?

AMPELISCA: Soaked to death, I should think. Neptune was free with his liquor last night.

TRACHALIO: I bet he was, and no heeltaps. Oh Ampelisca, my darling honey-love, your words are like sugar. But how did you and Palaestra escape drowning?

AMPELISCA: I'll tell you. We jumped into the boat, frightened to death, when we saw the ship being driven on to the rocks. I got the rope untied as quick as I could, while all the other passengers were in a panic, and we were carried away in our boat, away from everybody else. Then we had a terrible night of it, wind and waves like I don't know what. And at last we were carried up on the shore this morning half dead.

TRACHALIO: Trust old Neptune, like a keen customs officer, to throw any *dubious baggage* overboard.

AMPELISCA [*piqued, but playfully*]: Damn your eyes, Trachalio.

TRACHALIO: And yours, my darling. I knew this would happen. I knew what the old pimp would do. I said it. I shall have to let my hair grow long and set up as a fortuneteller.

AMPELISCA: You and your master didn't do much to stop him getting away, then?

TRACHALIO: What could he do?

AMPELISCA: What could he do? And he supposed to be her lover? He ought to have kept his eye on her night and day. It doesn't say much for what he thinks of her.

TRACHALIO: I don't see that.

AMPELISCA: Well, it's obvious.

TRACHALIO: Ay, but you see – say a chap goes to the baths, he keeps a sharp look-out for his clothes, he gets them stolen just the same. And why? Because he doesn't know which man to watch. But the thief can easily spot the man who's trying to watch out for *him*. The man on his guard doesn't know which is the thief, see? Come on, take me to her.

AMPELISCA: She's in that temple; just go in and you'll see her sitting there crying her eyes out.

TRACHALIO: Oh dear, I am sorry. What's she crying for?

AMPELISCA: She's in despair, you see, because our master took away a little box she had, in which she kept the things that would help to make her known to her parents. She's afraid it's lost for ever.

TRACHALIO: Where was the box?

AMPELISCA: In the ship with us. The old man locked it up in his trunk so that she would never find her parents.

TRACHALIO: Dirty swine. Trying to make a slave out of a free girl.

AMPELISCA: Now I suppose it will be at the bottom of the sea with the ship. All the old devil's gold and silver is there too.

TRACHALIO: Someone will have dived down and fetched it up by now, I expect.

AMPELISCA: So that's why she's so miserable, poor girl, having lost all those things.

TRACHALIO: Ah well, all the more reason I should go in and cheer her up, before she dies of despair. Every cloud has a silver lining, is my motto.

AMPELISCA: There's many a slip, is mine.

TRACHALIO: Very well then – a brave heart is the best sauce for sadness. I'll go in, then, shall I? Unless you want anything else.

AMPELISCA: Go on.

[*He goes into the temple.*]

AMPELISCA: I must go and get this water, like the priestess said. She said they'd give it me, if I said it was for her. She's a nice old lady, I will say. I've never seen a nicer. I'm sure she deserves all the best of heaven and earth. She took us in so kindly and hospitably and willingly when she saw us poor miserable dripping half-dead castaways; never made a grumble, but took us in as if we were her own children. And then tucking up her skirts to get our baths ready! . . . She'll be waiting; I must get the water, as she said. [*She goes to the cottage door.*] Anyone in? . . . Can I come in? . . . Anyone there?

[SCEPARNIO *comes out.*]

SCEPARNIO: Now then, who's knocking our door to pieces?

AMPELISCA: Oh, it was me.

SCEPARNIO: Well!! What a bit of luck! A woman, and a pretty one, by God!

AMPELISCA: Good morning, young man.

SCEPARNIO: Good morning to you, young lady.

AMPELISCA: I've come –

SCEPARNIO: Come again this evening and you'll be right welcome. Morning's not much good. Eh, what do you say, pretty beauty?

AMPELISCA: Not so free with your hands, if you please.

SCEPARNIO: The very image of Venus, by all the gods. What a twinkle in her eye, what a shape, what a nice rusty – no, russet – brown skin, what pretty paps, what luscious lips –

AMPELISCA: Take your hands off me. I'm not public property.

SCEPARNIO: Nothing wrong with a nice little cuddle with a nice little girl, is there? ·

AMPELISCA: We'll see about that, when I've time to spare for fun and games. Now will you please tell me whether you can or can not give me what I came for?

SCEPARNIO: What did you come for?

AMPELISCA [*indicating her jug*]: If you have eyes you can see what I want.

SCEPARNIO: If *you* have eyes you can see what *I* want.

AMPELISCA: The priestess of Venus here sent me to ask you for some water.

SCEPARNIO: Ah well, I'm the priest in charge here. You'll have to ask me nicely or you won't get a drop. Besides, we dug that well at our own expense, and with our own tools, I may tell you. Go on, say your prayers nicely or you can't have a drop of our water.

AMPELISCA: Do you grudge me a little water? Can't you give me what even enemies give to enemies?

SCEPARNIO: Can't you give me what friends give to friends?

AMPELISCA: Oh all right, honey, I'll do anything you want.

SCEPARNIO: Yippee! I'm in luck. Honey she calls me. You shall have your water, love. I don't expect nothing for nothing. Give us your jug.

AMPELISCA: There you are. As quick as you can, please.

SCEPARNIO: Wait here. I'll be back in a jiffy, honey. [*He goes in.*]

AMPELISCA: The old woman will be thinking I'm taking a long time. What shall I tell her? . . . Oh that sea, it gives me the horrors. But what's that? Oh my goodness, what do I see down on the shore there? My master, the old pimp, and his Sicilian friend. Oh dear, I thought they were both drowned. More trouble, and just when we thought we were safe. I must run and tell Palaestra, and we must take refuge at the altar before the wicked old devil comes and catches us here. There's not a minute to lose. [*She runs into the temple.*]

[*SCEPARNIO comes out of the cottage with the water.*]

SCEPARNIO: Oh ye immortal gods, what a wonderful thing is water. I never knew I could love it so much. It was a pleasure to draw it. The well didn't seem nearly as deep as usual. No trouble at all. . . . Fancy me falling in love like this! I am a one, aren't I, though I says it. [*Not noticing Ampelisca's absence, and making a pantomime of carrying the jug*] Here's your water, lovely. Carry it nicely, like I'm doing, won't you? . . . [*Looking round*] Where are you, sweetheart? . . . Hey, here's your water. . . . She's hiding; naughty, naughty. I'm sure she loves me. . . . Where are you? Don't you want your jug? Where are you? Having a game with me, are you? . . . Come on, now, that's enough. Don't you want your water? . . . Where the hell are you? Well, I don't know where she is. She's got me guessing. All right, then, I'll leave the jug out here. [*Puts it down in the middle of the road.*] . . . Nay, that won't do, though; what if someone pinched it? That's a sacred jug of Venus, that is. I should get into trouble if anything was to happen to that jug. . . . 'Struth, I believe the old woman is setting a trap for me, to get me caught with one of Venus's holy jugs! If I'm caught with this I shall be in jug, and off with my head, and quite right too. [*He examines the jug again.*] Why, it's got writing on it! It says who it belongs to, as plain as plain. Hey, I'm going to get this priestess out here and make her take her jug back. . . . Hey, Miss, Ptolemocratia, I've got your jug here. Some girl brought it to me. . . . [*There is no reply.*] I shall have to take it in. The jobs I have to do! Fetching water for this lot now! [*He goes into the temple.*]

[*Up from the sea comes* LABRAX, *the pimp, with his friend* CHARMIDES *following slowly. They are both soaked and shivering.*]

LABRAX: Anyone looking for wrack and ruin, he'll get it quick enough if he puts his body and soul into Neptune's hands. Have anything to do with that old sod and he'll send you home in – this state. They say Liberty would never be a fellow-passenger with Hercules; I don't blame her. Where's that messmate of mine? He's the one that got me into this mess. Oh, here he comes.

CHARMIDES: Where the devil are you hurrying to, Labrax? I can't keep up with you at this pace.

LABRAX: I wish you'd been hung out to dry in Sicily before I ever set eyes on you. If it wasn't for you I wouldn't be in this damned pickle.

CHARMIDES: I wish I'd been safely tucked up in jail before you invited me to your place. I hope the everlasting god will send you none but the sort of guests you're fit for, for the rest of your mortal life.

LABRAX: Inviting you into my house was the damnedest

unlucky thing I ever did. And wasn't I a bloody fool to listen to you, to leave home, to embark on that ship? I've lost all I ever possessed, and more.

CHARMIDES: I don't wonder the ship was wrecked, with a crook like you and your ill-gotten gains aboard.

LABRAX: It was you that persuaded me, blast you.

CHARMIDES: Your supper was about as fatal to me as those given to Thyestes or Tereus.

LABRAX: Oh god, I feel awful. Hold my head, quick.

CHARMIDES: Heave ho! . . . You can heave your lungs out, as far as I am concerned. . . .

LABRAX [*better*]: Ooh . . . Hey, I wonder what's happened to Palaestra and Ampelisca.

CHARMIDES: Feeding the fishes at the bottom of the sea, I expect.

LABRAX: A damned good turn you did me with all your untruthful twaddle. Making me listen to all that magniloquent mendacity.

CHARMIDES [*amused*]: Your dip in the briny has salted your sense of humour. You can thank me for that, anyway.

LABRAX: Oh go to the devil and be damned.

CHARMIDES: I'm quite happy here, thanks; but don't let me stop you.

LABRAX: Oh . . . if ever a man suffered more than I. . . .

CHARMIDES: I'm suffering more than you, my dear fellow.

LABRAX: Why?

CHARMIDES: Because I don't deserve it; you do.

[*They sit and shiver in company for a few moments.*]

LABRAX:

> 'Oh blessed bull-rush, how I envy thee
> For thy invincible aridity. . . .'

CHARMIDES [*his teeth chattering*]: My w-words are g-galloping like a regiment of soldiers in t-training.

LABRAX: I wish Neptune would provide something more than a cold plunge. I can't get warm even with my clothes on, after a visit to his bath-house.

CHARMIDES: If he'd serve hot drinks it would be very pleasant, instead of nothing but iced salt and water.

LABRAX: I wouldn't mind a blacksmith's job; nice and cosy round the fire all day.

CHARMIDES: I wouldn't mind being a duck; dry the minute you come out of water.

LABRAX: How would I do as a bogey-man at a fair?

CHARMIDES: Why that?

LABRAX [grimacing]: Look at the way my teeth chatter.

CHARMIDES: Well, it served me right, I suppose, getting washed up like this.

LABRAX: Why served you right?

CHARMIDES: For being such a fool as to travel with you. You brought the fury of the ocean against me.

LABRAX: I like that! I was following your advice. You promised we should make our fortunes in whores. All I had to do was to rake in the shekels, according to you.

CHARMIDES: And you expected to glut your belly with the whole of Sicily.

LABRAX: I'd like to know what whale's belly is digesting my portmanteau, with all my gold and silver packed in it.

CHARMIDES: Probably the same one that's eating the wallet I had in my pocket with all my money in it.

LABRAX: Look at me! Reduced to this one shirt and this remnant of a cloak. I'm ruined, ruined!

CHARMIDES: We might go into partnership; we've both got the same amount of capital.

LABRAX: If only the women were safe, there'd be some hope for us. That young Plesidippus will have it in for me, if he finds me; he paid me a deposit for Palaestra.

CHARMIDES: Well, don't cry, baby. As long as you can talk, you won't want. You can talk anything out of anybody.

[SCEPARNIO *comes out of the temple.*]

SCEPARNIO: I'm damned if I know what's going on here. Two women in that temple, crying and clinging to the statue, scared stiff of somebody or other. They say they were shipwrecked last night and cast ashore this morning.

LABRAX: What's that, young 'un? Where are they, where are these women?

SCEPARNIO: In there.

LABRAX: How many of them?

SCEPARNIO: About . . . as many as . . . you and me.

LABRAX: Well then, they're mine . . . aren't they?

SCEPARNIO: I wouldn't know.

LABRAX: What are they like?

SCEPARNIO: All right. I'd take on either of them myself, if I were drunk enough.

LABRAX: You're sure they're young girls?

SCEPARNIO: I'm sure you're an old nuisance. Why don't you go and see for yourself?

LABRAX: Charmides my lad, my women are in there. It must be them.

CHARMIDES: God rot you, whether they are or whether they aren't.

LABRAX: I'm going into that temple if I have to break in.

CHARMIDES: Go and break into hell. . . .

[LABRAX *storms into the temple.*]

Look, my friend, can you possibly give me some place to sleep?

SCEPARNIO: Sleep where you are; anywhere you like. It's public property, nobody will stop you.

CHARMIDES: But you see what a state I'm in, in these wet clothes. If you could take me into your house, and give me something to wear while my things are drying, I'd repay you somehow or other.

SCEPARNIO: Here's this bit of matting; it's the only dry thing I've got. You can have it if you like. It's what I use for an overcoat when it rains. Give us your clothes; I'll see that they're dried. [*Lays hands on Charmides' clothes.*]

CHARMIDES: Hey, no you don't! After being cleaned out at sea, I suppose you'd like to see me stripped down on land?

SCEPARNIO [*turning away, and taking back the matting*]: I don't give two pips whether you're stripped down or swabbed out. I wouldn't trust you with anything of mine without a receipt. As far as I'm concerned you can sweat or freeze to death, go to bed or go to hell. We aren't having any wild foreigners in this house – and I can't stand here arguing any longer. [*He goes in.*]

CHARMIDES: Oh must you go? . . . I don't know who he is – slave-trader, I should think; he has no pity for anyone. Well, it's no use standing here wet and woebegone. I might as well go into the temple and sleep off the night's carouse – a thicker night than I bargained for! Old Neptune must have thought we needed an infusion of brine, like Greek wines – or a dose of salts to purge our bellies. A little more of his hospitality and we should have been under the table; as it is, we've just managed to stagger home. I'll go and see what my fellow-toper the whoremaster is up to in there. [*He goes into the temple.*]

*

[*Only a few moments later,* DAEMONES *comes out of his cottage.*]

DAEMONES:
Strange, how the gods delude the minds of men

And cannot even let us sleep in peace
But trouble us with curious dreams. Last night
I had a most extraordinary dream.
I can't think what it means. I saw a monkey
Clambering up towards a swallow's nest
And trying to pull it down. She couldn't reach it,
From where she was, so then she came to me
To borrow a ladder! 'Certainly not,' I said,
'I cannot let you harm my countrymen;
Swallows are children of Philomela and Procne.'
She then grew angry, and seemed to be threatening me
With dire calamity; and after that
She brought an action against me! In my rage
I somehow managed to grab her round the waist
And got the nasty creature put in chains.
What that could mean I've no idea, and so far
I haven't thought of a solution. . . .

   [*A noise of disturbance from the temple.*]
Good gracious! What's all that noise in the temple?
Extraordinary thing! . . .

   [TRACHALIO *rushes out of the temple, broadcasting an appeal
   for help.*]

TRACHALIO: Help, help, help, Cyrenian citizens, help!
Farmers, neighbours, countrymen, help for the helpless,
vengeance on a vile villain! Rescue the innocent, impotent,
and inoffensive from the power of the proud potentate.
Castigate unchastity and let righteousness be rewarded.
Let life be lived lawfully and none be frightened by fear or
force. To the temple of Venus hasten one and all; help, all
that are here to hear! Bring aid to those who by right of
ancient custom have committed their lives into the care of
Venus and the ministress of Venus! Root out wrong or
wring its neck before wrong wrings yours.

DAEMONES: What does all that mean?

TRACHALIO: Father, I beseech you by your knees, whoever you are –

DAEMONES: Kindly leave my knees alone and tell me briefly what you're shouting about.

TRACHALIO [*still grovelling and gabbling*]: Sir, I implore and adjure you, as you hope for a bounteous harvest of laserwort and asafoetida and comfortable conveyance of the same without let or loss to Capua and for everlasting immunity from hay fever –

DAEMONES: Are you crazy?

TRACHALIO: – or alternatively a satisfactory season of silphium seed, that you will not disdain to hearken to my prayer – O father.

DAEMONES: Then by your legs and ankles and backside, and in expectation of a bumper bundle of birchrods and a satisfactory harvest of bruises, have the goodness to tell me what the devil you're shouting about.

TRACHALIO [*returning to normal*]: What are you cursing me for? And after I've wished you all the good I could think of.

DAEMONES: I'm not cursing you. I'm wishing you all that's good for you.

TRACHALIO: Well, for the gods' sake, just listen to this, will you.

DAEMONES: Listen to what?

TRACHALIO: There are two innocent females in there, and they need your help. They've been illegally, outrageously, and indubitably ill-treated, in there, in the very temple of Venus – and it's still going on. The priestess has been assaulted too.

DAEMONES: No! Who could be so bold? Assaulting the priestess? Who are the other women? What's happening to them?

TRACHALIO: I'll tell you if you'll listen. They're clinging to the statue of Venus, and a wicked fellow is trying to abduct them. He's no right to touch them anyway.

DAEMONES: Who is the god-defying villain? Quick!

TRACHALIO: He's a most accomplished trickster, criminal, parricide, perjurer, the most infamous, insolent, impudent, indecent – well, he's a pimp, that's the long and the short of it.

DAEMONES: He seems to qualify for every kind of punishment.

TRACHALIO: He does, a scoundrel who could try to strangle a priestess.

DAEMONES: We'll make him suffer for it, by Hercules we will. Hey, Turbalio, Sparax! Where are you?

TRACHALIO: Go in and help them, sir, for pity's sake.

DAEMONES: Do you hear me?

[*Two of his strongest slaves appear.*]

Come with me.

TRACHALIO: Look, sir, tell them to beat his eyes out, like cooks do with cuttle-fish.

DAEMONES: Fling him out by the heels like a stuck pig.

[*He and the slaves go into the temple.*]

TRACHALIO [*listening*]: They're at it. The pimp's getting a pummelling. I hope they knock all the bastard's teeth out. Hullo, here are the women coming out, poor creatures.

[PALAESTRA *and* AMPELISCA *escape from the temple.*]

PALAESTRA:

What will become of us now?
Nothing is left.
All that we hoped for, all that we had,
Is lost.
All that could help us,
All that could save us,

Gone.
Gone is our only chance
Of safety and life.
Where can we go?
We do not know
Which way to turn.

So roughly and so brutally
Our cruel master treated us,
There is no spirit left in us.
And the poor priestess – how he threw
And pushed and pulled the poor old dame
In that outrageous way;
Then dragged us by main force
Down from the sacred shrine.

If this must be our lot,
If this our fate,
'Twere better far to die.
Ay, death is best;
In our great misery
'Tis best to die.

TRACHALIO: Nay, that's no way to talk. I must try and console them. Hey, Palaestra!

PALAESTRA [*not looking*]: Who's that?

TRACHALIO: Ampelisca!

AMPELISCA: Oh mercy, who can that be?

PALAESTRA: He called our names.

TRACHALIO: Look round and see.

PALAESTRA: Oh life and hope!

TRACHALIO: Now stop crying and be brave. Just leave it all to me.

PALAESTRA: I could if I had no force to fear; force which forces me to do violence to myself.

TRACHALIO: Ah, give over that silly talk.

PALAESTRA: And you give over trying to talk me into comfort after all I've suffered. Just find some protection for us, Trachalio, or there's no hope.

AMPELISCA: I know I'm ready to die rather than let that old pimp get his hands on me again. But I've only a woman's spirit; when I think of death I go cold all over. Oh, what a plight to be in!

TRACHALIO: You must be brave.

PALAESTRA: Oh god, where can I find strength to be brave?

TRACHALIO: Just stop being afraid, I tell you. Sit here by the altar.

AMPELISCA: Will this altar protect us any more than the statue in the temple? We were clinging to it just now, and we were dragged away by force.

TRACHALIO: Sit here anyway; I'll be your protector here. This altar is your camp, and I'll stand guard on your ramparts. With the aid of Venus I will boldly defy the power of the pimp.

AMPELISCA: Yes, Trachalio, we will. Kind Venus, we beseech thee, as we cling weeping to this thy altar, kneeling before thee we beseech thee to take us under thy care and protect us. May it please thee to take vengeance on the wicked men who have held thy shrine in contempt, and permit us to rest at this altar under thy peace. And pray you scorn us not, nor hold us guilty if you think we are not as cleanly washed as we should be; we were both well washed by Neptune last night.

TRACHALIO: Fair enough, Venus, don't you think so? You can't refuse them your forgiveness. They've been frightened into doing this. Eh, Venus? You came out of a shell yourself, I'm told; don't be hard on these two little shell-fish . . . Oh good, here comes our friend the kind old gentleman.

[DAEMONES *comes out of the temple, followed by the two slaves taking charge of* LABRAX.]

DAEMONES: Come on, out of it, you son of sacrilege. You girls can go and sit at the altar. . . . Where are they?

TRACHALIO: They're there already.

DAEMONES: Good; that's what I wanted. Now let him attempt to approach them if he dare. Now let's see you try any more lawbreaking. Let him have it.

[*A slave punches Labrax's face.*]

LABRAX: I'll get even with you for this.

DAEMONES: Still defies us, does he?

LABRAX: I want my rights. They're my girls and you've no right to take them away from me.

TRACHALIO: We'll see about that. Let's have any respectable Cyrenian senator here, and let him tell us whether these are free girls or your girls, and whether you ought not to be locked up in a cell for the rest of your life or until you've worn out every stone of it.

LABRAX: I didn't expect to have to talk to a gallows-bird. It's you I'm addressing, mister [*to Daemones*].

DAEMONES: Have it out with *him* first; he knows your kind.

LABRAX: It's *you* I'm talking to.

TRACHALIO: But it's me that's talking to you. Are these your girls?

LABRAX: Yes, they are.

TRACHALIO: Go on, then; touch one of them; either of them; with the tip of your little finger.

LABRAX: So what?

TRACHALIO: So that I can use you as a punch-bag, hang you, and thump you, you lying lump of sin.

LABRAX: Can't I take my own women away from that altar?

DAEMONES: You can't; the law says –

LABRAX: I don't give a damn for your laws. I'm going to

take them away, both of them. Of course, if you've taken a fancy to them, old cock, that would be a matter of hard cash. For the matter of that, Venus can have them if she likes them, at a price.

DAEMONES: Venus pay you for them? Just let me tell you what I think about it. You attempt to do any violence or even a pretence of violence to those girls, and I'll send you away in such a state you won't know yourself. And see here, you [to slaves], when I tip you the wink, you knock the eyes out of him, unless you want me to wrap you round with whips like bundles of tied myrtle.

LABRAX: Who's using violence now?

TRACHALIO: Have you any objection to violence, you abysmal abomination?

LABRAX: That's enough from you, gallows-bait.

TRACHALIO: All right, gallows-bait am I, and you're a gentleman. Is that any reason why these girls shouldn't be free?

LABRAX: Free? These women?

TRACHALIO: Free, and fit to be your owners. Greek born they are, one of them of free Athenian parents.

DAEMONES: What's that you say?

TRACHALIO: This girl is a freeborn Athenian.

DAEMONES: Good gracious! A compatriot of mine?

TRACHALIO: I thought you were a Cyrenian?

DAEMONES: No indeed. I was born and bred and brought up in Athens of Attica.

TRACHALIO: Then for goodness' sake, my old friend, you must protect your fellow-citizens.

DAEMONES: Ah, my dear lost daughter! How my sorrow comes back to me when I look at this young girl. Three years old when I lost her, and now she would be just this girl's age if she were alive.

LABRAX: I tell you I paid good money to their owners for the two of them. What do I care whether they were born in Athens or Thebes or anywhere else, so long as I have them in my service?

TRACHALIO: You wicked old woman-trapper, do you think we're going to let you keep free children stolen from their parents and work them to death for your filthy profit? I admit I don't know where this other girl comes from; all I know is she's better than you, you scum of the earth.

LABRAX: You seem to know a lot about them; are they your property?

TRACHALIO: Which of us is the liar, then? Come on, strip and I'll prove it to you. If there aren't more blisters on your back than bolts in a battleship, never believe me. And when I've inspected your back, you can look at mine; if it's not as smooth as the finest skin any bottle-maker could desire for his trade, I give you leave to . . . to . . . to let me tan your hide till I'm tired of it. It's no use looking at those girls; if you touch them, I'll tear your eyes out.

LABRAX: Say what you like, they're coming with me. [*He moves towards the cottage.*]

DAEMONES: Now what are you going to do?

LABRAX: Get Vulcan on the job; he hates Venus.

TRACHALIO: Where's he going?

LABRAX [*at the door*]: Hey there! Anyone in?

DAEMONES: You dare to touch that door, you'll have my fingers making hay in your stubble.

A SLAVE: He won't find any fire in there, we never eat anything but dried figs.

DAEMONES: I'll give you fire, once I can strike a light on your head!

LABRAX [*turning away*]: I'll get some fire from somewhere.

DAEMONES: And then what?

LABRAX: Make a bonfire here.

DAEMONES: To burn the devil out of you?

LABRAX: I'll burn those two wenches alive at the altar, that's what I'll do.

DAEMONES: I'll have you by the beard and throw you into the middle of it, then toss you half-cooked to the vultures. . . . Now I think of it, of course, this must be the monkey I dreamed of, that wanted to pull the swallows out of their nest.

TRACHALIO: Tell you what, grandfather – you look after the girls, don't let anyone touch them, while I fetch my master.

DAEMONES: Yes, do, go and bring him here.

TRACHALIO: Watch this fellow –

DAEMONES: It will be the worse for him, if he touches them, or tries to.

TRACHALIO: Be careful, then.

DAEMONES: I'll be all right. Off you go.

TRACHALIO: And don't let him escape either; if we don't set him up today we owe the hangman a hundred pounds.

DAEMONES: Get along with you. I can manage.

TRACHALIO: I'll be back. [*He goes.*]

DAEMONES: Well, pimp, will you keep quiet quietly, or have we got to make you?

LABRAX: I don't give a toss for you, professor. I'll have my girls, and I'll drag 'em away by the hair, and not you or Venus or Jove Almighty can stop me.

DAEMONES: Touch them, then.

LABRAX: I mean to.

DAEMONES: Go on, then; there they are.

LABRAX: Just tell those two big devils to move out of the way.

DAEMONES: Perhaps you'd like them to move in your direction?

LABRAX: They'd better not try.

DAEMONES: What would you do if they did?

LABRAX: I'd − I'd − I'd keep out of their way. But by the gods, old gaffer, next time I meet you in town, if I don't make you laugh on the other side of your face, my name's not Pimp Labrax.

DAEMONES: I hope you keep your word. In the meantime, touch those girls and you'll be sorry for it.

LABRAX: How sorry?

DAEMONES: As sorry as any pimp deserves to be.

LABRAX: A fig for your threats. Say what you like, I shall take those two women.

DAEMONES: Touch them, then.

LABRAX: I'm going to.

DAEMONES: You are? You know what you're doing? . . . Quick, Turbalio, a couple of clubs from the house.

LABRAX: Eh, clubs?

DAEMONES: The thickest you can find. At the double.

[TURBALIO, *one of the slaves, goes into the house.*]
We'll have you treated to a royal reception.

LABRAX: Just like me to lose my helmet in the ship; I could have done with it here. . . . I suppose I can speak to the girls, can't I?

DAEMONES: You can't. . . .

[TURBALIO *returns with two cudgels.*]
Ah good, here's our ace of clubs.

LABRAX: Lord, my ears are tingling already.

DAEMONES: Now then, Sparax, kindly take that other club [TURBALIO *keeping one of them*]. One of you stand *here*, the other *there*. . . . A little closer, please, both of you. . . . That'll do. . . . Now pay attention. If this gentleman lays a finger on these girls against their will, you will deal with him with your instruments so effectively that he won't be able to find his way home – if you don't I'll kill you. If he tries to speak to either of them, *you* will answer instead of her; if he attempts to escape, you will as promptly as possible wrap those sticks round his legs.

LABRAX: What, not even allowed to run away?

DAEMONES: That is what I said. [*To slaves*] When Trachalio comes back with his master, whom he has gone to fetch, you can go off duty. Those are my instructions; carry them out with all diligence.

[*He goes into the cottage.* LABRAX *stands checkmated, with a slave behind each shoulder; he ponders the situation ruefully.*]

LABRAX: Blimey, these temples change hands pretty quickly here. This one used to be Venus's and now it's Hercules' – with the old man's two club-swinging statues on guard. Gods, I don't know where to make for now, shipwrecked on sea and hamstrung on land. . . . [*He tries to attract the attention of the girls.*] Hey, Palaestra!

SPARAX [*answering, as bidden, behind his right ear*]: What do you want?

LABRAX [*startled at the gruff voice, looking round*]: Eh, what's that? Some mistake; that's not Palaestra answering. . . . [*He tries again.*] Ampelisca!

TURBALIO [*behind his left ear*]: Watch it!

LABRAX [*exasperated*]: Oh, clear off! . . . These talking statues are looking after me very carefully. . . . Say, fellows, listen: any objection if I go a little closer to them?

TURBALIO: None whatever, as far as we are concerned.

LABRAX: I shan't get into trouble?

TURBALIO: None whatever – if you're careful.

LABRAX: Careful of what?

TURBALIO [*swinging club*]: Of what's coming to you.

LABRAX: Oh, for holy Hercules, let me get away.

SPARAX: No one's stopping you.

LABRAX: I can go? Really? Oh . . . good. Thanks very much.
I think I'll go *this* way [*via the altar*].

TURBALIO: Get back from there!

LABRAX: Oh damn, foiled again. There's only one thing to
do and that's to starve them out. [*He sits down to wait.*]
[*Presently* TRACHALIO *comes back, with* PLESIDIPPUS.]

PLESIDIPPUS: That pimp is trying to drag my girl away from
Venus's altar?

TRACHALIO: That's about it, sir.

PLESIDIPPUS: Why didn't you kill him there and then?

TRACHALIO: Well . . . I hadn't a sword, sir.

PLESIDIPPUS: You could have finished him with a stick or a
stone.

TRACHALIO: Would you have me throw stones at a man
like a dog – a dirty dog?

LABRAX: Now I'm done for. Here's Plesidippus. He'll
sweep me up to the last crumb.

PLESIDIPPUS: Were the women sitting at the altar already,
when you came to look for me?

TRACHALIO: They were, and they still are.

PLESIDIPPUS: Who's there to keep an eye on them?

TRACHALIO: Some old gentleman I've never seen before;
lives next door to Venus. He was very helpful. He's guard-
ing them now with his slaves. I saw to all that.

PLESIDIPPUS: Where is the pimp? Take me to him at once.
[*This conversation, of course, has taken place at the extremity
of the stage; now they move in to the centre.*]

LABRAX: Good day to you, sir.

PLESIDIPPUS: I don't care whether it's a good day or not.
Take your choice, quick – be dragged off by the neck or
hauled off by the heels. Which is it to be?

LABRAX: I don't fancy either.

PLESIDIPPUS: Trachalio, run down to the shore and tell those men to come up and meet me at the harbour – those friends I brought with me to hand this fellow over to the hangman. Then come back here and keep guard. I mean to bring this damned outlaw to justice.

[TRACHALIO *goes*.]

Come on, you; into the dock with you.

LABRAX: What am I charged with?

PLESIDIPPUS: You want to know? Didn't you take a deposit from me on the woman and then abduct her?

LABRAX: I didn't take her away.

PLESIDIPPUS: You didn't take her away?

LABRAX: I took her a *little* way; I failed to take her *right* away, worse luck for me. Look, mister, I said I'd meet you at the Venus shrine, didn't I? Well, haven't I done so? I'm here, ain't I?

PLESIDIPPUS: You can tell that to the magistrate; we've had enough argument. Quick march! [*Slips a rope round his neck*.]

LABRAX: Help, mercy, help, Charmides! Come here! I'm being dragged by the neck!

[CHARMIDES *comes out of the temple, half asleep*.]

CHARMIDES: Did someone call me?

LABRAX: Look, look what they're doing to me.

CHARMIDES: Oh, so they are. . . . I'm delighted to see it.

LABRAX: Haven't you got the guts to help me?

CHARMIDES: Who is the gentleman with the rope?

LABRAX: Young Plesidippus –

CHARMIDES: Congratulations, sir; mind you don't lose him. [*To Labrax*] The best thing you can do is to creep quietly into prison. Not many people are as lucky as you.

LABRAX: What the hell do you mean?

CHARMIDES: – getting exactly what you asked for.

LABRAX: Come with me, for god's sake.

CHARMIDES: Another of your invitations? On your way to jail, and pressing me to join you. [*To Plesidippus*] Have you got him tight, sir?

LABRAX: He's strangling me.

PLESIDIPPUS: I wish I were. Palaestra, my love, and Ampelisca, don't you move from there till I come back.

TURBALIO: If I might suggest, sir, they'd better come over to our house, and you can call for them there.

PLESIDIPPUS: Very good. Thanks.

LABRAX: Thieves!

TURBALIO: Thieves, are we? Take him along, sir.

LABRAX: Palaestra! Pity me!

PLESIDIPPUS: Come on, offal!

LABRAX: My old friend –

CHARMIDES: I'm not your old friend. I've had enough of your old friendship.

LABRAX: You throw me over like that?

CHARMIDES: Yes, just like that. Once bitten –

LABRAX: God rot you.

CHARMIDES: Pray for yourself.

[LABRAX *is removed; the girls are escorted into the cottage.*]
I've heard of men being changed into animals;
I rather think it's true. This pimp, perhaps,
Is going to be a pigeon; at any rate
He'll soon be in his pigeon-hole, cooped up
In a cosy nesting-box. I'll go along
And offer to conduct his case; my services
Should get him sentenced all the sooner!

[*Exit*]

*

[DAEMONES *comes out of the cottage.*]

DAEMONES:

I've done a good day's work today, I think,
Saving two damsels in distress. And now
I've got two charming lodgers in the house,
The prettiest pair you ever saw – delightful. . . .
My wife, of course, has got her eye on me,
The wretch, in case I might as much as nod
Or wink at the women. . . . Ah well. . . .

[*He looks out to sea.*]

Gripus is late; I wonder what's happened to him.
He went out fishing last night. He'd have done better
To stay at home in bed. With all that storm,
And blowing still, he's only wasting his time,
And losing his nets too, I shouldn't wonder.
I'll fry on my fingers anything he catches
In a sea like this. . . . Ah, there's my wife
Calling me in to dinner. Back we go,
To listen to a torrent of idle chatter.

[*He goes in.*
His boy GRIPUS *is a sturdy and honest youth, normally
good-tempered but pugnacious in defence of his rights. Just now
he is on top of the world as he comes up from the sea dragging
a net loaded with a strange catch.*]

GRIPUS [*singing*]:

O thank you, Father Neptune, O king of the fish in the
     sea;
O thank you, Father Neptune, for what you've done for
     me.
My nets are heavy, my coble is safe from the raging of
     the main;
O thank you, Father Neptune, for bringing me home
     again.

My, but I've had some marvellous wonderful fishing;
if you call it fishing; not an ounce of fish did I catch
all night, but my net's full all the same! . . .

> I was out of my bed at midnight, with never a thought of
>   sleep;
> And into the howling storm I went, to earn my master's
>   keep;
> To brave the billowy ocean, with never a thought of rest;
> For a slave has got to earn his bread, so I always do my
>   best.

Ay, a lazy man is worse than useless. I never could abide a
lazy man. If there's work to be done, you've got to get up
early, and that's all there is to it. Not lay there doing nothing
till your master comes to turn you out. Long sleep means
short profit and trouble in store. . . .

Take me, now; by working hard I've done myself so much
good that I need never work again if I don't want to.
That's the prize I've fished out of the sea. [*He examines the
treasure in his net – a wooden trunk.*] I don't know what's in it
but whatever it is, it's heavy. It'll be gold, I reckon. And
nobody knows about it but me. Now then, Gripus,
here's your chance to be as free as the freest man in the
world.

And this is what I'm going to do. I've made my plan.
I shall go up to my master, choosing my time carefully
and cautious like. Then I shall offer him a price for my
freedom – work it up gradually, till he accepts. When I'm
free, I'll invest in some land, house, slaves, and all that, set
up a merchant-shipping business; I'll be famous, a prince of
princes. I shall build a yacht, for my own amusement; like
Stratonicus; sail around from port to port. When I'm really
well known, I'll build a big new town, and give my name
to it, Gripopolis; it'll be a monument to my famous

T – P – E

achievements and the capital of a mighty empire. Oh yes,
I've big ideas in my head. . . .

But the first thing to do is to hide this trunk. . . . For the
time being, this prince will have to make his dinner off sour
wine and salt water, and no trimmings. [*He begins to drag
off the net with the trunk, trailing ropes and tackle.*]

[TRACHALIO *comes along.*]

TRACHALIO: Hey you. Wait a minute.

GRIPUS: What for?

TRACHALIO: You're losing one of your ropes. I'll wind it up
for you. [*He helpfully picks up one end of the rope.*]

GRIPUS: You let that rope alone, mate.

TRACHALIO: I'm only trying to help you. One good turn –

GRIPUS: It's no use your asking me for any fish, son; I
haven't one; it was too rough last night. See, a soaked net
and not a flipper in it.

TRACHALIO [*eyeing the net suspiciously*]: I'm not looking for
fish. Just passing the time of day with you.

GRIPUS: I've no time to spare for the likes of you, whoever
you are.

TRACHALIO [*hanging on to the rope*]: Not so fast. There's no
hurry.

GRIPUS: Just watch what you're doing, my lad. What's the
idea, hanging on to me like this?

TRACHALIO: Listen, and I'll tell you.

GRIPUS: I don't want to listen.

TRACHALIO: Ah, but you will.

GRIPUS [*trying to get the rope away*]: Well, what?

TRACHALIO [*hanging on*]: Hold on a minute. This will
interest you.

GRIPUS: Come on, then; what is it?

TRACHALIO: Are you sure we're not overheard?

GRIPUS: Should I worry if we were?

TRACHALIO: Indeed you should. Can you keep a secret?

GRIPUS: Just tell me, for god's sake, what this is all about.

TRACHALIO: All right, all right. I'll tell you. Only promise me you won't break your promise.

GRIPUS: I don't know who you are, but I promise I won't break my promise.

TRACHALIO: Right, then; listen. I saw a robber robbing – I knew the man he robbed from – I went up to the robber – I offered him a bargain – 'I know the man you robbed,' I said – 'you give me fifty-fifty – I'll say no more about it.' He wouldn't listen to me. Well, I ask you, wasn't half a fair share? Go on, say yes.

GRIPUS: You should have asked more than half. If he won't give it you, I'd say you ought to tell the owner.

TRACHALIO: Thanks, I will. Now see here: this is where you come in.

GRIPUS: What do you mean?

TRACHALIO: You've got a trunk there. I know who it belongs to. I've known him a long time.

GRIPUS: What are you talking about?

TRACHALIO: And I know how it was lost.

GRIPUS: Do you, then? And *I* know how it was found, and I know who found it, and I know who it belongs to now; and it's no bloody business of yours – no more than your story is any business of mine. You may know whose property it *was*, but I know whose it is now. Nobody's going to take it away from me, and don't you try it.

TRACHALIO: What if the owner were to come along?

GRIPUS: Don't be silly. No man alive owns that stuff but me; I fished it out of the sea.

TRACHALIO: Did you indeed?

GRIPUS: Look, you wouldn't call any particular fish in the sea mine, would you, as long as it's in the sea? But those that I catch, supposing I do catch any, are mine – right? They're my property; nobody else can meddle with them or claim any share in them. I sell 'em in the market as my own stock – right? Of course I do. The sea's common ground to everybody.

TRACHALIO: Quite right; then why isn't this trunk as much my property as yours? It was found in the common sea.

GRIPUS: Well, of all the bloody cheek! Good-bye to fishermen, if the law were what you make it out to be. Set your stuff out in the market and you'd never get a buyer; everybody would be asking for free shares of what was caught in the common sea!

TRACHALIO: Oh no, you can't get away with that. You can't compare a trunk with a fish. Surely you can see it's quite different.

GRIPUS: I can't help it if it is different. I let down a net or a hook, I pull up whatever it catches. And whatever it catches, it's damn well mine.

TRACHALIO: It damn well isn't. For instance, if you were to pull up some vase or jar.

GRIPUS: Philosopher, are you? [*He attempts to move on.*]

TRACHALIO [*still on the end of the rope*]: Hold on, stinker. Tell me, did you ever see a fisherman catch a fish in the form of a trunk, or offer such a thing for sale? You can't set up in any number of trades at once; you are trying to be a fisherman and a carpenter at the same time, you greedy devil. Go on, then, explain to me how a trunk can be a fish, or I can't let you carry off what was never born in the sea and doesn't look like it.

GRIPUS: You never heard of a trunk-fish, then?

TRACHALIO: There's no such thing, damn you.

GRIPUS: Oh yes ... oh yes, there is. ... I'm telling you,

I'm a fisherman and I know. Of course they're very rarely caught. They hardly ever come near land.

TRACHALIO: Do you think you can pull my leg with that yarn, crossbones? What colour are they?

GRIPUS: You get 'em different colours; little ones mostly this colour; some are redskins, big 'uns; or black –

TRACHALIO: I'm sure you do. You'll find yourself turning into several sorts of trunk-fish, if you're not careful -- first a redskin, then black, and blue.

GRIPUS: You're in an ugly mood, aren't you?

TRACHALIO: We can't stop here all day talking. What we'll have to do is to choose an arbitrator to settle the dispute between us.

GRIPUS: Let the trunk settle it. [*Meaning, 'Have a tug of war for it'. He prepares to pull harder.*] Come on.

TRACHALIO: Oh, you've no brains at all.

GRIPUS: Thanks, learned master.

TRACHALIO: You're not getting away with this. You've got to name a trustee or arbitrator to give a decision.

GRIPUS: Are you off your nut?

TRACHALIO: Yes, and dangerous.

GRIPUS: Well, I'm hopping mad, and I'm not letting go of this net.

TRACHALIO: Say another word and I'll punch your brains out. See? Drop it, or I'll wring the guts out of you like water out of a wet sponge.

GRIPUS: You touch me, and I'll bash you to pieces on the ground like an octopus. If you want a fight, come on.

TRACHALIO [*since Gripus is very probably the stronger*]: Do you think that's really necessary? Wouldn't you rather go shares in the swag?

GRIPUS: The only share you're going to get is a share of

trouble, I can promise you that. I must be going [*He tries to make a move.*]

TRACHALIO [*manoeuvring with the rope*]: Haul away there. Hard astern. Easy all.

GRIPUS: Think you're skipper, do you? Well, I'm at the helm. Drop that rope, ye lubber.

TRACHALIO: Not till you drop that trunk.

GRIPUS [*relaxing again*]: Look, for god's sake, you'll never be a penny the better for this lot of salvage.

TRACHALIO: It's no use trying to talk me out of it, chum. Equal shares, or find an arbitrator or trustee.

GRIPUS: But damn it, I caught the thing in the sea –

TRACHALIO: And I saw you catch it.

GRIPUS: You did, did you? With my own skill, my own hands, my own boat and net – well, there you are, then.

TRACHALIO: Would you say – if the owner came along now – would you say I was just as guilty as you, for having seen you in possession of it?

GRIPUS [*thoughtlessly*]: 'Course you are.

TRACHALIO [*jumping on it*]: Am I, rope's end? Come on, then, explain your reasoning. How do you make out I can be guilty of theft without being a sharer in the profits? Go on, explain; I want to know.

GRIPUS [*defeated*]: Oh hell, I don't know. I don't go for all that legal stuff. All I know is, this trunk is mine!

TRACHALIO: And I say it's mine.

[GRIPUS, *after a pause for thought, lays what he hopes is a trap for Trachalio, but not clever enough.*]

GRIPUS: Just a minute, though. . . . I think I see how you can get out of being either a thief or an accessory.

TRACHALIO: Oh, how?

GRIPUS: Just let me go my way, and you go yours and say no more. You give nobody any information about me, and I give you none of the stuff. You say nothing, and I won't let on about you. Fair enough?

TRACHALIO [*not so green*]: *You're* going to offer terms now, are you?

GRIPUS: I *am* offering; like I said; [*trying to twitch the rope away*] you clear off, drop that rope, and not bother me any more.

TRACHALIO: Just a minute, just a minute; it's my turn to make an offer.

GRIPUS: I wish you'd offer to remove yourself.

TRACHALIO: Do you happen to know anyone around here?

GRIPUS: I ought to know my own neighbours, I suppose.

TRACHALIO: Do you live here? Where?

GRIPUS [*prevaricating*]: Over there; a good long way; across them fields.

TRACHALIO: What about getting the man who lives in this house to be our referee?

GRIPUS: Ah well, that's an idea. Pay out the rope a bit, while I think it over by myself. [*He moves farther off.*]

TRACHALIO: Granted.

GRIPUS [*aside*]: Well, what do you know! That does it; my prize is safe now. He wants to make my own master the referee – here, on our own ground! The fellow doesn't know what he's offering; master'll never award sixpenn'orth of damages against his own estate. I'll take his offer.

TRACHALIO: Well, how about it?

GRIPUS: I'm perfectly certain I'm in my rights, mind you; still, rather than fight about it, I'll do as you say.

TRACHALIO: Sensible fellow.

GRIPUS: I don't know anything about this referee you're taking me to; but that don't matter; if he's on the level, I'll recognize him, even though I never saw him before; if he isn't, even if I know him, I'll never speak to him again.

[DAEMONES, *now obliged to get the girls off his hands,
comes out with them. The two guardian slaves are still in
attendance.*]

DAEMONES: I assure you, my dear girls, I'd gladly make
myself responsible for you, and make everything nice and
comfortable for you. But I'm afraid my wife wouldn't like
it. She'd probably turn me out of the house and say I was
flaunting my women in front of her face. If anyone is going
to have to take refuge at the altar, I'd rather it were you than
me.

PALAESTRA and AMPELISCA: Oh dear, whatever shall we
do!

DAEMONES [*caressing them*]: I'll see that you come to no harm,
never fear. [*Then, seeing the slaves*] . . . What are you out
here for? They are in no danger while I am present. Get
along inside; guard, dismiss. [*The slaves go.*]

[GRIPUS *and* TRACHALIO *arrive at the cottage.*]

GRIPUS: Morning, master!

DAEMONES: Oh hullo, Gripus; what luck?

[*He joins Gripus, leaving the girls to make their way to the
altar.*]

TRACHALIO [*astounded*]: Is this boy your slave?

GRIPUS: And proud of it.

TRACHALIO: I wasn't addressing you.

GRIPUS: Then flip off.

TRACHALIO [*to Daemones*]: Begging your pardon, sir, is
this boy your slave?

DAEMONES: He is.

TRACHALIO: Well, that's wonderful news. I'm delighted to
hear it. Good morning to you again, sir.

DAEMONES: Good morning to you. Wait a minute, aren't
you the man who went away from here to look for his
master a little while ago?

TRACHALIO: That's me.

DAEMONES: Well, what's your business now?

TRACHALIO: This fellow is really your slave, is he?

DAEMONES: Yes, he is.

TRACHALIO: Splendid ... that's really wonderful ... your
slave ... fancy that!

DAEMONES: What the devil are you talking about?

TRACHALIO: That boy is a criminal.

DAEMONES: Oh? And has he committed any crime against
you?

TRACHALIO: I should like to see his legs broken.

DAEMONES: What on earth – ? What are you two quarrelling
about?

TRACHALIO: I'll explain.

GRIPUS: No, I'll explain.

TRACHALIO: My move first, I think.

GRIPUS: You'd move off, double quick, if you had any shame.

DAEMONES: Shut up, Gripus, and pay attention.

GRIPUS: What, and let him speak first?

DAEMONES: Yes, listen. Go on, young man.

GRIPUS: Well ... fancy letting someone else's man speak
first.

TRACHALIO: He's irrepressible, isn't he? Well, as I was about
to say, you know that fellow you threw out of the temple
this morning – that pimp – your slave has got his trunk,
and here it is.

GRIPUS: I haven't.

TRACHALIO: Do you think I'm blind?

GRIPUS: I wish you were. I've got it, or I haven't got it.
What I'm doing is no business of yours, is it?

TRACHALIO: The question is, *how* you got it, rightly or
wrongly.

GRIPUS: Look, sir; what's in that net I caught with my own

hands, crucify me if I didn't. [*To Trachalio*] And is what I caught in the sea yours any more than mine?

TRACHALIO: He's just quibbling, sir. I'm giving you the plain facts.

GRIPUS: If you think –

TRACHALIO: I'm speaking, I believe. [*To Daemones*] Would you kindly tell your boy to lie down?

GRIPUS: My master's not that kind of man; yours may be.

DAEMONES [*amused*]: He's got you there, I think. Well, go on with your story.

TRACHALIO: Whatever's in that trunk, I'm not claiming any share of it. I've never said it was mine at all. But, as a matter of fact, it contains a little box belonging to that young lady, the one I have already told you is free-born.

DAEMONES: What, the one you said was a compatriot of mine?

TRACHALIO: That's right. And in the box, which is in that trunk, there are some little trinkets, rattles and things that she used to play with when she was a baby. They can be of no possible use to him, and he'll be doing the poor girl a good turn if he gives them back to her, to help her find her parents.

DAEMONES: Well of course I'll see that he does.

GRIPUS: Sir –

DAEMONES: You keep quiet.

GRIPUS: I won't give him a thing.

TRACHALIO: I'm only asking for the box and the toys.

GRIPUS: They might be gold.

TRACHALIO: And what if they are? We'll get you the value for them, gold for gold and silver for silver.

GRIPUS: Show us your gold first, and then I might let you see the box.

DAEMONES: You hold your tongue or there'll be trouble. Anything else?

TRACHALIO: Only this, sir. Please do your best for the girl, if it really is the pimp's trunk, as I suspect. Mind you, I don't know for certain, I'm only guessing.

GRIPUS: Watch him, sir; he's setting a trap for you.

TRACHALIO: Shut *your* trap, and let me finish. If the trunk does belong to that old sinner, the women will be able to recognize it. Tell him to let them see it.

GRIPUS: Let them see it? I'll –

DAEMONES: It's perfectly fair, Gripus. You must produce the trunk.

GRIPUS: It's *not* bloody well fair.

DAEMONES: Why isn't it?

GRIPUS: Because as soon as I show it to them, they'll immediately say they recognize it, naturally.

TRACHALIO: You damned crook, do you think everybody's as dishonest as you – lousy liar?

GRIPUS: All that sort of talk doesn't worry me, as long as my master here is on my side.

TRACHALIO: He may be on your side, but the evidence is now coming from my side.

DAEMONES: Patience, Gripus, and just listen. Tell me briefly what you propose.

TRACHALIO: I've told you once, but in case I didn't make myself clear I'll tell you again. These two girls, I said, have a right to be free; one of them – this one – was stolen from Athens as a child.

GRIPUS: I can't see what it's got to do with the trunk, whether they were free girls or slaves.

TRACHALIO: We shall be here all day, blast you, if you want everything said twice over.

DAEMONES: All right, cut the abuse, and finish your explanation.

TRACHALIO [*patiently*]: Inside that trunk there should be a wooden box, and in the box those mementoes by which the girl can be made known to her parents, since the poor child had them with her when she disappeared from Athens; *as* I said before.

GRIPUS: Jupiter strike you stiff! See here, poison-mouth, these women aren't dumb, are they? Can't they speak for themselves?

TRACHALIO: A woman's silence is always worth more than her speech.

GRIPUS: You're no use as man or woman, then.

TRACHALIO: What exactly do you mean by that?

GRIPUS: You're not to be trusted, speaking or silent. . . . Say, am I ever going to get a chance to talk?

DAEMONES: Another word, and I'll brain you.

TRACHALIO: As I was saying, sir – I beg you to make this man restore the box. If he wants a reward for it, let him have it, as well as whatever else is in the trunk.

GRIPUS: Now you're talking – since you realize I'm in the right. Just now you were all for having a half share.

TRACHALIO: I still am.

GRIPUS: Very likely. I've seen kites after their prey, and not getting it.

DAEMONES: Have I got to *make* you keep quiet?

GRIPUS: He keeps quiet, I keep quiet; he talks, I'm talking too.

DAEMONES: Gripus, let me have that trunk.

GRIPUS: I'll give it to you, sir, on condition I have it back if none of that stuff is in it.

DAEMONES: You shall have it back.

GRIPUS: There you are, then.

[*The trunk is exhibited on the ground.*]

DAEMONES: Now then, Palaestra and Ampelisca, I have something to tell you.

[*They approach.*]

You said your little box was in a trunk. Is this the trunk?

PALAESTRA: Oh, it is, it is!

GRIPUS: Well I'll be beggared, she says it's hers without hardly giving it a look.

PALAESTRA: I can easily prove it. In the trunk there should be a little wooden trinket-box. And I'll tell you what should be in the box, article by article. Don't show me anything. If I make a mistake, disqualify me and keep whatever is there for yourselves. If I am right, then please, please, let me have my things back.

DAEMONES: Agreed. That's perfectly fair, in my opinion.

GRIPUS: It's not fair in *my* opinion, by Herc'les. She may be a witch or a clairvoyant and able to reel off every damn thing that's in it. Are you going to give this box to a fortune teller?

DAEMONES: Not unless she gets them all right; and I don't think she'll be able to do that by magic. Get the trunk open, so that I can see immediately what is really there.

GRIPUS: Here goes, then. [*He unropes the trunk.*] It's open.

DAEMONES: Lift up the lid. [*He finds the box in the trunk.*] A box! Is this the one?

PALAESTRA: It is, it is! O my beloved parents, this is you in here. Here I have kept all my help and hope of finding you.

GRIPUS: You'll be punished at the day of judgement, lady, for keeping your parents shut up in that little box.

DAEMONES: Stand here, Gripus. You are concerned in this. Now, my girl, you stand over there, and tell us what is in the box; describe each article, and don't omit anything. One slip and you're out; no corrections or second guesses.

GRIPUS: I agree to that.

TRACHALIO: He's not asking you, quarrelsome.

DAEMONES: Begin, girl. Gripus, listen, and *keep quiet*.

[*A pause;* PALAESTRA *concentrates.*]

PALAESTRA: A chain of toys.

DAEMONES: Correct.

GRIPUS: Knocked out first round. Hey, don't show it to her yet.

DAEMONES: What kind of toys? Name them in the right order.

PALAESTRA: A little gold sword, with an inscription on it.

DAEMONES: And what is the inscription on the little gold sword?

PALAESTRA: My father's name. Next to it, a little double-headed axe, also of gold, and also with an inscription; it has my mother's name on it.

DAEMONES: Just a minute. What *is* the name on the sword, your father's name?

PALAESTRA: Daemones.

DAEMONES: Good gods, is there yet hope for me?

GRIPUS: Is there any for me?

[*A pause,* DAEMONES *deeply affected.*]

TRACHALIO: Well, why don't we get on with it?

GRIPUS: Why don't you drop dead?

DAEMONES: And your mother's name, on the little axe?

PALAESTRA: Daedalis.

DAEMONES: The gods are good to me!

GRIPUS: Not to me they aren't!

DAEMONES: She must be my daughter! Gripus, she's my daughter!

GRIPUS: Have I said she isn't? God damn your eyes that they ever saw me here today! And wasn't I a god-damned fool not to make sure and certain there was nobody spying on me before I pulled that net out of the water!

PALAESTRA [*continuing blithely*]: The next article is a tiny silver sickle; then comes a pair of clasped hands, and a spinning top or whirligig.

GRIPUS: I'd like to see you spinning to hell, with your whirligigs and piggy-wigs!

PALAESTRA: And the gold locket which my father gave me on my birthday.

DAEMONES: It is she, it is she! I cannot wait to embrace her. My daughter, my daughter! I am your father, I brought you up, I am Daemones, and your mother Daedalis is in this house.

PALAESTRA: The father I never thought to see again! O father!

DAEMONES: To have you in my arms again!

TRACHALIO: Permit me to congratulate you, sir. It is delightful to see your long affection so rewarded.

DAEMONES: Come, Trachalio, can you lift this trunk and take it indoors?

TRACHALIO: Poor old Gripus. He doesn't come very well out of this – I'm glad to say.

DAEMONES: Come along, my child, and see your mother. She will be able to verify all the details. She had more to do with you, and knows every mark on your body.

TRACHALIO: Let's all come, shall we? We're all in this.

PALAESTRA: Come, Ampelisca.

AMPELISCA: I'm so happy for your blessed good fortune.

[All but GRIPUS go into the house.]

GRIPUS: I could hang myself for fishing up that damned trunk. Or for not having the sense to hide it somewhere when I'd got it. Ye gods, with a prize like that out of a storm like that, I reckoned I'd have a whale of a time. I bet it's packed full of gold and silver, too. Well, there's nothing for it but to go inside and quietly hang myself – at least for the time being, until I get over it. [He goes off.]

[DAEMONES *comes out again, very pleased with himself.*]
DAEMONES:

Bountiful heavens! What a lucky man I am!
To find my daughter after all these years,
So unexpectedly. Well, it just shows,
When the gods above decide to help a man
They find a way of answering his prayers.
This blessing was more than I could ever hope for,
More than I could ever believe; yet here I am
With a daughter suddenly restored to me.
Now I shall marry her to a fine young man,
From a fine old family, an Athenian family,
My own in fact. I'm going to send for him
Without delay. . . .

            Where is that slave of his?
I want to send him to the market-place. . . .
What *is* the fellow doing? I've told him once
To come out here. . . . I'll have to go and see. . . .
  [*He goes to the door.*]
Oh there's my wife . . . hugging and clinging
Around the poor girl's neck . . . really, these women
Carry affection to ridiculous lengths,
The tiresome creatures. . . . [*Calls in*] Now then, haven't
   you finished,
Woman, with all that kissing? Get things ready
For a thank-offering, will you, to the household gods,
As soon as I come back. We ought to celebrate
The increase in our family. We've got some lambs
And pigs for the purpose. . . .

              What are you girls doing
With Trachalio there? . . .

            Oh, here he comes,
About time too.

[TRACHALIO *comes out.*]

TRACHALIO [*with great readiness*]: I'll find him, sir. I'll find him, wherever he is. Wherever he is, I'll find him, I'll bring him to you. I'll get Plesidippus here.

DAEMONES: Tell him all that has happened about my daughter. Tell him to drop everything else and come here.

TRACHALIO: All right.

DAEMONES: Tell him I'm going to let him marry my daughter.

TRACHALIO: All right.

DAEMONES: And here – say I know his father and am related to him.

TRACHALIO: All right.

DAEMONES: Don't waste any time.

TRACHALIO: All right.

DAEMONES: Get him here as soon as you can, so that we can have supper.

TRACHALIO: All right.

DAEMONES: You've got all that all right?

TRACHALIO [*about to dash off*]: All right – oh, there's just one thing . . . if you remember, you promised to get me freed today.

DAEMONES [*off-hand*]: All right.

TRACHALIO: You won't forget to ask Plesidippus to release me?

DAEMONES: All right.

TRACHALIO: Your daughter might put in a word for me; he'll do anything for her.

DAEMONES: All right.

TRACHALIO: And when I'm free I want to marry Ampelisca.

DAEMONES: All right.

TRACHALIO: I want the reward I deserve after all I've done.

DAEMONES: All right.

TRACHALIO: Everything's all right, then?

DAEMONES: In your own words – *all right*! Get a move on, away to the city and back.

TRACHALIO: All right. I'll be back in a jiffy. . . . You'll see that everything here's all right?

DAEMONES: All right!

[TRACHALIO *at last goes.*]

All right, all right, nothing but 'all right'. He'll find all right's all wrong one of these days, I hope.

[GRIPUS *comes back in chastened mood.*]

GRIPUS: Will it be all right [DAEMONES *jumps*] if I have a word with you, sir?

DAEMONES: Eh? Oh hullo, Gripus, what's up now?

GRIPUS: About that trunk, sir. If you had any sense you'd . . . have some sense, and keep what the good gods send you.

DAEMONES: You think it fair, do you, for me to lay claim to something which isn't mine?

GRIPUS: What, when I found it in the sea?

DAEMONES: That was a bit of luck for the man who lost it. It doesn't give us any more right to it.

GRIPUS: No wonder you're poor; you're too bloody honest.

DAEMONES:

O Gripus, Gripus, in the sea of life
There are many baited snares to catch us men.
Grasp at the bait too greedily, and lo,
You're trapped in the net of your own avarice.
The moderate, cautious, patient, prudent man
May long enjoy what he has rightly won.
It may be worth our while to lose that gain
Whose loss may be more profit than the keeping.
Should I conceal what has been given to me,
Well knowing it is another's? God forbid
That Daemones should do so. Wisest men,

No matter what their slaves may do, do well
To have no part in their dishonesty.
For my part, I desire no partnership
In crime, nor profit from conspiracy.

GRIPUS: Huh! I've heard actors in comedies spouting that sort of stuff, telling people how to behave, and getting applause for it. But I never heard of any of the audience behaving any the better for it, after they got home.

DAEMONES: Oh go away, I'm sick and tired of you. I don't want to hear any more. And you needn't think I shall give you any reward, because I shan't.

GRIPUS: Then whatever is in that trunk, gold or silver or what – please Almighty God, make it all crumble into dust. [He goes.]

DAEMONES: You see what rascals we have to put up with as slaves. If he had gone into partnership with some other slave, he'd have had him and himself involved in theft. Thinking he'd got a fine prize in his net, he'd have been led captive by his own capture. Well, now for that sacrifice – and then for that supper. [He goes in.]

*

[An hour or so may have passed, when PLESIDIPPUS comes along from the town with TRACHALIO, both in high spirits.]

PLESIDIPPUS: Oh Trachalio my boy, my love, my freedman, my master, my very father! Tell it me again. Palaestra has found her parents?

TRACHALIO: She's found them.

PLESIDIPPUS: And she's an Athenian?

TRACHALIO: I believe so.

PLESIDIPPUS: And she's going to marry me?

TRACHALIO: I expect so.

PLESIDIPPUS: Do you think we shall be betrothed today?

TRACHALIO: I do.

PLESIDIPPUS: Do you think I should congratulate the old man on finding her?

TRACHALIO: I do.

PLESIDIPPUS: And the mother?

TRACHALIO: I do.

PLESIDIPPUS: You do what?

TRACHALIO: I do think.

PLESIDIPPUS: You do think what?

TRACHALIO: I do think what you think.

PLESIDIPPUS: Don't you think you could think for yourself?

TRACHALIO: I do.

PLESIDIPPUS: Do you think I should run into the house?

TRACHALIO: I do.

PLESIDIPPUS: Or go in sedately, like this?

TRACHALIO: I do.

PLESIDIPPUS: Do you think I should greet her as I go in?

TRACHALIO: I do.

PLESIDIPPUS: And her father?

TRACHALIO: I do.

PLESIDIPPUS: And ... her mother ... do you think?

TRACHALIO: I do.

PLESIDIPPUS: Should I ... kiss ... do you think ... her father?

TRACHALIO: I don't.

PLESIDIPPUS: Or her mother?

TRACHALIO: I don't.

PLESIDIPPUS: Or herself?

TRACHALIO: I don't.

PLESIDIPPUS: Bother, now you're on the opposition side; we had better close the debate.

TRACHALIO: I think – you're off your head. Come along.

PLESIDIPPUS: Lead me, dear master, whither you will.

[*They go into the house.*

LABRAX *has meantime been brought to justice and defeated, but released from custody. He comes back in melancholy mood.*]

LABRAX: Everything's going wrong for me today. Now Plesidippus has got a verdict against me from the magistrates, and I've got to lose Palaestra. I'm finished. It must be right to call us whoremasters sons of joy; everybody seems to get a lot of fun out of our misfortunes. Well, I'm going into this temple to see how my other little property is getting on, and fetch her away at any rate; she's all the capital I've got left.

[GRIPUS *comes out of the cottage, carrying a rusty spit which he has been told to clean; he sits down to the job,* LABRAX *keeping an eye on him from a distance.*]

GRIPUS: I've made up my mind. If I don't get that trunk back, Gripus dies tonight – on my living oath.

LABRAX: Trunk! The sound of the word kills me dead. Like a stake through my innards.

GRIPUS [*aware of Labrax*]: You see? He's a free man – that criminal. And me, for catching and pulling out that trunk from the sea, I don't get a bean.

LABRAX: Eh, what's that? I must listen to this.

GRIPUS: But you won't get away with it, my fine friends. What I'm going to do, I'm going to stick up notices everywhere, in letters a yard high. Anyone who's lost a trunk full of silver and gold to apply to one Gripus.

LABRAX: Well blow me, this fellow knows who's got my trunk, I do believe. I must tackle him. Gods, help me.

GRIPUS [*in answer to a call from the house*]: What do you want? I'm out here, cleaning up this spit. . . . It's more rust than iron too; the more I rub the thinner it gets, and still red;

the bloody thing's got a wasting disease – it's falling to pieces in my hands.

[LABRAX *approaches him.*]

LABRAX: Good afternoon, sonny.

GRIPUS: God bless you, curly-locks.

LABRAX: What's going on here?

GRIPUS: Spit – and polish.

LABRAX: I hope you are quite well.

GRIPUS: Do you? Are you a medical man, then?

LABRAX: Not *medical*, no; a word something like it, though.

GRIPUS [*with unusual acumen*]: Medical – oh, mendicant, perhaps?

LABRAX: You've hit it.

GRIPUS: You seem to be dressed for the part. How come?

LABRAX: I was washed out in the sea last night. Ship lost, all my possessions lost; cleaned out.

GRIPUS: Really? What did you lose?

LABRAX: A trunk with a lot of gold and silver.

GRIPUS: Did you now? Can you remember anything particular that was in this trunk?

LABRAX: What's it matter? It's all gone now. Let's talk of something else.

GRIPUS: What if I know who found it? If you could give me some identification marks –

LABRAX [*eagerly*]: It contained eight hundred gold pieces in a wallet, and a hundred Philippic minas in a separate bag.

GRIPUS [*aside*]: Phew! That's a nice haul! I'm in for a handsome profit. Bless you, gods; I shall clean up after all! It's his trunk all right. . . . Anything else?

LABRAX: A talent of good silver in a purse; and a bowl, tankard, pitcher, an urn and a ladle –

GRIPUS: Corks! You had a pretty juicy fortune, then?

LABRAX: *Had* – that's the misery of it – *had* and not *have*.

GRIPUS [*stealthily*]: How much would you give a chap for knowing where it is and showing you how to get it back? Quick, sharp! How much?

LABRAX: Three hundred.

GRIPUS [*dismissing it with contempt*]: Peppercorns.

LABRAX: Four hundred.

GRIPUS: Fleabites.

LABRAX: Five hundred.

GRIPUS: Peanuts.

LABRAX: Six hundred.

GRIPUS: Maggots, little ones.

LABRAX: Well, seven hundred.

GRIPUS: You've got a cool cheek, for a man with a parched tongue.

LABRAX: I'll make it a thousand.

GRIPUS: You're dreaming.

LABRAX: Not a penny more.

GRIPUS: Good day, then.

LABRAX: No, look – if I leave you, I'll never be here alive again. Eleven hundred?

GRIPUS: Wake up.

LABRAX: Well, you tell me what you want.

GRIPUS: Two thousand would cover it. Not a penny less. Yes or no.

LABRAX: Oh . . . oh, all right. I've no choice. You shall have two thousand.

GRIPUS: Come this way, please. I want Venus to be our witness.

LABRAX: Anything you like.

GRIPUS: Touch the altar.

LABRAX: I'm touching it.

GRIPUS: Swear by Venus.

LABRAX: What shall I swear?

GRIPUS: What I tell you.

LABRAX: Say the word. [*Aside*] As if swearing wasn't second nature to me!

GRIPUS: Hold on to the altar.

LABRAX: I've got it.

GRIPUS: Swear you will give me the money on the day you get possession of the trunk.

LABRAX: I'll do that.

GRIPUS: Like this: 'Venus of Cyrene, I take thee to my witness, if I recover the trunk which I lost at sea, complete with the gold and silver therein and receive it again into my hands, then I will give to this man Gripus' – touch me as you say that –

LABRAX [*repeating and continuing*]: . . . Then I will give to this man Gripus – can you hear me, Venus – two thousand on the nail.

GRIPUS: Now add, that if you double-cross me, you pray Venus will wipe you out of your profession, body and soul . . . which I hope will happen to you anyway, oath or no oath. . . .

LABRAX: All right – Venus, if I slip up, you can damn all pimps to hell.

GRIPUS: She will, whatever you do. Now then, you wait here, and I'll get the old man. All you have to do is to ask him for your trunk. [*He goes into the house.*]

LABRAX: Once I get that trunk back, he can whistle for his two thousand. My tongue hath sworn – the rest is up to me. Quiet now; here he comes with the old fellow.

[GRIPUS *and* DAEMONES *come out.*]

GRIPUS: This way please, sir.

DAEMONES: Where is he?

GRIPUS [*to Labrax*]: Hey you, this gentleman has your trunk.

DAEMONES: That is so, I believe I have; if it is really yours,

you shall have it. [*Nods to Gripus to fetch the trunk.*] I think
you'll find it complete with all its contents. . . . There, if it's
yours, take it.

LABRAX: Gods above, it is mine. Welcome, old friend.

DAEMONES: You are sure it's yours?

LABRAX: It can be Jupiter's, for all I care; it's mine now.

DAEMONES: Everything is safe inside; except for one thing –
a little box of trinkets, thanks to which I have today been
reunited with my daughter.

LABRAX: Daughter? What daughter?

DAEMONES: This girl Palaestra, who used to be in your
employ, turns out to be my daughter.

LABRAX: Oh . . . splendid . . . wonderful. How very fortunate for you. I am glad.

DAEMONES: I'm not so sure that you are.

LABRAX: Oh but I am. To show you how glad I am, I won't
take a penny for her. I'll let you have her as a gift.

DAEMONES: Really, that's too kind of you.

LABRAX: Not at all, don't mention it. I'm deeply obliged to
you. [*He shoulders his trunk and moves off.*]

GRIPUS [*stopping him*]: Pst! You've got your trunk, then.

LABRAX: That's right.

GRIPUS: Come on.

LABRAX: Come on, where to?

GRIPUS: I want my money.

LABRAX: No fear. I don't owe you anything.

GRIPUS: You what? Not owe me anything?

LABRAX: Not on your life.

GRIPUS: Didn't you swear?

LABRAX: I may have done; and I'll swear some more if I
feel like it. Oaths are for protecting property, not losing it.

GRIPUS: You dirty villain, give me my money please.

DAEMONES: What money is that, Gripus?

GRIPUS: The money he swore to give me.

LABRAX: I can swear or not as I like. You're not the high priest; I'm not answerable to your reverence for perjury.

DAEMONES: What did he promise you money for?

GRIPUS: He promised me two thousand if I got his trunk back for him.

LABRAX: All right, then, give us an arbitrator; it may turn out that you made an illegal bargain – or that I'm a minor!

GRIPUS [indicating Daemones]: Let him settle it.

LABRAX: I'd rather have someone else.

DAEMONES [aside]: It's going to be difficult to deprive Gripus of the money, if I give a decision in his favour. [To Labrax] You say you promised the money?

LABRAX: I did, I admit.

DAEMONES: Anything promised to my slave is, of course, due to me; and you can't procure yourself out of that, so don't try, Mr Procurer.

GRIPUS: That's right; you mistook your man, if you thought you could swindle me. I want my money in full, and I'm going to buy my freedom with it.

DAEMONES [waving Gripus aside]: In consideration of my kindness to you and my efforts in recovering your property –

GRIPUS: I like that – your efforts, what about mine?

DAEMONES: I advise you to keep your mouth shut, boy. . . . [Continuing to Labrax] I think I can expect you to return my good offices with similar generosity.

LABRAX: Do I understand you to be asking a favour of me?

DAEMONES: I'm doing you the favour of not insisting on my rights at any cost.

GRIPUS [seeing hope]: Good for me; the pimp's weakening; freedom is in sight.

DAEMONES: My slave found your trunk, and I kept it for you, with all that money of yours.

LABRAX: It was very kind of you; and I see no reason why you shouldn't have the sum of money I promised to your man.

GRIPUS: Then kindly hand it over, to *me*, or else –

DAEMONES: Are you going to hold your tongue?

GRIPUS: What, with you pretending to act for me, and just filling your own pocket? You're not going to do me out of this lot, by heck, even if I did lose the rest.

DAEMONES: One more word, and a thrashing.

GRIPUS: You can throttle me for all I care. Two thousand smackers it'll take to keep me quiet.

LABRAX: I'm sure your master will oblige you. Do be silent.

DAEMONES: Come over here a minute, Mr – Procurer.

LABRAX: With pleasure.

GRIPUS: No whispering and mumbling, please. Let's hear you.

DAEMONES [*away from Gripus*]: Tell me, how much did that other girl, Ampelisca, cost you?

LABRAX: A thousand I paid for her.

DAEMONES: May I make you a handsome offer?

LABRAX: Name it.

DAEMONES: I'll halve the two thousand.

LABRAX: Good enough.

DAEMONES: You get a thousand for that girl's freedom, and give me the other thousand.

LABRAX: Done.

DAEMONES: In exchange for which I'll give Gripus his freedom; it's to him you owe the recovery of your trunk and I my daughter.

LABRAX: It does you credit, sir, and I'm grateful.

GRIPUS [*not having heard these details*]: Well, when do I get my money?

DAEMONES: It's all settled, Gripus. I've got the money.

GRIPUS: But damn it, *I* want the money.

DAEMONES: It's no use your expecting any of it, I'm afraid. You'll have to absolve him from his oath.

GRIPUS: I knew it! By heck, I'll hang myself, may I die if I don't! No one will ever swindle me again in this world.

DAEMONES: Perhaps you will join me for supper, Mr –

LABRAX: I shall be very happy to oblige.

DAEMONES: Then come in.

[*To the audience*] Friends, I would gladly invite you to my supper too; but I have nothing to give you; there is no rich entertainment in my house. Besides, I am sure you all have other invitations. However – give us your loud applause, and you will be welcome to my hospitality . . . after another sixteen years have passed.

Come in to supper – [*giving his hand to Gripus*] – both of you.

LABRAX: We will.

DAEMONES: Now – your applause.

EXEUNT

A Three-Dollar Day

(TRINUMMUS)

INTRODUCTORY NOTE TO
A THREE-DOLLAR DAY

THE Prologue informs us that this play is derived from the Greek of Philemon, and there are reasons for believing it to be a more than usually faithful translation to which Plautus has contributed less than his usual exuberance of comic invention.

It was probably from Philemon also that Plautus derived his play *Mostellaria*, in which, as it happens, a similar basic situation sets the plot in motion. A young man is taking the opportunity of his father's absence to squander the family fortune in riotous living; what will happen when the father returns? What happens in *Trinummus* happens only in the last few minutes of the play in a tame conclusion of reconciliation and opportune marriages. In *Mostellaria*, on the other hand, the father arrives on the scene early, to be made the butt of a series of practical jokes organized by a resourceful slave with the object of delaying his entry into his house.

How much of the difference between these two basically similar plays is due to Philemon and how much to Plautus is anybody's guess. For whatever reason, what we miss in *Trinummus* of the Plautine comic energy is replaced by a full measure, almost to excess, of moral edification; although nearly all of it, it must be acknowledged, is quite aptly integrated into the plot.

No less than four elderly gentlemen, three of them fathers, are eloquent, in this play, with advice or reproof for their contemporaries or their juniors or society in general. Of the young men also, one, the son of a martinet father, after having on occasions rebelled against strict discipline and sampled the pleasures of freedom, has now opted for virtue and is anxious to reform his libertine friend; but the latter too, with all his weakness and waywardness, shows a gentlemanly sense of honour and some sign of affection for his father. The only slave to appear in the play is also a decent character and he too, though he is allowed some of the traditional 'cheek' and artfulness of his kind, gives vent to indignant strictures on the corrupt morality of the day.

With all these conscientious individuals on his hands, the author – one author or the other – was hard put to it to introduce the 'deception' necessary to create a comic situation. The mild deception is in fact the work of two of the respectable old gentlemen, planned for entirely altruistic ends and entrusted for its execution to the only unscrupulous character in the play, a hired impostor who would have faithfully carried out his instructions – for a fee of 'three dollars' – had not events made his errand abortive.

It was a characteristic quirk of Plautus to choose a title having reference to this episode, a minor one but one which he perhaps would have liked to elaborate if he had been inclined to improve upon his model.

The play thus stands out as exceptional in mood – its nearest match is *Captivi* – and shows us a Plautus capable of restraint and at the same time (since the shape and tone of the dialogue must be largely his) shrewd and sympathetic as ever in the delineation of character even in the utterance of fairly commonplace sentiments. He allows himself some traditional joke-cracking, such as the ungallant remarks of Megaronides and Callicles about their elderly wives; but, taken as lighthearted badinage, these irrelevances do not seriously blemish the portraits of the amiable pair of cronies.

The women, though essential to the story, are absent

from the stage. We are not shown, as in *Mostellaria*, any of the partners in the libertine's debauches, nor either of the marriageable virgins who would in any case only appear as exchangeable chattels. This has the effect of keeping realism at a distance and maintaining the abstract and theoretical air which is felt in the male pronouncements on vice and virtue, obedience and independence, duty and expediency. The result is a cool and leisurely comedy, which offers an agreeably convincing, if partial, picture of Graeco-Roman family problems.

No translation of the term '*trinummus*' is very satisfactory. *Nummus*, a 'coin', had differing values at different stages in the currency; it is said to have been used in Plautus's time as the equivalent of two Greek drachmas; in that case, since 4,000 drachmas is in this play the price of a house, a *nummus* should be worth from £1 to £2. In *Aulularia* (448) and in *Pseudolus* (809) a *nummus* is the day's wage for a hired cook, and in *Menaechmi* (290) it is the price of a pig. Something of this order would seem to be a more suitable remuneration for the Impostor in *Trinummus*, than the 'three bob' of pre-inflationary translators.

CHARACTERS

LUXURY	*as Prologue*
POVERTY	*her daughter*
MEGARONIDES	*an elderly gentleman*
CALLICLES	*his neighbour*
LESBONICUS	*a spendthrift youth*
CHARMIDES	*his father*
LYSITELES	*friend of Lesbonicus*
PHILTO	*his father*
STASIMUS	*slave to Charmides and Lesbonicus*
AN IMPOSTOR	

*

The scene is at Athens, outside the houses of Megaronides and Callicles

A THREE-DOLLAR DAY

[*Enter* LUXURY, *introducing her daughter* POVERTY, *who follows reluctantly.*]

LUXURY: Come along, my child; come this way and play your part.

POVERTY: I'm coming. But I'd like to know where we're going.

LUXURY: This is where we are going. Do you see that house? I want you to go in there . . . yes, now.

[*The girl creeps unwillingly into the house, the one from which Callicles will later appear.*]

LUXURY: I can see you are wondering what all this is about. If you will promise to pay attention, I will briefly put you on the right track. My name, according to Plautus's instructions, is Luxury; and that girl is my daughter Poverty. The reason why I have sent her into that house is as follows – if you will listen carefully while I explain. There is a young man living in that house; and this young man, with my assistance, has been squandering his father's estate. Now that it has come to the point when I can see he can't afford to keep me any longer, I have sent my daughter to live with him instead. But I am not going to give you a synopsis of the play; there are two old gentlemen coming on presently, and they will tell you all about it. The play has been translated by Plautus from the Greek play of Philemon entitled *Thesaurus*, or *The Treasure*. Plautus calls it, in our barbarian language, *Trinummus*, and hopes that you will allow it to be known by that name. That is all. Farewell. Be silent and give ear.

[*Exit.*]

[*An elderly gentleman,* MEGARONIDES, *comes out of his house; he is about to pay a visit to the house next door, but he pauses doubtfully outside.*]

MEGARONIDES: It's a very disagreeable thing to have to castigate a friend whose faults deserve it; but as things are in this life, it is sometimes a necessary and salutary thing to do. That is what I have got to do today; remonstrate with a friend for something he has done wrong. I don't want to do it, but my conscience forces me to do it. There is a plague of wickedness rife in this city, destroying all the laws of morality; indeed most of them are by now a dead letter, and while morality withers wickedness flourishes like a well-watered plant. Wickedness is the cheapest thing you can find round here; you can pick a peck of it for nothing; there are far too many people who think more of pleasing a few friends than of what is best for the majority. Thus what is desirable takes second place to interest, and interest is everywhere a confounded plague, and an obstacle to private and public good.

[*His neighbour* CALLICLES *comes out of his house, turning back to speak to his wife within.*]

CALLICLES: Wife, go and say a prayer to our household god. Put a garland on him, and pray that our house may be ever righteous, happy, fortunate, and blessed ... and that your death may be not long delayed.

MEGARONIDES: This is the man I spoke of; this is the old fool who has been acting like a child and deserves a whipping for it. I'm going to speak to him.

CALLICLES: Who's that I hear?

MEGARONIDES: A well-wisher, if you are what I would wish you to be; if not, an enemy who has a bone to pick with you.

CALLICLES: Oh, it's you, my old friend and contemporary. How are you, Megaronides? I hope you're well.

MEGARONIDES: And the same to you, Callicles.

CALLICLES: You are well, I trust? You've not been ill?

MEGARONIDES: I am quite well, thank you; I have not been ill.

CALLICLES: And your wife? How is your wife? Is she well?

MEGARONIDES: Too well.

CALLICLES: Splendid. I'm glad she's well. I'm glad you've still got her with you.

MEGARONIDES: You're glad at anything that plagues me, I don't doubt.

CALLICLES: I always like my friends to enjoy what I have to enjoy.

MEGARONIDES: I bet you do. And how is your wife?

CALLICLES: She's immortal. Oh yes, she's still alive, and always will be.

MEGARONIDES: Excellent. I pray the gods she'll live as long as you do.

CALLICLES: I'd say the same – if she were your wife.

MEGARONIDES: Would you like to exchange, then? You take my wife and I take yours? I promise I wouldn't complain of the bargain.

CALLICLES: I should think not. You'd have done very well out of it. I should be the mug.

MEGARONIDES: You'd soon find that out, to be sure.

CALLICLES: We must keep as we find; better the devil we know. ... Lord, yes – if I took on a new wife now, I wouldn't know myself.

MEGARONIDES: Ah well, contentment is the secret of long life. But enough of this nonsense; I have come here especially to say something to you.

CALLICLES: Have you? What have you come to say?

MEGARONIDES: I have come to say something very unpleasant; to give you a thorough scolding, in fact.

CALLICLES: Me?

MEGARONIDES: Do you see anyone else here but us two?

CALLICLES: No.

MEGARONIDES: Then why ask whether it is you I have to scold? You don't think I want to scold myself, do you? Let me tell you, then, if you are going to let yourself fall away from your old principles, if you mean to change your nature, to give up your former manners and take to new ones, you will be causing great pain to all your friends, in fact they will soon be sick of the sight or sound of you.

CALLICLES: Whatever do you mean by that, Megaronides?

MEGARONIDES: I mean that it is a good man's first duty, and a good woman's too, to steer clear of wrong-doing or the suspicion of it.

CALLICLES: You can't do both those things.

MEGARONIDES: Why can't you?

CALLICLES: Don't you see? To keep clear of wrong-doing, that's up to me; my conscience is in my own keeping; but as for suspicion, that's something in another man's mind. For instance, if I were to suspect you of stealing the crown off the head of Jupiter on the top of the Capitoline temple – supposing you haven't done it, that is, but I choose to suspect you of having done it – well, you can't stop me suspecting, can you? But I would be very glad to know what all this is about.

MEGARONIDES: Have you a friend or acquaintance on whose discretion you can rely?

CALLICLES: Good heavens, I really couldn't say for certain. There are some whom I know to be my friends; others I think to be; and some whose natures and intentions I can't be sure of, whether to call them friends or enemies. But I

have no doubt that you are one of my truest friends. Therefore, if you know of anything foolish or ill-natured that I
have done, and fail to charge me with it, you yourself will
be very much to blame.

MEGARONIDES: You are right; and if I hadn't come to you
for that very purpose, your reproof would be timely.

CALLICLES: Speak on, then; I am all attention.

MEGARONIDES: First, let me tell you, you are the object
of much ugly gossip; people in this town are calling you an
unprincipled money-grubber; some have been heard to call
you a vulture; and to say that you don't care two straws
whether it be citizen or stranger whom you get into your
clutches. To hear you thus spoken of is exceedingly painful
to me.

CALLICLES: Well, Megaronides, that is something partly in
and partly out of my control. I can't stop people saying such
things; but I can make sure they have no ground for saying
them.

MEGARONIDES: Was my neighbour Charmides a friend of
yours?

CALLICLES: He was and he still is. If you don't believe me,
I can give you facts to prove it. After his son began squandering the family fortune and the old man saw himself on the
verge of bankruptcy – having a grown-up daughter on his
hands too, her mother his wife being dead – he had to make
a voyage to Seleucia, so he asked me to keep an eye on the
daughter, and the property, and the scapegrace son. He
wouldn't have done that, would he, if he hadn't considered
me his friend?

MEGARONIDES: Well, then; there was this young man, going
to the bad as you knew, entrusted to your care and protection. Why on earth aren't you trying to control him, why
aren't you trying to teach him thrift? Wasn't it your duty to

do all you could to improve him, instead of going the same
discreditable way yourself and adding your own misdeeds
to his?

CALLICLES: Why, what have I been doing?

MEGARONIDES: You have been acting like a scoundrel.

CALLICLES: I couldn't do such a thing.

MEGARONIDES: Didn't you buy this house from the young
man?

[CALLICLES *is silent and embarrassed.*]

Well, didn't you? This house which you are now living in?

CALLICLES: You are quite right, I did buy it, and I paid cash
for it. Four thousand drachmas I gave the young man for it.

MEGARONIDES: You actually gave him the money?

CALLICLES: I did, and I don't regret it.

MEGARONIDES: And a fine way that was of carrying out
your responsibility to the young man put in your charge!
You might as well have given him a sword with which to
kill himself, as put money into the hands of a youngster
in love, a mere boy with no self-control, giving him the
wherewithal to put the finishing touches to his own
demoralization.

CALLICLES: You think I shouldn't have paid him what I
owed him?

MEGARONIDES: You should not. You had no business to
buy or sell anything from or to him, nor give him the
means to ruin himself. You are just pandering to the boy
who was put under your care, and turning his father, who
entrusted him to you, out of house and home. A nice way
of performing your obligation to both parties! Put a man
in the position of guardian and he turns it to his own
advantage!

CALLICLES: Well, Megaronides, those are hard words, I
must say, and so unlike you that I feel obliged to impart

to you a secret that was entrusted to me, to my safe keeping, under the seal of silence, never to be revealed or made known to a single soul.

MEGARONIDES [*smugly*]: Any secret entrusted to me is safe with me.

CALLICLES: Look round carefully and make sure we are not overheard ... and again, please, to make quite sure.

MEGARONIDES [*having looked*]: There's no one.... Now I'm ready to hear what you have to say.

CALLICLES: Listen, and don't interrupt me. When Charmides was on the point of leaving for his trip abroad, he showed me, in this house, in a certain room in this house, a hoard of money.... Is anyone there? Look round again. ...

MEGARONIDES: No, there's no one about.

CALLICLES: A hoard, of about three thousand Philippics. He took me aside, just the two of us, and with tears in his eyes he conjured me never to reveal this secret hoard to his son; by our faith and friendship he bound me never to tell any single person from whom his son might get to know of it. And now, when he comes home, if he does come home safe, I shall be able to hand over this treasure intact; or if anything should happen to him, I shall at least have the money safe to provide a dowry for his daughter and so get her suitably married.

MEGARONIDES: Gods above! My friend, in those few words you have made me a different man from what I was when I came to speak to you. But tell me more.

CALLICLES: Alas, what can I tell you of that young rascal who has almost scattered to the winds his father's prudence and my loyalty and all the hidden treasure?

MEGARONIDES: How has he done that?

CALLICLES: Why, when I was away for a few days in the

country, without my knowledge or consent he put the house up for sale.

MEGARONIDES: Ah, so the wolf was growing hungrier and more ravenous, waited until the watchdogs were asleep, and hoped to devour the whole flock.

CALLICLES: And would have done, by Jove, but this watchdog got wind of him. But now it's my turn to ask you a few questions. I'd like to know what you think I ought to have done. Was I to tell him about the treasure, after having been sworn to secrecy by his father – or to let another purchaser take possession of the house, and the money with it? Anyway, what I did was to buy the house myself, and pay the young man for it, so as to keep the treasure intact for my friend. I didn't buy it for my own use or profit; I just bought it back to keep it for its owner, and paid the purchase price out of my own pocket. Well, there it is; right or wrong, that's what I did, Megaronides; that is what my wickedness and avarice amount to; and that is why I have to endure all this back-biting.

MEGARONIDES: Say no more. You have convinced your mentor; you have silenced me, I have nothing more to say.

CALLICLES: Ah, but you have. Now I want your help and advice; you must share this responsibility with me.

MEGARONIDES: I will do all I can.

CALLICLES: Where will you be, later on this morning?

MEGARONIDES: At home.

CALLICLES: I'll see you then.

MEGARONIDES: I hope you'll keep your word.

CALLICLES [going]: You can depend on me.

MEGARONIDES [calling him back]: Oh, tell me –

CALLICLES: What now?

MEGARONIDES: Where is the young man living now?

CALLICLES: In the annexe behind the house; which was not
included in the sale.

MEGARONIDES: I see. That's all I wanted to know. Good-bye.
... Oh, one thing more; what about the girl? Is she living
with you?

CALLICLES: That's right. I'm looking after her with my own
daughter.

MEGARONIDES: Good idea.

CALLICLES: Anything else before I go?

MEGARONIDES: That's all. Good-bye.

   [CALLICLES *goes*.]

MEGARONIDES: Of all the stupid, fatheaded, mendacious,
chattering, self-confident, unprincipled liars, there are none
worse than those town-trotting busybodies the scandal-
mongers. And I'm as bad as any of them for having listened
to their wicked gossip – people who know nothing and
pretend they know everything, know what everybody else
is thinking or about to think, know what the king has
confided privately to the queen, what Juno whispered to
Jupiter last night. They know; they know what never is
and never will be. They distribute their praise and blame as
they choose, without the slightest regard for truth. They
don't care two pins for anybody, as long as they can
pretend to know whatever it pleases them to know. Now
they've all been saying that my friend Callicles is not fit to
live in this city, because, as they say, he has been corrupting
this young man with his wealth. And I have been misled by
their scandal into giving my innocent friend a dressing-
down. There ought to be a strict inquiry into such rumours,
to find out where they come from; and if the scandal-
monger couldn't produce his authority he ought to be
heavily punished. If that were done, it would be a jolly
good thing for everybody; I warrant there'd be fewer people

professing to know what they don't know, and a lot of silly
talkers would learn to keep their mouths shut. [*He goes
away.*]

*

[*From along the street comes the young man* LYSITELES,
*on his way to visit his friend in the house which now belongs
to Callicles.*]

LYSITELES:

My mind is in a ferment
With all I have to think of,
And thinking makes me tired;
My mind's a tough drill sergeant
Who puts me through it, makes me sweat
And boil and pant
And faint from sheer exhaustion.

And still there's no solution,
I haven't found the answer,
I cannot tell which way to choose,
Which rule of life to follow.

Is love to be my master,
Or property? In which of these
Is one to find
His lifelong satisfaction?

I can't make up my mind. The only way,
It seems to me, is to be judge and prisoner
At once in the same court. That's what I'll do –
Examine both sides of the case.

First then

Let's see how Love deploys his art:
It is only the willing victim
He hopes to lure into his net.
He seeks him out, he hunts him down,
He charms him cunningly with soft persuasion.
Oh, he's a fascinator, a specious liar,
A lad of delicate and elegant tastes,
A shark, a thief, a miser,
A subtle tempter into shady places,
An indefatigable searcher-out of secrets.
Then, the first moment when the lover tastes
The sting of arrow-pointed kisses, *presto*,
Property vanishes, wealth is gone with the wind.
Then it's 'Honey sweetheart, won't you give me a present?
If you love me, buy me something – please.'
And the silly cuckoo must reply 'Of course,
Light of my eyes, I'll buy you anything,
Anything you want, just name it and you shall have it.'
He's down, and she hits him again. She asks for more,
Not content with the mischief she's done, she wants more;
More to eat, more to drink, more anything
As long as it costs money. The party is on;
She moves in with an army of camp-followers –
The dresser, the masseur, the mistress of jewels,
The maids with the slippers, the maids with the fans,
The maids with the trinket-boxes, musicians and messenger-
    boys,
And lackeys and runners –
And all of them eating their heads off
At the house's expense.
The poor young lover – he's ruined
But cannot say 'No.'

No – when I think of what it means
To be reduced to poverty – no, thank you.
No, thank you, Love, you're not for me.
Eating and drinking are very enjoyable,
But Love – that's where you pay for it.
No, it's not worth it.
Love makes a fellow a recluse;
He shuns the town, he shuns his family,
His friends shun him; he grows to hate
The sight of his own face. No, no,
There's nothing to be said for Love.
Don't touch it; keep away from it.
Once fall in love, you might as well
Fall off a precipice.
So farewell, Love;
Pack up your traps and leave my house,
And never call yourself a friend of mine.
Go plague and ruin those whom you have lured
Into your net. Thrift – that's the thing –
Yes, thrift shall be my watchword.
From now on I shall live a virtuous life –
Though it will take some doing.
What are a good man's aims? Honour and probity,
Substance and rank and credit and good repute,
These are an honest man's rewards; and I
Would always choose to live with honest friends,
Not knaves and double-talkers.

[*He is turning towards his friend's house when his father*
PHILTO *comes along the street, muttering to himself.*]

PHILTO: I wonder where that young man of mine has sneaked
off to . . . he left the house –

LYSITELES: Oh hullo, father. Yes, it's me. Can I do anything for you? I'm quite at your service. I'm not trying to avoid you or –

PHILTO: I should hope not. I wouldn't expect it of you. Regard for your father is what I should expect of a well-behaved son like you. I hope you never get into bad company, my boy; I hope you never exchange a single word with any undesirable person, in the street or in the forum or anywhere else. I know what people are like these days; I know what things are coming to. The knaves all want to turn good people into bad, so that everyone will be like them. They turn morality upside down, call black white. I know 'em – destructive, avaricious, malicious people who treat sacred things as profane, public property as their own private property; nothing's safe from their rapacious appetites. It's a great sorrow to me, my boy; it grieves me intolerably; that's why night and day I never cease from warning you to be on your guard against such things. These villains, they know no law; the only things they think they oughtn't to steal are the things they can't reach; anything else – pinch it, pocket it, clear off, and don't get caught. Oh, it makes me weep to think I should have lived to see such a generation. Would that I had joined the great majority before this day. . . . Yes, and these youngsters, if you please, actually praise the virtues of their ancestors even while they are besmirching their memory. I'll thank you never to have anything to do with such manners nor form your character after that pattern. Stick to the good old ways, my boy, and do as I tell you. I hate to see a good man corrupted by the filthy perverted manners that pass for morality nowadays. You just take my words to heart and you'll be blessed with a clear conscience.

LYSITELES: I have always been obedient to your commands, father. From my earliest boyhood until now, your word has been my law. For my conscience I count myself a free man, but where your orders are concerned I am content to make my inclination your slave.

PHILTO: Very well; but when a young man brings his inclination into the question, begins to ask himself whether he wants to be the sort of man his inclination chooses or the sort of man his parents and family wish him to be – why then, if his inclination wins, that's the end of him, he has made inclination his master. Only if he can conquer his inclination, then he has won a life-long triumph. If you can say you've conquered your inclinations and not been conquered by them, you can congratulate yourself. It is a far far better thing to be what you ought to be than to be what you want to be. The best men in the world are masters of their inclinations, not slaves to them.

LYSITELES: And haven't I always dressed myself in that fashion, father? Haven't I resolutely taken care to avoid bad company, stay home at nights, keep my hands from picking and stealing, and do nothing to upset your digestion? I have been scrupulously careful to keep the roof of your discipline in good repair over my head.

PHILTO: Well, don't hold it against me. It's for your own good, not mine. My time is nearly done; it's your interest I'm thinking of. The only virtuous man is the man who knows how far he falls short of virtue and honesty; the self-satisfied man is neither virtuous nor honest. Only when a man thinks little of himself has he got the true spirit of righteousness. You must reinforce your good deeds with more good deeds or they won't keep the rain out.

LYSITELES: If I am putting a case for myself, father, it is because I have a favour to ask of you.

PHILTO: Oh; well, what is it? I'm in a forgiving mood.

LYSITELES: I have a friend here, of my own age, a young

man of good family, who has been behaving with too little prudence or caution. I want to give him a helping hand, father, if you have no objection.

PHILTO: To help him out of your own pocket, I presume?

LYSITELES: Of course; that is, my own, so far as what is yours is mine, and whatever is mine is yours.

PHILTO: Well, what about him? He's broke, I suppose?

LYSITELES: He's broke.

PHILTO: Although he was quite well off at one time.

LYSITELES: He was.

PHILTO: And how did he run through his money? Was he in public contracts, or shipping? If he had a fortune and lost it, perhaps it was in commerce or slave-trading?

LYSITELES: Nothing of that sort.

PHILTO: What then?

LYSITELES: It was simply his open-handedness, father. And perhaps a little extravagance on his personal tastes.

PHILTO: Well, there's a nice friend you've found for yourself. Broke and beggared for no honest reason. I won't have you making friends with characters of that sort.

LYSITELES: But I assure you there's no vice in him whatever; and that is why I want to help him.

PHILTO: It's no kindness to keep a beggar alive. It's only throwing your own money away and helping to prolong his life of misery. Mind you, I don't say I might not wish to do the same as you and do it gladly; if I refuse in this case, it is as an object lesson to you to beware lest your being sorry for other people may end in other people being sorry for you.

LYSITELES: I should be ashamed to desert him or deny him help in his trouble.

PHILTO: Better be ashamed than sorry.

LYSITELES: But in heaven's name, father, we're well off,

thanks to the gods and your own and your forefathers' prudence; surely you couldn't regret helping a friend; you ought rather to be ashamed not to help him.

PHILTO: Do you think great wealth grows any greater, or smaller, if you subtract from it?

LYSITELES: Smaller. But do you know what they say of a non-contributor:

'May your gain be your loss, and your profit hard labour,
 If you can't help yourself and you won't help your
     neighbour.'

PHILTO: Yes, I know. But what is usually meant by a non-contributor is a man who is too poor to pay his share.

LYSITELES: Well, by the grace of the gods, we have sufficient means for our own requirements and the means to be of use to our friends as well.

PHILTO: All right, all right. I find it impossible to deny you anything you wish, my boy. Who is this man whose destitution you want to relieve? You needn't be afraid to tell me.

LYSITELES: It's young Lesbonicus, Charmides' son, who lives in that house.

PHILTO: That fellow! Why, he has consumed all he ever had and more than he ever had.

LYSITELES: Don't blame him, father; many a man has had all he asked for from fate, and more than he asked for.

PHILTO: You're wrong, my boy; and it isn't like you. A prudent man is the architect of his own fate; things don't happen to him which he hasn't planned for – unless he's a bad architect.

LYSITELES: He'd have to be an uncommonly good architect to plan his whole life successfully. Anyway, Lesbonicus is only a youth.

PHILTO: Prudence isn't a matter of age, but of character. Age is a seasoning to prudence, but prudence is the nourishment of life. However, tell me how much you want to give him.

LYSITELES: I don't want to give him anything, father. I only ask you not to forbid me to accept anything from him.

PHILTO: Accept something from him? Is that how you propose to relieve his poverty, by accepting something from him?

LYSITELES: That's right.

PHILTO: I should be obliged if you would tell me what the devil you mean.

LYSITELES: I will. You know his family?

PHILTO: I do; and I know it to be an excellent family.

LYSITELES: Well, he has a sister, grown-up, unmarried. I want to marry her, father, without a dowry.

PHILTO: Marry a wife without a dowry!

LYSITELES: Yes, father. This is the way in which you can do him a real kindness, and it won't cost you a penny. You couldn't find a more convenient way of helping him.

PHILTO: You want me to let you marry a wife without a dowry?

LYSITELES: You can't refuse; you'll be adding lustre to our own family at the same time.

PHILTO: Well ... I could read you a fine and eloquent lecture, my boy, out of the hoarded wisdom of my experience. But, since it's clear you mean to add a tie of friendship and gratitude to our house ... well, I have opposed your wishes before now, but this time I say Yes; have it your own way; ask for her; marry her.

LYSITELES: God bless you, father. There *is* one other thing you could do for me.

PHILTO: Is there? What's that?

LYSITELES: If you would go to the man yourself and do the asking; persuade him if you can.

PHILTO: I knew it.

LYSITELES: You'll be able to settle the matter more quickly than I should. Nothing will go wrong if you handle it. One word from you will be worth more than a hundred from me.

PHILTO: I knew it. That's what I get for my kindness – more trouble. All right, I'll see to it.

LYSITELES: You're a brick, father. This is where he lives. Lesbonicus is the name. You'll see to it, then? I'll wait for you at home. [*He goes.*]

PHILTO: I don't altogether like it, I must say. However, it's better than what might be worse. And one thing I will say, for my comfort: a man who does nothing but oppose his son and insist on having his own way, is wasting his time; not doing himself a bit of good; merely asking for trouble. He only brings a storm about his own head and lays up a hard winter for his old age. Well, there's the door opening . . . and yes, it's Lesbonicus coming out, with his servant.

[*LESBONICUS appears, with the slave* STASIMUS *– an elderly and responsible member of the household – with whom he is having an argument.* PHILTO *remains aside.*]

LESBONICUS: Why, it's less than a fortnight since you had four thousand drachmas from Callicles, in payment for this house. Isn't that so, Stasimus?

STASIMUS: Yes, now I come to think of it, it is.

LESBONICUS: Well, where has the money gone?

STASIMUS: Eaten, drunk, burnt . . . washed down the drain. The fishmonger's had it, the baker's had it, the butchers, the cooks, the greengrocer, the perfumier, the poulterer have had it. Oh, money soon disappears, I can tell you, with so many mouths waiting for it – like poppy-seed on an ants' nest.

LESBONICUS: All those things can't have cost more than six hundred.

STASIMUS: Can't they? What about the girls?

LESBONICUS: Including them.

STASIMUS: Perhaps I've pinched some of it?

LESBONICUS: That would account for most of it, I've no doubt.

STASIMUS: What you spend you can't have. Money isn't everlasting.

PHILTO [aside]: Too rash, and too late . . . instead of being cautious beforehand, spend first and tot up the account afterwards.

LESBONICUS: There's nothing to account for the deficit.

STASIMUS: The account's there all right; it's the money that's missing. Four thousand you had from Callicles, didn't you, when he took over the freehold of the house?

LESBONICUS: That is correct.

PHILTO: Good heavens! My future son-in-law must have sold his house. His poor father, when he comes home, will have to sit and beg at the gate, or disappear down his son's throat too!

STASIMUS: Then there was the thousand you owed the banker Olympicus.

LESBONICUS: Yes, I had offered to go bail for that amount.

STASIMUS: And had to pay up, unfortunately, when it was called in; all on account of that young friend of yours who was rich enough to pay you back any time, so you said.

LESBONICUS: I know, I know.

STASIMUS: So that's gone down the drain.

LESBONICUS: Yes, yes, I know it has. He was in difficulties and I was sorry for him.

STASIMUS: You're always being sorry for someone, never for yourself, nor ashamed neither.

PHILTO: I must go and speak to him.

LESBONICUS: Isn't that Philto coming this way? It is, by Jove.

STASIMUS: I wouldn't mind having him for my slave, with all the cash he's got put away.

PHILTO: Greetings to you both, master and slave. Greetings, Lesbonicus and Stasimus.

LESBONICUS: May the gods give you all you desire, Philto. How is your son?

PHILTO: He sends you his good wishes.

LESBONICUS: I return them.

STASIMUS [aside]: Good wishes ain't much good without good deeds. I've a good wish to be free and what good does it do me? My master may wish to be a careful man; he might as well wish for the moon.

PHILTO: My son has asked me to call on you, in the hope of effecting a union of love and esteem between you and our family. He wishes to marry your sister; and I entirely concur with his wish.

LESBONICUS [seemingly affronted]: It is not what I would expect of you, sir, if you mean to flaunt your prosperity and insult my poverty.

PHILTO: Oh come now, as man to man . . . I have no intention of insulting you. God love me, I wouldn't dream of it. I mean exactly what I say. My son has asked me to request you to give him your sister in marriage.

LESBONICUS: I am sorry, sir, but I must recognize the position in which I find myself. Our family has not the same status as yours. You should look elsewhere for a match.

STASIMUS [aside to Lesbonicus]: Man, are you out of your mind or off your head; to refuse a good offer like that?

Here's someone to help you carry the load, it seems to me.

LESBONICUS: Go and hang yourself.

STASIMUS: As if you'd let me!

LESBONICUS: So that is my answer, sir, if you will excuse me.

PHILTO: No, no, Lesbonicus. I feel sure I can persuade you into a more reasonable frame of mind. I cannot allow a young man to talk so foolishly and act so foolishly too.

STASIMUS: Hear, hear.

LESBONICUS: Another word from you and I'll knock your eye out.

STASIMUS: That won't stop my mouth. I can talk as well with one eye as with two.

PHILTO: You say, do you, that your means and status are not equal to ours?

LESBONICUS: I do.

PHILTO: But that's nonsense. Suppose you went to a festival dinner, where the banquet was, as they say, free for all – and happened to be sitting next to some rich man – and suppose that this man's retainers gathered all the good things round him. Well, if you had a fancy for some of the delicacies heaped round his plate, would you help yourself or sit hungry alongside this rich guzzler?

LESBONICUS: I suppose I would help myself, if he didn't object.

STASIMUS: I'd help myself, by Jove, whether he objected or not, and have a good old tuck-in, starting with the titbits he'd got his eye on for himself. I wouldn't stint myself for him, not likely. No use being bashful at a banquet; it's a matter of life and death.

PHILTO: You put it admirably.

STASIMUS: And I'm not kidding. In the street, in a passage, or in a matter of promotion to public office, of course I'd give way to the gentleman; but at bellywork, no, I wouldn't budge an inch – unless he was a better fighter than me. With the cost of living what it is, a free meal's as good as a tax-free legacy.

PHILTO: Never forget, my dear Lesbonicus, the best thing is to be one of the best sort of people yourself; failing that, the next best thing is to keep up with the best sort of people. Now then, I am both offering you and asking you for a contract of marriage; I very much hope you will grant my request and accept my offer. The only truly rich people are the gods; they are entitled to their wealth and status; we are but poor mortal creatures, and once we have breathed out our little puff of breath, beggar or king, we all count for the same in the book of the dead.

STASIMUS: You can't take it with you, that's a fact. When dead you're dead and there's an end of it.

PHILTO: And to show you that there's no question of status or wealth in this matter, and that it is your goodwill we value, I propose to accept your sister as a bride for my son without any dowry. So may the gods prosper it. Well, have you no answer? Is it a betrothal?

STASIMUS: By golly, that's a wonderful offer!

PHILTO: Nothing to say? Can't you utter the words 'I agree; may the gods prosper it'?

STASIMUS: Look at him; he's said 'I agree' often enough when he shouldn't have done. Now, when he should, he won't.

LESBONICUS: I am grateful, Philto, to you and your family for thinking me worthy to be connected with it. My own fortune, thanks to my own folly, is in ruins, but we still have an estate not far from the city. I shall insist on making this my sister's dowry. It is all, save my life, that my reckless-ness has left me.

PHILTO: But I tell you I want no dowry.

LESBONICUS: And I say I mean to give it you.

STASIMUS [*aside to Lesbonicus*]: Hey, master, steady on; do you want to give away the only nurse we have to keep us alive? Think what you're doing. What are we going to live on after that?

LESBONICUS: Hold your tongue. I don't have to submit my accounts to you, do I?

STASIMUS: We're done for, that's a fact, unless I can think of something. . . . [*To Philto*] Sir, if I might have a word –

PHILTO: What is it, Stasimus?

STASIMUS: Come a bit further this way. . . .

PHILTO: Very well.

STASIMUS: This is confidential; don't tell him I told you – nor anyone else for that matter.

PHILTO: You can depend on me.

STASIMUS: For the love of God, sir, never let that farm become your property, nor your son's. I'll tell you why.

PHILTO: Yes, do, for goodness' sake.

STASIMUS: In the first place, whenever that land is ploughed, the oxen drop dead in every fifth furrow.

PHILTO: You don't say so?

STASIMUS: I do. That farm of ours is just over hell's mouth. Then the grapes rot on the vines before ever they ripen.

LESBONICUS [*apart*]: He seems to be persuading the old man. He's a rascal, but a loyal one.

STASIMUS: I'll tell you something else. When every other farm has got bumper harvests, that land will give you back one third what you put into it.

PHILTO: A good place for sowing wild oats, if there's a chance of their being nipped in the bud!

STASIMUS: No one that ever owned that land has had anything but loss out of it. Of those that have tried it, some have gone abroad, others died of exhaustion, other hanged themselves. And now, as you see, its present owner is bankrupt.

PHILTO: Heaven preserve me from an estate like that!

STASIMUS: You may well say so. You'll say it again when I've told you the whole truth. Every other tree has been struck by lightning, the pigs are dying of quinsy, the sheep are scabby and bare as the palm of my hand. And as for the slaves, the Syrians, toughest lot there are, not one has been able to stand six months of it. They all die of fever.

PHILTO: That may well be, Stasimus. You should use Campanians; they'll put up with things that Syrians won't stand for, I'm told. However, from your account, that farm would seem to be an ideal place for a penal settlement. Like the fabled Isles of the Blessed, where all the good men go, this place, by the sound of it, is where all the criminals should be sent to.

STASIMUS: That's right, sir, it's a home of the damned; that's all there is to be said about it. If you're looking for trouble of any sort, that's where you'll find it.

PHILTO: Not but what *you* would find it anywhere, I'd say.

STASIMUS: You promise not to tell anyone I told you this?

PHILTO: Your secret is safe with me.

STASIMUS: My master himself would be glad to get rid of it, if he could find anyone mug enough to take it.

PHILTO: Well, I'm not taking it.

STASIMUS: You'd be a fool if you did. . . . That's done it nicely, I think; I've choked the old man off taking the farm. We shouldn't have a thing to live on if we lost that.

PHILTO: Well, Lesbonicus?

LESBONICUS: Would you mind telling me what he has been saying to you?

PHILTO: Oh, just what you'd expect. It's only natural, poor fellow, he wants his freedom, but hasn't the wherewithal to get it.

LESBONICUS: Like me! I want to be comfortably off, but now it's no use wanting.

STASIMUS: You could have been if you'd liked; now you can't because there's nothing left.

LESBONICUS: What are you muttering about, Stasimus?

STASIMUS: About what you just said; if you'd wanted to be well off, you could have been; now you want to be and it's too late.

PHILTO: Well, evidently we can't come to an agreement about the dowry; settle it as you please with my son. Once again, I ask you to give your sister to my son, and may the gods prosper it. Now what is your answer? Not made up your mind yet?

LESBONICUS: Oh very well. If you insist. May the gods prosper it; I give my consent.

STASIMUS: Good oh! That consent gives me as much joy as a newborn baby to its parents. God bless the marriage.

PHILTO: And so say I.

LESBONICUS: Stasimus, run in to Callicles' place, and tell my sister what we have arranged.

STASIMUS: I will.

LESBONICUS: And give her my congratulations.

STASIMUS: Of course I will.

PHILTO: If you'll come along to my house, Lesbonicus, we'll confirm the contract and settle a day for the wedding. [*He goes.*]

[STASIMUS *remains, watching Lesbonicus.*]

LESBONICUS: Go and do as I told you, Stasimus. And ask Callicles to see me here. I'll be waiting for him.

STASIMUS: But you *will* go to Philto's?

LESBONICUS: I must see what can be done about this dowry first.

STASIMUS: Yes, but you *will* go?

LESBONICUS: She's not going to be married without a dowry, that's flat.

STASIMUS: But you'll go –

LESBONICUS: I don't intend to let her suffer –

STASIMUS: Do go –

LESBONICUS: – for my recklessness.

STASIMUS: Yes, but go.

LESBONICUS: It's only right that my sins should fall on my head –

STASIMUS: Are you going?

LESBONICUS: – and no one else's.

STASIMUS: Go, sir, go.

LESBONICUS: Oh father, shall I ever see you again?

STASIMUS: Go now, go, go!

[*At last* LESBONICUS *goes, in great distress.*]

I've got him off at last. God preserve us! One thing is saved from the wreck, anyway, if the farm's still ours; but that's none too certain as yet. But by golly, if it is given away, I might as well be a dead man; it'll be marching orders for me, carrying his shield, helmet, and pack. He'll be off to the wars somewhere or other, as soon as this wedding's over – off to blazes in Asia, Cilicia, God knows where. Well, I'd better go and carry out my orders; though I can't stand the sight of this house, since we were turned out of it . . . turned out of our own house and home. . . . [*He goes grumbling into Callicles' house.*]

*

[*After an interval,* CALLICLES *comes out of his house with* STASIMUS.]

CALLICLES: Now then, what's all this, Stasimus?

STASIMUS: As I said, my young master Lesbonicus has betrothed his sister. What do you think of that?

CALLICLES: Betrothed her to whom?

STASIMUS: To Lysiteles, Philto's son, and without a dowry.

CALLICLES: Marry her without a dowry into a wealthy family like that? I can't believe it.

STASIMUS: Well, don't believe it, then. If you don't believe it, then I don't believe –

CALLICLES: Don't believe what?

STASIMUS: Don't believe I care a damn.

CALLICLES: How long ago did this happen, and where?

STASIMUS: Where – in front of this doorstep; and how long ago – 'not long since', as they say at Praeneste.

CALLICLES: Has Lesbonicus grown more canny in his downfall than he ever was in his prosperity?

STASIMUS: It wasn't his idea; it was Philto himself that came to make the proposal for his son.

CALLICLES: The poor girl must have a dowry; it would be a sin to deny her one. Yes, by Jove, I must do something about this. I'll go and find my mentor and ask his advice. [*He hurries off to Megaronides' house.*]

STASIMUS: I bet I know what he's after, too; I know what he's up to; he wants to do Lesbonicus out of the farm, like he's done him out of the house. Oh my poor master Charmides, they're tearing your property to pieces here; I hope you'll soon get home safe and sound, to chastise your enemies – and to reward me for the good service I've given you and am giving you. It's the hardest thing in the world to find a friend worth the name, one to whom you can trust your property and sleep sound afterwards. Here they come, though – our future son-in-law and his future brother-in-law ... doesn't look as if things were going too well between them . . . both walking fast, our chap in front and t'other dragging at his cloak. . . . Now they've stopped . . . that makes a prettier picture. I must hear what these two brothers-in-law have got to say to each other. I'll keep out of sight over here. [*He retires to a corner.*]

[*The young men appear.*]

LYSITELES: Wait a minute, please; don't try to avoid me.

LESBONICUS: Can't you let me go my own way?

LYSITELES: If it were to your own interest, your honour or good name, I would.

LESBONICUS: It's easy enough to do what you're doing.

LYSITELES: What am I doing?

LESBONICUS: Playing a dirty trick on your friend.

LYSITELES: That's not the way I've been taught to behave.

LESBONICUS: You do it well enough without teaching. Heaven knows what you could do to annoy me if you *had* been taught. You're just pretending to help me, and doing me all the harm, and giving me the worst advice you possibly could.

LYSITELES: I am?

LESBONICUS: You are.

LYSITELES: How am I harming you?

LESBONICUS: You're trying to do exactly what I don't want.

LYSITELES: I'm trying to do what I think best for you.

LESBONICUS: And do you know better than I what is good for me? I'm not an imbecile, I can see for myself what is best for me.

LYSITELES: Only an imbecile would refuse a favour from a good friend.

LESBONICUS: It's no favour to do something for a person against his will. I'm perfectly clear as to what I ought to do; I am in my right mind; I know what public opinion is and I intend to respect it, and nothing you can say will prevent me.

LYSITELES: So that's it, is it? Then it's high time for me to tell you a few home truths. Your forefathers left you a fine and honoured name; was it for you to dissipate in vicious living all that their virtuous efforts had won? You could have carried on the torch of honour to your descendants, by the straight and open way which your father and grandfather had prepared for you, the way to advancement and distinction; but you preferred to make it a hard way with your weakness and sloth and folly. You preferred to put affairs of love before your duty. And now you hope to cover up your misdeeds by this one act of generosity. You cannot. What you must do is to school your mind to honourable things and cast out idleness from your nature. Be of service to your fellow men in the city, not, as has been your habit, to your women in bed. As for that farm of yours, the reason I am determined that you shall keep it is that you may have the means to reform, and that your poverty shall not continue to be a byword to all your ill-natured neighbours.

LESBONICUS: Yes, I know. I admit everything you say. I will write out and sign a confession, if you like, of how I have ruined my father's estate and disgraced the name of my ancestors. I knew quite well what sort of man I ought to be, but unfortunately I was incapable of being it. I was enslaved by love and by my disposition to idleness, and now I am paying for it. I owe you all my thanks, and I offer them to you sincerely.

LYSITELES: But that won't do. I can't let you turn my efforts aside and treat my advice with the contempt which you evidently feel for it. I'm sorry, too, that you are not more truly ashamed. If you won't listen to my advice, the end of it will be that you'll have lost all hope of distinction, skulking behind your own miserable self; sunk without trace, at the age when you would most like to be a person of some consequence. Come, Lesbonicus, I know your real nature better than that; I know you never wilfully chose the path of error; love made you blind. Oh yes, I know all about the ways of love. Love – it strikes like a flying bombshell; it's the fastest weapon yet invented. It changes a man's character, robs him of all sense and sanity, makes him detest what's good for him and run after what is forbidden, covet what is scarce and despise what is common. Urge a lover one way and he'll take the opposite way, give him good advice and he'll act to the contrary. You're lost and damned once you take lodgings at Love's hotel. Think – I repeat again and again – think what you're doing. If you insist on your own way, you'll burn your house down over your head, and not know where to turn for a drop of water to put out the blaze; and even if – with a lover's artfulness – you find it, there won't be a spark or cinder left from which to rekindle your family's life.

LESBONICUS: That will be no trouble; even an enemy will oblige one with a light. Don't you see that your sermons against my misdeeds are only urging me into worse error? You are asking me to give my sister away without a dowry. A nice thing that would be – I, having frittered away a fortune, to go on living in comfort on the land, while she is turned off, penniless. She would hate me for the rest of her life, and rightly. A man who has forfeited the respect of his own family is not likely to command respect outside it. It's no use; I shall do as I have said, and you can save your breath.

LYSITELES: Do you really prefer to accept poverty for your sister's sake and let me take the land, instead of keeping what might be your only means of paying your way?

LESBONICUS: I'd rather you thought less about my poverty and how to relieve it, and more about my reputation. Am I to be disgraced as well as beggared? Is it to be said that I gave you my sister as a mistress, not a wife, if she is to have no dowry? Wouldn't I be called an unspeakable cad? All the gossip would glorify you, for nobly accepting her without dowry, and throw mud at me; bouquets for you and brickbats for me. No, thank you.

LYSITELES: I suppose you think they'd make you Head of the State, if you persuaded me to take the farm?

LESBONICUS: I don't think anything of the kind; and I wouldn't want it either. But a man has some self-respect, and a wish to do the right thing.

LYSITELES: I know very well what is at the back of your mind. Yes, I see; I get it; I can guess what you're up to. As soon as you've got our two families united by this marriage, and handed over the farm to me, and left yourself nothing to live on – the moment the wedding is over, you mean to become an exiled pauper, cut yourself off from home, family, friends, and relations. Then what? Everybody will say it was my doing, my stinginess that drove you out of the country. Oh no, I'm not going to let myself be put in that position, so don't imagine it.

STASIMUS [*interrupting*]: Good for you, Lysiteles! Excuse me, but I can't help cheering. Bravo, sir, bravo; you win hands down; your performance easily beats his. [*To Lesbonicus*] He gets into the spirit of the part, sir, better than you do; and his elocution is better too. In fact, I think I'll have to fine you a hundred drachmas for incompetence.

LESBONICUS: Who asked you to interfere? I don't know how you got here at all.

STASIMUS: I got here by the same way as I'm . . . going away again.

LESBONICUS: Come in with me, Lysiteles, and we'll continue the discussion behind closed doors.

LYSITELES: No, thank you; I've nothing to hide. Here is my
offer: let me marry your sister, on the terms I think
proper, that is without a dowry; remain here yourself; and
all that is mine I will share with you. If that is not to your
liking, then I can no longer be your friend; do what you
will, and good luck to you. That is my last word. [*He goes.*]

STASIMUS: He's gone. Hey, Lysiteles, come back! [*He turns
to find that* LESBONICUS *has also disappeared.*] And now he's
gone too. That leaves me. What am I going to do, then?
Nothing for it but to strap up my pack and sling on my
shield and get my boot-heels well shod. There'll be no
stopping here. I can see I shall be a soldier's batman by this
time tomorrow. I expect he'll be earning his keep under
some royal potentate. There won't be a soldier in the world
to beat him at . . . running; there'll be no counting the
spoils that his . . . enemy will win. And where shall I be?
With my bow in my hand . . . and my quiver at my side . . .
and my arrows in my quiver . . . and my helmet on my
head . . . I shall be . . . fast asleep in my tent! Well, now I'll
just pop down to the forum. I lent a chap six thousand
drachmas last week; I must get it back from him, so that I
shall have something to take with me on my travels. [*He
goes.*]

[MEGARONIDES *comes out of his house with* CALLICLES.]

MEGARONIDES: From your account of the matter, Callicles,
I should say it is unthinkable that the girl should not be
given a dowry.

CALLICLES: Of course it is. It's the only decent thing to do.
I can't allow her to get married without a dowry, when I've
got that money of her father's in my possession.

MEGARONIDES: Exactly; the dowry is there waiting for her.

Of course you could, if you like, let her brother give her away without it, and then go to Philto and say you'd like to give her something yourself – say you're doing it as a mark of your friendship with her father. I'm not sure, though, that such an offer might not expose you to ugly accusations from the public; there must be good reasons, they'd say, for your generosity to the girl. Or else they'd assume that the dowry had been entrusted to you by the father, and you had been kind enough to bestow it upon her – or part of it, keeping the rest for yourself. On the other hand you can't wait for Charmides to come home; that would be too late; the young man might have changed his mind by then and not want to marry; we don't want her to lose such an excellent match.

CALLICLES: I know, I know. I've thought of all those things myself. Look, do you think this would be a good and feasible plan: suppose I go to Lesbonicus and tell him exactly how matters stand? And yet I don't know; he's a reckless young fellow, with no thought for anything but love and indulgence. Can I let him know there's a buried treasure waiting for him? No, no, I'm sure I can't. He'd get his hands on the place where it's hidden, as sure as you're born. I daren't dig it up, lest he should hear me at it; and if I mention a word about giving a dowry, he's quite likely to ferret out the secret for himself.

MEGARONIDES: I don't see how you're going to get the stuff out of storage without anyone knowing.

CALLICLES: I could wait for a favourable opportunity and meanwhile ask some friend to lend me the money.

MEGARONIDES: You think you can get some friend to lend you the money?

CALLICLES: I think I can.

MEGARONIDES: Not on your life! You'd only get the usual

answer: 'Sorry, I simply haven't the money to lend you.'

CALLICLES: To which I would reply: 'I'm much more sorry that you're a liar than that you can't lend me the money.'

MEGARONIDES: H'm ... Well, here's an idea; what do you think of this?

CALLICLES: What is it?

MEGARONIDES: I think I've hit on an ingenious plan.

CALLICLES: Let's hear it.

MEGARONIDES: We should have to hire some fellow looking as much like a foreigner as possible.

CALLICLES: And what's he going to do for us?

MEGARONIDES: We'd have him dressed up convincingly in foreign style; he'd have to be someone unknown to the folk around here; and a good liar –

CALLICLES: Yes, but what is he going to do?

MEGARONIDES: Some bluff chap with a gift of the gab –

CALLICLES: To do what?

MEGARONIDES: He comes to young Lesbonicus, pretending to be a messenger from his father in Seleucia – gives him his father's greeting and all that – tells him the old man is alive and well and prospering and will be home very shortly. He brings with him two letters – which we shall have prepared – seeming to come from his father; gives one of them to the boy, and says the other is for you and he's going to give it you personally.

CALLICLES: Good, good, go on.

MEGARONIDES: He will also say that he has brought a sum in gold from the father for the girl's dowry, and that the father's instructions are that the gold is to be handed over to you. Do you get the idea?

CALLICLES: I do indeed; it appeals to me immensely.

MEGARONIDES: Then finally you will give the money to Lysiteles when the girl is married.

CALLICLES: It's a wonderful scheme, it really is!

MEGARONIDES: This way Lesbonicus won't suspect anything when you produce the treasure which you have dug up; he'll think it's the gold sent to you by his father, but you'll have got it out of the hidden hoard.

CALLICLES: It's a brilliant notion! Though I must say I'm sorry to lend myself to such a deception at my time of life. But wait a minute – when this fellow of yours brings the sealed letters, surely Lesbonicus must know his father's seal and wonder why –

MEGARONIDES: Oh nonsense; don't make objections; one could think of a hundred explanations – he lost the signet he had and got a new one made ... anything like that. For that matter the man could bring the letters unsealed and say they were opened and examined at the customs. But come, in this sort of business it's sheer waste of time to spend the whole day talking; there'd be no end to it. Get along as quick as you can to that treasure, and don't let anyone see you. Get all your slaves and women out of the way. . . . And one other thing –

CALLICLES: What?

MEGARONIDES: Don't let your wife know anything about it. She's incapable of holding her tongue about anything. Well, don't stand there; get a move on. Open up the cache and get out the gold, or as much of it as we need, and then close it up again immediately. And, I repeat, keep it a secret. Send everybody out of the house first.

CALLICLES: I will.

MEGARONIDES: But here we are still talking too much; wasting time when we ought to be getting to work. The business about the seal won't give us any trouble; just leave it all to me; the excuse I mentioned – that the letters were opened at the customs – will do splendidly. Anyway, look at the time; it's easy to guess what state the young man will be in by now, with his tastes and inclinations – dead drunk long ago. He'll believe anything, especially as our friend will say that he's bringing him something, not asking him for something!

CALLICLES: Yes, it should be all right.

MEGARONIDES: I'll go down to the forum and pick up a suitable impostor, and I'll get the two letters written out, then I'll brief the messenger carefully and send him up here to the boy.

CALLICLES: Very good. You do that, and I'll be about my job in here. [*He goes into his house.*]

MEGARONIDES: This is going to be a rare old lark! [*He goes off to the town.*]

*

[*About an hour later,* CHARMIDES, *the father of Lesbonicus, arrives home from his travels abroad. Before reaching his own front door, he looks back in the direction of the harbour, and addresses a salutation to Neptune.*]

CHARMIDES:
O Neptune, Neptune, brother of Jove and Nereus,
Omnipotent, salt-ipotent . . . to thee
My thanks and homage here I gladly vow. . . .
And to thy briny billows, in whose hands
Lay all my life, my goods, my destiny,
And who have now restored me from their realms
Back to my own, my own dear native land. . . .
Yea, Neptune, thee above all other gods
I thank with all my heart . . . thee whom men call
The cruel god, the stern, the avaricious,
The most destructive, most inhuman god,
The unendurable, the ravenous fiend. . . .

Not so to me, for I have found thee kind
And gentle as I could wish, out on the main.
Oft had I heard – 'tis common among men –
That thy especial virtue was to show
Compassion to the poor, and to the rich
Death and damnation. Not a bit of it.
My compliments to thee . . . thou art a just
And truly generous god, treating all men
Fairly and squarely, as the good gods should.
So may they ever spare the poor. Treacherous
They call thee? Nay, to me thou hast been loyal.
But for thy saving hand, thy satellites
The demons of the deep had torn in pieces,
Scattered asunder all that I possessed,
And my poor self, athwart the dark grey waters. . . .
What time, like yelping hounds, the whirling winds. . . .
Ay, like mad dogs . . . encompassing my ship,
With rains and waves and angry hurricanes,
Were like to rend our sails, smash yards,
And tear down topmasts . . . had it not been for thee
And thy propitious grace. But now farewell.
Now for a quiet life. The toils I've borne
To seek a fortune for my only son
Are over. I am rich . . . and I can rest.

  [*Satisfied with this exordium, he is about to turn towards
  home.*]

But who is that, I wonder, coming across the square? He's
very oddly dressed. I must wait and see what he's up to,
even though I am anxious to get home.

  [*He waits aside, while the* IMPOSTOR *comes into view,
  curiously arrayed in a medley of foreign garments.*]

IMPOSTOR: Three dollars! This is my three-dollar day.
That's what I get for lending my services in some kind of

a carnival caper. I'm supposed to have come from Seleucia, or Macedonia, or Asia, or Arabia. . . . I don't know, I've never set eye or foot on any of 'em. What a job! Well, beggars can't be choosers. Anyway, for three dollars I've got to say these letters were given to me by somebody I've never seen, never heard of, may never exist at all for all I can be sure of.

CHARMIDES: He looks like some kind of a mushroom in that enormous hat. An Illyrian possibly, from his dress and appearance.

IMPOSTOR: This party I'm working for, the chap who hired me, he takes me off to his house, tells me what he wants me to do, gives me full instructions and demonstrations, how I'm to behave and all that; anything over and above, what I put in for myself – well, he's getting so much a better performance for his money, isn't he? These togs I'm wearing, he provided them; wonderful what money can do, isn't it? He got them from the stage wardrobe, as a matter of fact, at his own risk. With a bit of luck I can make off with them; that'll show him what an expert impostor I am, won't it?

CHARMIDES: The more I see of him, the less I like his looks. Some night-prowling cutpurse, I shouldn't wonder. He's probably spying out the land and getting to know the houses round here; yes, that's it, I bet he's reconnoitring with a view to robbing us later on. I must certainly keep an eye on him and see what he's about.

IMPOSTOR: And this is the place my employer described to me. That house there is the one where I'm to do my impersonation act. I'll knock at the door. . . .

CHARMIDES: Bless me if he isn't making straight for my house. By Jove, it looks as if I shall have to spend my first night at home as a night-watchman.

IMPOSTOR: Open the door, please. Hey! Anyone in charge of this door?

CHARMIDES: Now then, young fellow, what do you want there? Why are you knocking at that door?

IMPOSTOR: I'll tell you, old fellow; and I'm an honest man, my tax returns are all in order. I'm looking for a young man named Lesbonicus, who lives somewhere around here, I believe; and another gentleman, white-haired like you, name of Callicles, so I was told by the man who gave me these letters.

CHARMIDES [aside]: He must be looking for my son Lesbonicus and my friend Callicles, whom I left as guardian of my children and property.

IMPOSTOR: I should be glad if you would inform me, if you can, as to the residence of these gentlemen, oh father.

CHARMIDES: What do you want of them, sir? Who are you? Where do you live? Where have you come from?

IMPOSTOR: That's too many questions at once. I'm not sure which you'd like answered first. If you would kindly make your inquiries calmly and one by one, I shall be happy to supply you with my name, my business, and an account of my travels.

CHARMIDES: Very well. First tell me your name.

IMPOSTOR: That's asking a lot, to begin with.

CHARMIDES: Is it? Why?

IMPOSTOR: Because my name is that long, if you were to start from the beginning of it before dawn it would be bedtime before you got to the end of it.

CHARMIDES: Dear me; that would be an expensive journey, I should think.

IMPOSTOR: But I've got another one – a teeny weeny one – just a tot of a name.

CHARMIDES: And what is that, my boy?

IMPOSTOR: Flip – that's my name, my everyday name.

CHARMIDES: Sounds a dodgy sort of name; I can well imagine, if I asked you for something which I had lent you, 'Flip!' and it would be gone. [*Aside*] The man's a rascal, without a doubt. . . . Well, what about it, young man?

IMPOSTOR: What about what?

CHARMIDES: Just tell me what you want from those two people you're looking for.

IMPOSTOR: The young man's father, Lesbonicus' father that is, has given me these two letters. He's a friend of mine.

CHARMIDES [*aside*]: That's got him. I gave him letters, did I? I'll soon have him on toast.

IMPOSTOR: If you will kindly give me your attention, I will continue what I was saying.

CHARMIDES: I am all attention.

IMPOSTOR: *This* letter is the one the gentleman asked me to give to his son Lesbonicus, and *this* one is for his friend Callicles.

CHARMIDES [*aside*]: He, he! This is where I can have a bit of fun too, I think. . . . Where was this friend of yours when you left him?

IMPOSTOR: Oh, he was doing all right.

CHARMIDES: Yes, but where?

IMPOSTOR: In Seleucia.

CHARMIDES: And he gave you those letters himself?

IMPOSTOR: With his very own hands he put them into my very own hands.

CHARMIDES: Can you describe his appearance?

IMPOSTOR: Taller than you – about eighteen inches taller.

CHARMIDES [*aside*]: That's odd – if I'm taller abroad than at home. . . . You know him, do you?

IMPOSTOR: Well of course I know him; what a silly question. We often have meals together.

CHARMIDES: What did you say his name was?

IMPOSTOR: Oh ... he's got a good honest name ... a good honest fellow.

CHARMIDES: I'd like to hear it.

IMPOSTOR: It's ... it's ... let me see now ... ts, ts ... oh bother ... [*choking*] excuse me.

CHARMIDES: What's the matter with you?

IMPOSTOR: I just ... swallowed the ... name.

CHARMIDES: I don't like a man who bites his friends.

IMPOSTOR: It was on the tip of my tongue just now.

CHARMIDES [*aside*]: A good thing I got here before he did.

IMPOSTOR [*aside*]: He's got me, damn it.

CHARMIDES: Have you remembered the name yet?

IMPOSTOR: I'm sorry, by heaven and earth I am.

CHARMIDES: You don't seem to know the man very well.

IMPOSTOR: Oh but I do. I know him as well as I know myself. You know how it is ... when you can't find something and you're holding it in your hands before your own eyes all the time! ... I could work it out letter by letter, perhaps. It begins with a C.

CHARMIDES: Callias?

IMPOSTOR: No, that's not it.

CHARMIDES: Callippus?

IMPOSTOR: No.

CHARMIDES: Callidemides?

IMPOSTOR: No.

CHARMIDES: Callinicus?

IMPOSTOR: No.

CHARMIDES: Callimarchus?

IMPOSTOR: Nothing like it. Anyhow, what the hell does it matter? I can remember all I need to remember.

CHARMIDES: Yes, but there are several Lesbonicuses in this town. If you can't tell me the name of his father, I can't direct you to the people you are looking for. What sort of name is it? Let's see if we can get a bit nearer by guessing.

IMPOSTOR: It's something like ... Chares? ... Charmides? ...

CHARMIDES: Could it be Charmides, do you think?

IMPOSTOR: That's it, by golly – Charmides, and be damned to him.

CHARMIDES: I've told you before, you ought to speak well of your friend, not curse him.

IMPOSTOR: Well, the silly beggar shouldn't have hidden himself between my teeth and my lips.

CHARMIDES: Never speak ill of an absent friend.

IMPOSTOR: Why did he try to escape me, then, the coward?

CHARMIDES: He would have answered to his name if you had uttered it. However, where is he now?

IMPOSTOR: I left him with Prince Rhadamas on the Isle of Cecrops.

CHARMIDES [aside]: Asking for my own whereabouts now! Did you ever hear anything so crazy? Still, anything makes sense in this odd affair. . . . Tell me then, what places have you visited on your travels?

IMPOSTOR: All sorts of wonderful places, extraordinary places.

CHARMIDES: I'd like to hear all about them if you don't mind.

IMPOSTOR: Certainly, I'd love to tell you. First we went to Arabia, on the Black Sea.

CHARMIDES: Is Arabia on the Black Sea?

IMPOSTOR: Oh yes. Not the Arabia where the incense comes from, but where they grow wormwood and henbane.

CHARMIDES [aside]: He's a charlatan if ever I saw one. More fool me to be asking where I've come from – as if I didn't know better than he does. But I shall be interested to know where he'll end up. . . . Well, and where did you go next?

IMPOSTOR: I'll tell you, if you really want to know. We visited the source of the river that rises under the throne of Jupiter in heaven.

CHARMIDES: The river that rises under Jove's throne?

IMPOSTOR: That's right.

CHARMIDES: Up in heaven?

IMPOSTOR: The highest point of heaven.

CHARMIDES: You mean to say you actually ascended into heaven?

IMPOSTOR: Well, actually we sailed there, in a fishing boat, up the river, upstream all the way.

CHARMIDES: Fancy that! And you saw Jupiter, I suppose?

IMPOSTOR: He was away, as it happened. The other gods told us he'd gone to his place in the country to see about his slaves' rations. After that –

CHARMIDES: All right, after that you needn't tell me any more.

IMPOSTOR: Oh very well, grumpy.

CHARMIDES: No respectful man should speak lightly of having made the journey from earth to heaven.

IMPOSTOR: Just as you like. Now would you please direct me to these men I'm looking for, so that I can give them these letters?

CHARMIDES: Tell me this. If you were to meet this Charmides himself now, the man who gave you these letters, would you recognize him?

IMPOSTOR: Well, for heaven's sake, do you take me for a dumb animal? As if I wouldn't recognize a man I've known all my life. Or do you think he would be such a fool as to trust me with a thousand gold Philippics, which is what he has asked me to take to his son and to his friend Callicles, who I understand has been left in charge of his property here – would he have trusted me with all that money if he and I hadn't been bosom friends?

CHARMIDES [*aside*]: I've a good mind to try and beat this chap at his own dirty game, and get that thousand pounds off him. Saying I gave it him indeed, when I never heard of him or set eyes on him until this moment! Why in the world should I trust him with gold, I should like to know? I wouldn't trust him with a lead penny, not even if my life depended on it. I must handle him carefully. . . . Look here, Mr . . . Flip, I'd like a word or two with you.

IMPOSTOR: As many as you like.

CHARMIDES: Did you say you had some gold on you, entrusted to you by this Charmides?

IMPOSTOR: That's right – a thousand good golden Philippic sovereigns, personally counted out to me by his banker.

CHARMIDES: You're sure it was Charmides who gave them to you?

IMPOSTOR: It could hardly have been his grandfather or great-grandfather; they must both be dead by this time.

CHARMIDES: Young man, you had better hand over that money to me.

IMPOSTOR: Hand over – what money?

CHARMIDES: The money you acknowledge having received from me.

IMPOSTOR: Received from you?

CHARMIDES: From me.

IMPOSTOR: Who are you, then?

CHARMIDES: I am the man who gave you the thousand pounds; I am Charmides.

IMPOSTOR: You damn well aren't, and never will be – as far as this gold is concerned. Get away, you swindler! You can't swindle me; I'm a swindler, so I know.

CHARMIDES: I tell you I am Charmides.

IMPOSTOR: And much good may it do you, because I haven't got any gold, so there. You thought you saw a good chance to do me down, didn't you? I say I've got some gold on me, so you immediately become Charmides; which you never were until I mentioned the gold. Nothing doing, old boy. If you can charmidize yourself so easily, you'd better go and de-charmidize yourself.

CHARMIDES: Who am I, then, if I am not myself?

IMPOSTOR: What do I care? So long as you're not the man I don't want you to be, you can be whoever you like, as far as I'm concerned. First you weren't the man you really were; now you've turned into the man you weren't before.

CHARMIDES: Come on; do it now, if you're going to do it.

IMPOSTOR: Going to do what?

CHARMIDES: Give me back the gold.

IMPOSTOR: You're dreaming, old lad.

CHARMIDES: You have admitted that Charmides gave you the money.

IMPOSTOR: He gave me some papers.

CHARMIDES: You thieving footpad, you'd better get out of this neighbourhood double quick, before I have you roughly handled.

IMPOSTOR: What for?

CHARMIDES: Because, as I've told you, I am Charmides, the man you've been telling this tall story about, the man who you say gave you the letters.

IMPOSTOR: You are? Are you really?

CHARMIDES: Yes, really and truly.

IMPOSTOR: Honest? The very man?

CHARMIDES: The very man.

IMPOSTOR: You are?

CHARMIDES: Yes, I tell you, *I am* Charmides.

IMPOSTOR: You're the same person as . . . yourself, then?

CHARMIDES: I am the very same person. Now will you get out of my sight!

IMPOSTOR: Well! . . . Fancy that! . . . So you've come home at last, and we must welcome you . . . on behalf of myself and the new watch committee . . . to a first-rate . . . flogging!

CHARMIDES: Now, now, none of your threats.

IMPOSTOR [*as if about to compliment him*]: Not at all . . . my blessing. . . . Now that you are safe home again, may the gods . . . strike me dead if it mattered two straws to me whether you got lost on the way or not. I've got my money for this job, and to hell with you; as to who you are or who you aren't, I don't give a damn. I'll go and report back to the geezer who gave me three dollars and let him know he's wasted his money. Good-bye, and the worst of luck to you. [*And, as a parting benediction:*]

> Here on your safe return from overseas,
> Gods speed you to perdition, Charmides!

[*He goes away.*]

CHARMIDES: Thank goodness, he's gone at last; now I can breathe again, and speak my mind. I'm still on tenterhooks about what business he can have been up to at my house. That letter suggests hundreds of alarming possibilities to my mind; and the thousand gold pounds, what could be the meaning of them? A bell doesn't ring for nothing, by Jove. Well, it doesn't, does it? Unless somebody pulls or moves it, it remains dumb and silent. Hullo, who's this hurrying into the square? . . . I'll wait here and see what he wants. [*He retires aside.*]

[STASIMUS *comes trotting in, and continues doubling round the scene, chatting to himself breathlessly, while* CHARMIDES *comments from his concealment.*]

STASIMUS: Get along, Stasimus ... home to your master at the double ... if you don't want your back to pay for your stupidity. Step along, there ... look lively! You've been a nice long time away, haven't you? ... If you don't look out you'll have rawhides playing pat-a-cake on your backside, if you're not there when your master asks for you. Keep on running. ... [*He stops suddenly, looking at his hand.*] Well, you're a prize idiot, Stasimus ... you've gone and left your slave-ring in the pot-house, after calling in for a throat-warmer. You'd better run back and get it before it's too late.

CHARMIDES: Whoever he is, he seems to be under the orders of his gullet; it keeps him on the run!

STASIMUS [*stopping again*]: Clot! Aren't you ashamed if you've lost your memory after three pints? Or do you imagine they were honest men you were drinking with, who could keep their hands off other people's property? No, there was Truthus, and Cerconicus, and Crinnus, and Cercobulus, and Collabus, and a pack of other chain-rattlers and whip-scarred fetter-wearers; do you think you've a chance of getting your ring back from among that crowd? I've heard of one of them stealing the shoes off a running man.

CHARMIDES: A master-thief, by god!

STASIMUS: So what's the use of going to look for what won't be there? Only adding extra work to a dead loss. Hard astern, and back to your master. [*He turns back.*]

CHARMIDES: He's not a runaway, at all events; he knows where he belongs.

STASIMUS: Oh dear, I wish we were living in the good old days, when the old rules of life, the old plain living, were held in honour more than they are under our present perverted morality.

CHARMIDES: Good heavens, he's beginning to talk like a preacher! He must be a good old-fashioned type, the way he admires and longs for the old ways.

STASIMUS: Morality nowadays means taking no notice of the law and just doing what you please. Self-advancement is what morality now approves of, and the law does nothing to stop it. Morality now permits a man to drop his shield and run from the enemy. Seeking honour by corrupt means is morality nowadays.

CHARMIDES: Shocking morality, to be sure.

STASIMUS: Honest effort gets you nowhere.

CHARMIDES: Too true.

STASIMUS: This so-called morality has got the upper hand of law. Law has about as much control over morals as parents have over their children! You can see 'em, our poor old laws, nailed up on walls – which is where our wicked morals ought to be.

CHARMIDES: I'd very much like to go and speak to him; but I like listening to him too; I'm afraid he may change the subject if I interrupt him.

STASIMUS: Laws can't protect anything from this corrupt morality; they're slaves to it; it plays havoc with all sacred things and all public property.

CHARMIDES: Good! Sentence of death for corrupt morality.

STASIMUS: And who ought to punish this sort of thing if not the state? Characters like that are public enemies and a menace to the common people. Their dishonesty undermines the credit of even innocent men. Good men's characters are judged by the base standards of these criminals. And how has this been brought home to me now? Simply by my own experience. Let a man borrow something of yours, then it's no longer yours; it's lost. Ask for it back, and you find your kindness has turned a friend into an enemy. Ask him twice, and you can take your choice of two things: either lose what you lent, or lose your friend. . . .

CHARMIDES [*now seeing the man's face clearly for the first time*]: Well, upon my word, it's my own slave Stasimus!

STASIMUS: That's what has happened to me. As I told you, I lent a man six thousand drachmas; for that price I've bought myself an enemy and sold a friend. But Lord, what a fool I am, to be bothering my head about public morality when I ought to be looking after a much more important matter – the safety of my own skin! I must get along home.

CHARMIDES: Hey there! Stop a minute, I want to speak to you.

STASIMUS [*resuming his walk, or trot*]: Hey to you; I can't stop.

CHARMIDES: I want you.

STASIMUS [*not looking*]: Suppose I don't want you to want me?

CHARMIDES: You're very bad tempered today, Stasimus.
[STASIMUS *is not to recognize Charmides for some time yet; perhaps he continues marching round the stage with* CHARMIDES *at his heels.*]

STASIMUS: Buy your own slaves and give them your orders.

CHARMIDES: I've got one, bought and paid for. But if he won't listen to me, what can I do?

STASIMUS: Give him hell.

CHARMIDES: Good idea, I will.

STASIMUS: Unless you're afraid to touch him.

CHARMIDES: I shan't want to touch you if you behave properly; if not, I shall.

STASIMUS: Me? What's it got to do with me whether your slaves are good or bad ones?

CHARMIDES: Because the profit or loss in this case is partly yours.

STASIMUS: Well, you can keep the loss; put me down for a share in the profit.

CHARMIDES: I will, if you deserve it. Just look this way, will you. I am Charmides.

STASIMUS [*stopping*]: Eh? What's that? Did somebody mention the name of the best man alive?

CHARMIDES: The best man himself.

STASIMUS: Heaven and earth and sea! So help me, gods, can I believe my eyes? Is it really the master? It is, it is, it positively is! O my beloved master, after all this time, welcome home, sir.

CHARMIDES: Greeting to you, Stasimus.

STASIMUS: To see you safe and well again is –

CHARMIDES: Yes, yes; I'm sure it is. But first and foremost, tell me this: how are my children, my son and daughter whom I left behind me?

STASIMUS: Both alive and well, sir.

CHARMIDES: Both of them?

STASIMUS: Both of them, sir.

CHARMIDES: Then I am alive and well, thanks be to the gods. Anything else I want to ask you can be asked at our leisure indoors. Come along in. . . .

STASIMUS: Where do you think you're going, sir?

CHARMIDES: Where? Why, home, of course.

STASIMUS: You think this is your home?

CHARMIDES: Well, of course I do. Where else should it be?

STASIMUS: As a matter of fact . . .

CHARMIDES: What matter of fact?

STASIMUS: . . . this is not our house any longer.

CHARMIDES: What on earth do you mean?

STASIMUS: It's been sold . . . this house . . . your son has sold it.

CHARMIDES: Never! God help us!

STASIMUS: For cash down . . .

CHARMIDES: How much?

STASIMUS: Four thousand drachmas.

CHARMIDES: Damn it, who was the purchaser?

STASIMUS: Callicles – the man whom you left in charge of your affairs. And now he's moved in, and moved us out.

CHARMIDES: Then where is my son living?

STASIMUS: In the annexe here.

CHARMIDES: It's monstrous!

STASIMUS: I was afraid you'd be upset by the news.

CHARMIDES: Upset! After facing untold perils on the high seas, after barely escaping with my life from the hands of innumerable buccaneers, I come home safe at last, to find myself ruined and betrayed by the very persons for whose sake I have exposed my declining years to all these hazards. I am overcome. . . . I cannot get my breath. . . . Hold me up, Stasimus.

STASIMUS: Shall I get you some water, sir?

CHARMIDES: You should have . . . watered . . . the dying breath . . . of my departing . . . property.

[CALLICLES *appears from the house, wearing what might be his gardening clothes.*]

CALLICLES: What's all this caterwauling in front of my house?

CHARMIDES: Callicles? Callicles! O Callicles, is this the friend whom I left to take care of my property?

CALLICLES: It is, and your most faithful, loyal, true, and trusty friend. Welcome, welcome home; how good it is to see you safe and alive.

CHARMIDES: It may be, if you are what you say you are. What are you . . . why the working clothes?

CALLICLES: I'll tell you. [*Confidentially*] I was just digging up your buried treasure, to provide a dowry for your daughter. But come in, and I'll tell you all the news.

CHARMIDES: Stasimus!

STASIMUS: Sir?

CHARMIDES: Get along down to the Piraeus, as fast as your legs can carry you. You'll see the ship there in which I came home. Find a man named Sangario in charge of my baggage, and tell him to get it ashore, and then come back with him. The harbour dues have all been paid, there won't be any delay. Off with you, and be back as soon as you can.

STASIMUS: I'll be back before you know I'm there.

CALLICLES: Come along in.

CHARMIDES: I'm coming.

[*They go into the house.*]

STASIMUS: Well, there's the one honest friend the master ever had; one to stick to him through thick and thin. He's never budged an inch from his duty, though he must have had a deal of trouble in doing it. [*He goes off to the harbour.*]

*

[*After a few minutes,* LYSITELES *comes along from the town, in high spirits.*]

LYSITELES:

> Hurray, hurray, hurray,
> I'm the happiest man today!
> Everything's beautiful, everything's fine,
> Everything's going my way.

Yes, I've got all the luck I could ask for. Stasimus has just been to my place to tell me that his master Charmides has come home from abroad. I must see him now, as soon as possible, so that the old man can ratify the bargain I've made with his son. I'm going now. [*As he reaches the door, there are sounds from within.*] Bother, he's got someone with him. I shall have to wait. [*He stands aside.*]

[CHARMIDES *and* CALLICLES *come out, in conversation.*]

CHARMIDES: My dear fellow, I don't believe there is or ever was or ever will be a man more true and loyal to his friend than you have been. If it hadn't been for you, that lad would have pulled this house down over my head.

CALLICLES: I don't think I deserve all that much praise for having kept my word and done a good turn to a friend; I should have been much to blame if I had acted otherwise. After all, a man has a right to claim what has been lent for another's use; it is not like a gift outright, which once given is given for good.

CHARMIDES: Quite so, quite so. What astonishes me is that the boy should have been able to get his sister betrothed into such a well-established family.

CALLICLES: Yes, to Philto's son, Lysiteles.

LYSITELES [*aside*]: He's talking about me, then.

CHARMIDES: He couldn't have found a better family.

LYSITELES: I've a good mind to go and speak to them now. I'll wait a minute, though. He looks as if he has got more to say on the subject.

CHARMIDES: By the bye, Callicles –

CALLICLES: Yes?

CHARMIDES: There's something else I forgot to mention just now. The moment I arrived here I was confronted by a joker of some kind – a most accomplished liar, I should say. He informed me that he had a thousand pounds in gold on him, which *I* had given him to bring to you and Lesbonicus. I hadn't the faintest notion who he was – never seen him in my life. Well, what are you laughing at?

CALLICLES: My dear fellow, I sent him! He was to pretend

that he was bringing the gold from you so that I could give it to your daughter as her dowry, so that your son, when I handed over the money to her, would believe it came from you; this would make sure that he didn't tumble to the real truth, that your buried treasure was in my care, or try to sue me for the return of it as part of his patrimony.

CHARMIDES: Well, that was an ingenious scheme, by Jove!

CALLICLES: Wasn't it? It was our mutual friend Megaronides' idea.

CHARMIDES: Splendid; I congratulate you both.

LYSITELES: I can't stand here like a booby, afraid to interrupt their conversation. I must take the bull by the horns. I'll speak to them now.

CHARMIDES: Someone coming this way; who is it?

LYSITELES: It is Lysiteles, sir, and he greets his father-in-law Charmides.

CHARMIDES: Lysiteles! God bless you.

CALLICLES: Don't I get a greeting too?

LYSITELES: Certainly, Callicles; greeting to you. But he must come first, you know – 'the shirt is closer than the cloak', as the saying is.

CALLICLES: The gods be good to you both, say I.

CHARMIDES: My daughter is betrothed to you, I hear.

LYSITELES: If you have no objection, sir.

CHARMIDES: I have no objection at all.

LYSITELES: You give me her hand, then?

CHARMIDES: I give you her hand, and a thousand gold Philippics for dowry.

LYSITELES: I don't want the dowry.

CHARMIDES: Damn it, if you like the girl, you've got to like the dowry she brings you. You'll jolly well accept what you don't want, or else you won't get what you do want.

CALLICLES: Fair enough.

LYSITELES: All right, if you're his judge and advocate, he wins. You give me her hand on those terms, then?

CHARMIDES: I do.

CALLICLES: And so do I.

LYSITELES: Two fathers-in-law! Bless you both.

CHARMIDES: And now, my friend, I've a bone to pick with you.

LYSITELES: Why? What have I been doing?

CHARMIDES: You have been allowing my son to go to the bad.

LYSITELES: It was none of my doing. You'd have a right to scold me if it were. But may I beg a favour of you, sir?

CHARMIDES: It depends what it is.

LYSITELES: Just this: please forgive him all his follies. You shake your head?

CHARMIDES: I don't know what to say. I'm angry, and yet I should be sorry –

LYSITELES: Why so?

CHARMIDES: I am angry that my son should disappoint me so; but I should be sorry if my refusing your request made you think I undervalue your kindness. Well, I won't be obstinate. You shall have your way.

LYSITELES: That is good of you. I'll go and call him out.

CHARMIDES: It's a bad thing, though, if wrongdoing is not to be punished as it deserves.

LYSITELES [*at the door*]: Open this door; quickly, please; and send Lesbonicus out, if he's there. I want him here urgently. Look sharp!

[LESBONICUS *appears.*]

LESBONICUS: Who's calling me out with all this racket?

LYSITELES: A very good friend of yours.

LESBONICUS: You don't say so? And what have you to tell me?

LYSITELES: This is what I have to tell you. I am happy to say your father has come home, alive and well.

LESBONICUS: Who says he has?

LYSITELES: I say he has.

LESBONICUS: Have you seen him?

LYSITELES: I have, and so may you.

LESBONICUS: Father! O my dear father, welcome, welcome home!

CHARMIDES: Bless you, my boy.

LESBONICUS [*with some anxiety*]: I am afraid you must have had –

CHARMIDES: No trouble at all; set your mind at rest. Everything has turned out splendidly; now I'm home, and all's well – or will be, if you're a good boy. Callicles is going to let you marry his daughter.

LESBONICUS: I'll take her; and as many more as you like to mention, father.

CHARMIDES: Well ... I *was* going to punish you, but one penance is enough for one man.

CALLICLES: Not for him it isn't. A hundred wives would be no more than he deserves for all his misdeeds.

LESBONICUS: From now on, I'll turn over a new leaf.

CHARMIDES: So you say. I hope you will.

LYSITELES: Is there any reason why I shouldn't get married tomorrow?

CHARMIDES: None whatever; you shall. And you [*to Lesbonicus*] get ready to be married the day after.

OMNES: Friends, show your thanks.

EXEUNT

Amphitryo

INTRODUCTORY NOTE TO
AMPHITRYO

ONLY once did Plautus leave the common ground of human affairs for an excursion into divine mythology. We do not know what Greek original inspired this experiment, though it is fairly certain that the subject had been handled by more than one dramatist. It appealed to Plautus, we may guess, as an occasion not so much for raising his audience's eyes from the streets to Olympus as for bringing the Olympians down into the streets. Given the legend of the parentage of Hercules, offspring of the Father of Gods and a mortal married woman, the indignation of the deceived mortal husband clearly provided the most fruitful comic theme. Jupiter remains, in the play, only cautiously personalized, and that in so far as he assumes mortal disguise; too much licence was perhaps inhibited by fear of censorship or a shred of reverence; the mortal characters are the life of the comedy: Amphitryo the enraged cuckold, Alcmena the morally virtuous but unwittingly errant wife, and Sosia the long-suffering but ever cheerful slave. The play turns out, after all, to be another comedy of human errors. It would not be surprising if the creation of Sosia, and the doubling of Sosia and Mercury as a foil to that of Jupiter and Amphitryo, were Plautus's own invention. Certainly a good deal of the Roman flavour which has been strongly imported into the play is to be found in Sosia's language and behaviour, his nocturnal encounter with Mercury in the dark and dangerous streets, his epic battle-report. If it is correct to assign the play to a date about 195 B.C., the war currently in the minds of the Roman audience would be that of

Flamininus against Philip V of Macedonia, brought to a triumphant conclusion on Greek soil in 196 B.C.

The character of Alcmena has been admired by some critics as a wholly serious portrait of a model wife. Virtuous, technically, she may be, but also surely a figure of comedy? This is a matter in which a translator can easily tip the scales, by the nuance which he puts into certain lines. I give Alcmena credit for sincerity, but feel bound to observe, for its comic effect, a womanly inconsistency between her tearful farewell to a departing husband and her hardly concealed annoyance at his surprisingly sudden return ('Is he deliberately spying on me, to see whether I really miss him?'). It is the essence of the comedy that Amphitryo's censure of his wife should be literally justified but morally unjustified; additional piquancy is gained if Alcmena admits a little capricious naughtiness into her wifely rectitude.

It will be seen that whoever designed the construction of the play was little concerned with the literal probability of the events. If Hercules and his twin brother were to be born on the day of the action, are we to assume that Jupiter had been visiting Alcmena from at least seven months previously? If so, had Alcmena been under the impression that her husband was enjoying brief spells of leave from active service? Or was the gestation of Hercules an instantaneous miracle and the 'seven months' only a fiction or translation of supernatural timelessness into terms of human chronology? No; we are not to expect the laws of arithmetic or biology to apply to a tale of fantasy – nor, for that matter, the facts of geography, since the Thebes of this play has a harbour within easy walking distance.

The tale has survived, to be re-created in the theatre of later ages: by Molière (*Amphitryon*), by Dryden (*Amphitryon, or The Two Sosias*), and by Giraudoux (*Amphitryon 38*), as the most notable instances.

One more point must be mentioned. A hiatus of about three hundred lines in the text deprives us of the climax at which Jupiter and Amphitryo come face to face. I have supplied (between square brackets, from page 272 to page 278) a reconstruction based on the twenty-odd lines which, gleaned from grammarians and lexicographers, are believed to have formed part of this scene.

CHARACTERS

AMPHITRYO   *Commander of the Theban army*

ALCMENA   *his wife*

SOSIA   *his slave*

JUPITER   *impersonating Amphitryo*

MERCURY   *impersonating Sosia*

BLEPHARO   *a sea captain*

BROMIA   *a nurse*

Other Slaves of Amphitryo

★

The scene is at Thebes, outside the house of Amphitryo.

AMPHITRYO

[*Night.* MERCURY *appears – a young god, but at present dressed as a young slave. He begins in a tone of formal proclamation to the audience.*]

MERCURY: All people here that would have me prosper their affairs and bring them gain in the buying and selling of merchandise or any other business –

You that would wish me to forward your interests and undertakings at home or abroad, and bless with everlasting profit your present and future enterprises wheresoever and whatsoever –

You that expect me to bring to you and all your friends nothing but good news; to announce, report, and convey such information as will be to your greatest advantage (reports and profits being, as you are aware, the department specially entrusted to me by the company of the gods) –

You that desire all these benefits and services from me – have the goodness to listen to this play attentively, one and all, and judge it with fair and open minds.

So to my Prologue:

[*Grandiloquently*]

At whose command I come, and to what end,
What name I bear, my task is first to tell –

[*Abandoning this formal style*]

I come at Jove's command, if you want to know.
My name is Mercury; Jove is my father.
And why he's sent me, is, to intercede with you.
Of course he knows he has only to give you orders
And you'll obey him; he knows well enough

You're scared to death of him; and so you should be;
He's God Almighty. Still, the fact remains
In this case he has sent me here to *ask* you –
Most gently and politely – to do him a favour.
    Oh yes, great Jove, 'at whose command I come',
Is no more fond of trouble than any of you are.
His mother was human, and so, I believe, was his father;
So it's only natural he takes good care of himself.
Like me – his son. If anything upsets father,
I expect to catch it too!
        With great respect, then, and humbly begging your
            pardons,
I wish to submit a just and fair request.
Just, as you're just and fair, and I a fair,
Or just fair, speaker. Nobody, after all,
Would ask fairminded men for unfair favours;
Just as to ask for justice from the unjust,
Who just don't know what justice is, would be
Just silly! . . .
                Where was I? . . .
                Pay attention, please.
    You cannot refuse us, after all we've done –
My father and I – for you and for your country.
Shall I rehearse (they do it in tragedies,
With Virtue, Victory, Mars, Neptune, Bellona,
Blowing their trumpets) – shall I, I say, rehearse
The manifold benefactions of my father,
King of the gods, towards all men on earth?
Certainly not; it wouldn't be like my dad
To cast his goodness in good people's teeth.
He knows you're grateful and he loves to help
Such well-deserving people.
        But I still haven't told you

About this favour I came to ask of you –
Not to mention explaining the plot of this tragedy.
I must get on. . . .

           What's that? Are you disappointed
To find it's a *tragedy*? Well, I can easily change it.
I'm a god, after all. I can easily make it a comedy,
And never alter a line. Is that what you'd like? . . .
But I was forgetting – stupid of me – of course,
Being a god, I know quite well what you'd like.
I know exactly what's in your minds. Very well.
I'll meet you half-way, and make it a *tragi-comedy*.
It can't be an out-and-out comedy, I'm afraid,
With all these kings and gods in the cast. All right, then,
A tragi-comedy – at least it's got one slave-part.
    Now about this favour Jupiter wants me to ask:
He'd like to have some inspectors patrolling this theatre
To look out for planted supporters in anyone's interest,
And if they catch them, haul them out and fine them
One toga for each offence. The same for canvassing
On behalf of any artist or team of actors,
By letter, or personal or indirect back-scratching,
To obtain an award of merit. And, furthermore,
Any magistrate guilty of favour or corruption
In awarding a prize shall be subject (by order of Jupiter)
To the selfsame law as applicable in a case
Of illegal solicitation for public office.
    How do you win your wars? – says Jupiter.
Not by corruption or solicitation;
Merit makes men of war, valour wins victory.
The same should be true of the service of the stage.
Merit should earn applause, not hired hands.
Where there is merit, there'll be no lack of hands,
When honest judgement rules. And to this end,

I am also commanded by Jupiter to require
That actors, too, be subject to inspection.
Anyone organizing a claque for himself,
Or crabbing a fellow-actor – out he goes,
With strips torn off his rigging, and himself.
Perhaps you're surprised at Jupiter's taking an interest,
All of a sudden, in actors? It's perfectly simple:
He's going to appear in this comedy himself.
That *does* surprise you? Well, it's not so new;
There's a precedent for it. Wasn't there a play last year,
On this very stage, when somebody called on Jove,
And out he popped to save the situation?
Anyway, he's going to appear in person today,
And I shall be with him.

　　Now, I shall have to ask you
To bear with me for a few moments longer,
While I expound the ARGUMENT. The scene
Is laid in Thebes. *That* is Amphitryo's house.
He comes of an Argive family. His wife is Alcmena,
Daughter of Electrus. At the moment, Amphitryo
Is commanding the Theban army; Thebes is at war
With the Teleboians. Amphitryo went away
Leaving Alcmena pregnant. Jupiter . . . well,
You know, of course, how – what shall I say – *broad-
minded*
He has always been in these affairs, what a *wonderful*
Lover he is, when he comes across something he fancies.
He fancied Alcmena; and without informing her husband,
Took over the tenancy, as a temporary arrangement,
Of Alcmena's bed – and made her pregnant again!
I'll repeat that. Alcmena is with child twice over,
By her husband and by Almighty Jupiter.
The latter, in point of fact, is with her now,

In bed. And that is the reason this night,
By royal command, is somewhat longer than usual,
To enable his lordship to make the most of it,
Pretending, of course, that he is Amphitryo.

   And now I can see you are wondering what I'm doing
Dressed up as a slave like this. I suppose it's because
We're doing an old old story in modern dress;
So I'm rigged out in the latest fashion too.

   Well, there you are: Jupiter inside there
Looking exactly like Amphitryo,
And all the servants quite convinced it's he.
The old man can change his skin if he sets his mind to it.
And I'm the image of Sosia, the servant
Who has gone to the war with Amphitryo; thus I can help
My *loving* father, and none of the servants ask me
My name, when they see me in and out of the house.
No 'Who may you be?' or 'What's your business here?'
They simply take me for one of their fellow-servants.

   Father'll be having the time of his life in there,
In bed with his heart's delight. He'll be telling Alcmena
All his campaigning stories, and she'll never guess
That it isn't her husband but the old arch-fornicator.
He'll be giving her all the details, how he routed
The enemy's countless legions, and how he was given
Prodigious prizes out of the spoils of war.
By the bye, we've abstracted all Amphitryo's prizes;
A little job like that is no trouble to father.

   So this is the day Amphitryo's due back home,
With his servant Sosia, whose image I am assuming.
You see this little feather in my bonnet?
This is a sign to make it easier for you
To tell us apart. In the same way father will have
A little gold tassel on his; Amphitryo won't.

None of the household will notice this; but you will.
    Yes, here he is . . . the servant Sosia
Coming along from the harbour, carrying a lantern.
I've got to keep him away from the house.
Now watch!
This is going to be good.
Jupiter and Mercury on the stage together
Is something you don't see every day.
    [*He lurks near the house.*
    It is still dark in the street. SOSIA, *Amphitryo's slave,*
    approaches cautiously, carrying a lantern.]

SOSIA:
It's a job for a brave man, this is. All alone
On a pitch dark night. Well, don't you think I'm brave?
None braver, I give you my word. I know what it's like,
With these young thugs about, anything can happen.
I could be picked up by the police and clapped in quod.
Then out of the freezer first thing in the morning
And lined up for the rope's end, without so much as
'What have you got to say for yourself, young man?'
My master won't have a word to say for me.
No one to care a damn what happened to me.
Eight strong men on the anvil – and I'm the anvil.
That's the sort of reception I shall get –
A hero's welcome home.
    It's all my master's fault; he would have it
I must come from the harbour, at this time of night.
He could just as well have waited for daylight, couldn't
    he?
It's a dog's life, working for a man with money. . . .
I say it's no fun being a rich man's slave.
Work, work, work, from morning till night,
And night till morning. 'Do this, go there, say that' –

You can't get a wink of sleep.
While he, the rich master, never does a stroke of work.
Anything he happens to think of, he wants it done;
Just takes it for granted, never mind the trouble it gives you.
No, it's no fun being a slave. And it's not just the work,
But knowing you're a slave, and nothing can alter it.

[*Though they are some distance apart,* MERCURY *overhears
Sosia's soliloquies.* SOSIA *does not, till later, hear Mercury,
but he is vaguely aware of a hostile presence and may even
unconsciously echo his words.*]

MERCURY: I'm the one that should grumble. Look at me,
A free god this morning, and now my father's slave.
This fellow's a slave from birth. Why should he grumble?

SOSIA:
Slave from birth, and slave to the rope, that's me.
And I've said my prayers and thanked the gods already
For bringing me home. Rather too soon, perhaps.
Now I suppose they'll be thinking out a way
Of returning the compliment, sending someone along
To welcome me home with a jab in the jaw
For not being grateful enough for all they've done for me.

MERCURY:
He knows what he deserves; which is more than some do.

SOSIA:
Anyway, here we are, home safe and sound.
Which is more than I, or any one of my mates,
Had a right to expect. *We've won the war!*
Our troops are back victorious, enemy vanquished,
Huge battles ended, foemen slain in thousands.
The walls that sent sharp death to countless Thebans
Are crushed and captured by our valiant hosts,
Under the banner and bold leadership
Of my brave master, great Amphitryo.

With booty, fields, and fame he hath enriched
His fellow countrymen, and set King Creon
More firmly on his royal seat. He hath . . .
What else? . . . Oh yes, he hath sent me
Home from the harbour, like I said, before him
To tell his missis how our great commander
Has served and saved his country.
Now what am I going to tell her when I see her?
I shall have to invent a bit here and there, as usual.
I didn't see much of the fighting; I was too busy running.
I must use my imagination, and what I heard
From one or two others . . . I'd better have a rehearsal. . . .
How shall I begin? . . . Oh yes –

[*He makes a bow to the imaginary lady, and practises his
speech, adopting what he hopes is a suitably heroic and literary
style.*]

'Twas thus, my lady: Soon as we set foot on the shore of the
land to whither we were bound, our general's first care was
to summon and select his foremost captains and charge
them to deliver his challenge to the Teleboians, as thuswise:
'Be they willing, without blow or blood, to deliver up the
spoils, together with the spoilers, into Amphitryo's hands,
and to restore what they have pinched, well . . . and good;
he will forthwith lead his army home, the Argives will
quit the land and grant peace and tranquillity to the Teleboians. BUT . . . IF . . . they be not so willing, and if his
demands be not obeyed, thereupon he will assault their
city with all his might and men.'

Amphitryo's ambassadors having duly conveyed this
message to the Teleboians, the latter, proud warriors as
they are, bold in their might and boasting of their valour,
did make rude and angry answer to our embassy: by arms
they could well defend themselves and all what was theirs;

let Amphitryo *be off*, and remove his armies from their turf.

This answer being reported back, in the same instant did Amphitryo lead all his forces to the field. And from the Teleboian city out poured a like host in noble panoply. On either side vast armies, man by man and rank by rank, marched out to battle. Our legions were arrayed in customary form and order – and the enemy's legions . . . the enemy's legions . . . were arrayed on the opposite side. Forth strode the commanders, from this side and from that, and in the middle of the field, in front of the massed battalions, did hold their parley. And thus it was agreed: whichever side should lose the battle, should lose their city, their lands, their altars, their homes, and themselves.

After that, there was a flourish of trumpets, on either side, and a shout of battle, on either side, and the very earth did quake. The leaders, on either side . . . on this side and on that side . . . said their prayers to Jove, and addressed words of encouragement to their men . . . on either side. Then each man did what each man could, according to his valour, laying about him, on every side, with slashing sword and smashing spear. The skies re-echo to the shouts of men, their panting breaths congeal in clouds of mist, the ground is carpeted with bleeding bodies.

At length we gained the upper hand; our prayers were answered. The enemy's casualties were colossal. We, on the other hand, grew stronger and stronger. Nobody turned a hair, nobody ran, all stood to their posts, preferring death to desertion. And those that died fell where they stood, and left no gap in the line.

When our brave commander saw how things were going, he hesitated not a moment but gave the order for a cavalry charge on the right wing. They were off like a flash; with a

yell of delight they swooped from the right with all their
might, and trampled the foemen's forces into bloody dust –
and serve them jolly well right.

MERCURY: Word perfect. I was there myself at the time,
and so was my father.

SOSIA: The varlets broke and fled. Our men grew bolder.
And as the Teleboians turned their backs, their rears were
riddled with our weapon-points. Amphitryo himself cut
down King Pterelas.

So all day long the noise of battle rolled – I remember that,
because I missed my dinner – till night came on to part the
combatants. Next day, their chieftains came forth from the
city, weeping, to our camp. In suppliant fashion, they
besought us to pardon their transgressions, and surrendered
themselves, their possessions, profane and holy, their city,
and their children into the dominion and jurisdiction of the
Theban people. As a prize for valour my lord Amphitryo
was presented with a golden bowl, that same from which
King Pterelas himself was wont to drink.

Yes, that'll make a fine story for the mistress . . . Now
I'd better be about my master's business, and so to
bed.

MERCURY: He's coming this way now. I'll have to intercept
him. He's not setting foot in this house if I can help it.
My being got up as his twin brother will fox him. But if
I'm to be his double, I shall have to model my manners on
his. I shall need to use his weapons of craft, cunning, and
deceit to drive him from the door. . . . What is he doing
now? Staring up at the sky. . . . I wonder what his game is.

SOSIA [staring up at the sky]: That's funny. Looks as if old
Nocturnus went to bed drunk last night. There's the
Plough, still in the same place as last night, and the Moon
not moved an inch since she rose. . . . Orion . . . Evening

Star ... and the Pleiades nowhere near setting. Everything's at a standstill. It's no nearer dawn than it was six hours ago!

MERCURY: Well done, Night. You just go on as my father wants it. You're doing a fine job in a fine cause for a fine fellow, and you'll find it a fine investment.

SOSIA: Well, it's surely the longest night I've ever seen – barring the one when I was beaten and left trussed up for twelve hours. I believe this is longer, though. Sun must be still snoring ... drunk too, probably ... toasting himself too often.

MERCURY: The scoundrel imagines the gods in his own likeness. I'll show you what such talk deserves, you gallows-bait. Just step this way and see what happens to you. [*All this still aside.*]

SOSIA: What about it, you night-prowlers who never sleep alone if you can help it? You can get your money's worth tonight, eh, boys?

MERCURY: That's right. I'm sure he'd agree that my father is making good use of it, in Alcmena's bed, enjoying his heart's desire.

SOSIA: Well, I must get indoors and deliver my message. .... There's a man hanging round the door. Who is he, I wonder? I don't like the look of him.

MERCURY: Coward.

SOSIA: He looks as if he had a mind to pinch the cloak off my back.

MERCURY: I'll have some fun with the chicken-heart.

SOSIA: Oh ye gods, my teeth are tingling. This is the chap who's going to welcome me home with both hands, I'm sure it is. In the kindness of his heart he's going to oblige by putting me to sleep, after my master keeping me awake all night. I'm a dead man, for sure. Look at the size of him!

MERCURY: Wait till he hears me speak! I'll startle him. [*Loudly*] Come, fists of mine, it's time you found some meat for my stomach. You've done no work since yesterday, when you left four men flat out and stark naked.

SOSIA: Four men flat out. And I'm the fifth. From now on my name's Quintus.

MERCURY [*tightening his belt and squaring up*]: I'm ready for him.

SOSIA: He looks like business.

MERCURY: He's for it.

SOSIA: Who is?

MERCURY: The first man I meet gets this fist in his mouth.

SOSIA: Not me. Not at this time of night. I've had my supper, thanks. Give it to someone who's hungry.

MERCURY: That's a good fist, that is. Some weight in it.

SOSIA: I'm in for a pounding.

MERCURY: Shall I put him gently to sleep? Shall I?

SOSIA: Just what I need. I haven't had a shut-eye for three nights.

MERCURY: It'd be a shame, though, wouldn't it? It really would be a shame to spoil that lovely physiognomy. One knock of this knuckle and he'll be a changed man.

SOSIA: He's going to give me a beauty treatment.

MERCURY: Give him the full treatment and he won't have a bone left in his face.

SOSIA: Now he wants to fillet me. I don't think I like filleted face. If he sees me now, I'm done for.

MERCURY: I smell something evil.

SOSIA: It wasn't me, sir.

MERCURY [*weirdly*]: One that cometh from afar will soon be near. . . .

SOSIA: Crystal-gazer!

MERCURY [*soldierly*]: Up, fists, and at him!

SOSIA: Give 'em a bit of practice on that wall first, general.

MERCURY [*whimsically*]: Do I hear a little bird's voice winging its way hither?

SOSIA: So my voice is a bird, is it? I'm sorry I didn't clip its wings.

MERCURY [*contemptuously*]: This ass is just asking for a load of trouble.

SOSIA: What ass? I'm no donkey-driver.

MERCURY: I'll pummel his pommel.

SOSIA: I can't stand any more loading. I haven't recovered from that sea voyage yet. My stomach is heaving still. I can hardly carry *myself*, unloaded.

MERCURY: Surely someone spoke?

SOSIA: Someone. Then he hasn't seen me. I'm Sosia, not Someone.

MERCURY: Here on my right. Surely a voice hit my ear?

SOSIA: And he can't hit it back, so he'll hit me instead.

MERCURY: Good, he's coming this way now.

SOSIA [*in a hysterical gabble*]: Ooh, I'm frightened, I'm frozen, I'm flabbergasted, I don't know where I am, I'm stuck fast, I can't move, I can't speak, I've forgotten my name. This is the end; here lies poor Sosia and his message – [*Suddenly switching back to normal*] I know what I'll do. I'll go up and speak to him. If I put on a bold face, he may think I'm as brave as he is and let me alone.

[*He approaches the door;* MERCURY *intercepts him.*]

MERCURY: Whither away, lantern-bearer?

SOSIA: What's that to you, face-filleter?

MERCURY: Slave, or free man?

SOSIA: Whichever I please.

MERCURY: Really?

SOSIA: And truly.

MERCURY: You're on the way to a whipping, I think.

SOSIA: I think you're wrong.

MERCURY: I'll show you I'm right.

SOSIA: It's not that important, is it?

MERCURY: Tell me where you are going, and what is your business, and who is your master.

SOSIA: I'm coming here, I'm doing my master's business, and my master is the man I work for. Right?

MERCURY: I shall have to put that clever tongue of yours to bed.

SOSIA: You can't. She's not allowed out with strange men.

MERCURY: Funny, aren't you? Come on, what's your business with this house?

SOSIA: What's yours?

MERCURY: His Majesty's service. Special night watchman.

SOSIA: Fine; very kind of His Majesty to look after our house while we were away. Now you can knock off, and tell him the servants are back.

MERCURY: How do I know you're a servant? *You'd* better knock off, and double quick, or I'll serve you with the service you deserve.

SOSIA: I tell you I live here. I'm one of the family servants.

MERCURY: Do you know something? You're going to get a rise, if you don't take yourself off.

SOSIA: A rise? How's that?

MERCURY: You won't *take* yourself off; you'll be *lifted* off, shoulder-high, when this club has finished with you.

SOSIA: But I live here, I work here, I'm on the staff.

MERCURY: I'll staff you, if you don't clear off this minute.

SOSIA: It's a bit thick if a man can't get into his own home when he comes back from foreign parts.

MERCURY: Your own home, is it?

SOSIA: Of course it is.

MERCURY: Who is your master, then?

SOSIA: Amphitryo, commander-in-chief of the Theban army, husband of Alcmena.

MERCURY [*with a shout of laughter*]: Fancy that! And what is your name?

SOSIA: Sosia, the Thebans call me; Sosia, son of Davus.

MERCURY [*turning nasty again*]: I thought so. You'll be sorry for this, you summit of impudence – coming here with a tissue of lies, a patched tale –

SOSIA [*looking at his shirt*]: I may have come with a patched tail, but I've come on a true errand.

MERCURY: You haven't; you've come on your two feet. Ha! Ha! Ha!

SOSIA [*seriously*]: I suppose I have, really.

MERCURY: So you'll really get beaten this time, for lying.

SOSIA: But I really don't want to.

MERCURY: That really doesn't matter. And when I say *really*, I mean *really*.

[*The beating begins.*]

SOSIA: Mercy, mercy!

MERCURY: How *dare* you *say* you're *Sosia* when *I* am *Sosia*?

SOSIA: He's killing me!

MERCURY [*pausing*]: I'll do worse in a minute. Now who do you belong to?

SOSIA: Oh, you, sir. Now you've paid for me, hand over fist. [*Suddenly letting out a yell for help*] Help, Thebans, help!

MERCURY: Stop bellowing, carrion. And tell me what you're here for.

SOSIA: To give you someone to beat.

MERCURY: Whose slave are you?

SOSIA: I'm Sosia, Amphitryo's slave.

MERCURY: Lies again. . . . Take that. . . . I tell you I am Sosia.

SOSIA: I wish you were, by all the gods, then you'd be getting the beating.

MERCURY: What's that?

SOSIA: Nothing.

MERCURY: Who is your master, then?

SOSIA [giving it up]: You tell me.

MERCURY: And what's your name?

SOSIA: Any name that suits you.

MERCURY: I thought you said you were Amphitryo's Sosia.

SOSIA: My fault. I must have meant Amphitryo's *associate*.

MERCURY: That's better. I knew there was no Sosia in the household but me. A slip of the tongue, eh?

SOSIA: I wish you'd make a slip of the fist.

MERCURY [punching him]: *You* said *you* were Sosia, and *I* tell you *I'm* Sosia.

SOSIA: Look, mister, could I have a few minutes' peace to speak to you, and no more beating?

MERCURY: An armistice perhaps, if you have anything to say.

SOSIA: Nothing short of peace, or I won't talk. You've got the superior weapons.

MERCURY: Say what you want to say. I won't hurt you.

SOSIA: Promise?

MERCURY: Promise.

SOSIA: And if you break it?

MERCURY: Then may all the wrath of Mercury fall upon Sosia.

SOSIA: Well now, listen. Now I can get a word in – the fact is, I *am* Amphitryo's slave, Sosia.

MERCURY: That again!

SOSIA: Now, now. Pax. I've signed the treaty. And I'm telling the truth.

MERCURY: For which I'll thrash you.

SOSIA: Just as you like; I can't stop you. But whether you do or not, that's the truth and I'm sticking to it.

MERCURY: You can't tell me I'm not Sosia, not on this earth.

SOSIA: And you can't tell me I'm not a servant in this house; and there's no other servant called Sosia here but me.

MERCURY: He's raving.

SOSIA: It's you that's raving, man. [*To the audience*] Hell and damnation, don't *you* think I'm Amphitryo's Sosia? Didn't our ship arrive this very night from Perse Harbour, and me on it? Didn't my master send me here? Aren't I standing in front of our own house? Aren't I carrying this lantern? Isn't this me speaking? Am I awake? Hasn't this fellow beaten me black and blue? He must have; my face is still aching. What am I waiting for, then? Why don't I go home? [*Making for the door.*]

MERCURY [*intercepting him*]: Home?

SOSIA: Yes, home.

MERCURY: Just a pack of lies. [*To audience, calmly*] Of course I'm Sosia, Amphitryo's Sosia. We sailed from Perse Harbour yesterday afternoon, after sacking the city of King Pterelas and defeating the Teleboians. Amphitryo himself slew King Pterelas in battle.

SOSIA [*thunderstruck*]: Well I'll be damned. He's got it all pat. . . . Look, do you remember what was given to Amphitryo from the Teleboian spoils?

MERCURY: The golden bowl that Pterelas used to drink from.

SOSIA: Right too. And do you know where that bowl is now?

MERCURY: In a box, sealed with Amphitryo's ring.

SOSIA: What is the sign on the ring?

MERCURY: Sol rising in his chariot. Are you trying to catch me out, crossbones?

SOSIA: He's proved his case. I shall have to find another name. How he saw all this happen I don't know. . . . Damme, though, I believe I can catch him. . . . Let me see . . . something I did all alone, in the tent, with no one there to see me. . . . He can't possibly know that. . . . Look, mister, if you're Sosia, can you tell me what Sosia was doing, in his tent, while the battle was at its height? Tell me that and you win.

MERCURY: Oh yes; there was a cask of wine there; I drew a jugful.

SOSIA: Getting warm. . . .

MERCURY: And drank it. Beautiful wine too, fresh as the day it was born.

SOSIA: He's right; that's exactly what I did. He must have been hiding in the jug.

MERCURY: Are you convinced now that you're not Sosia?

SOSIA: You think I'm not?

MERCURY: Well of course you're not, since I am.

SOSIA: But I swear by Jupiter I am not lying.

MERCURY: And I swear by Mercury Jupiter doesn't believe you. He'd take my bare word against your oath, for that matter.

SOSIA: Well for Jupiter's sake, who am I, if I'm not Sosia?

MERCURY: You can be Sosia as much as you like, when I don't want to be. At the moment I am Sosia, and you can pack off, or take another thrashing – scum.

SOSIA: Well, I don't know. . . . Now I come to look at him, and look at myself – I mean I know what I look like, I've looked in a mirror before now – he *is* very like me. Hat . . . clothes . . . he might easily be me . . . leg, foot, height, haircut, eyes, nose, mouth, cheeks, chin, beard, neck . . . the lot. There's no denying it. If he's got a back striped with whip scars, he's me. But I can't understand it . . . I'm sure I'm the same man I always was. I know who my master is. I know this house. I can think . . . and feel . . . Well, damn it all, I don't care what he says, I'm going to knock at the door.

MERCURY: Where are you going now?

SOSIA: Home.

MERCURY: You won't get away from your fate, not if you were to climb into Jove's chariot and fly to Olympus.

SOSIA: Can't I go and tell my own mistress what my own master has told me to tell her?

MERCURY: You can tell *your* mistress anything you like, but you're not coming near mine. Provoke me once more, and you'll go home a bottomless ruin.

SOSIA [*giving in*]: All right, all right, all right. I'm going. . . . So help me gods, where did I lose myself? Where was I translated? Where did I shed my skin? Have I gone and left myself at the harbour by mistake? This fellow has certainly got hold of what used to be my likeness. My likeness being carried about while I'm alive! — as it never will be after I'm dead. I'll go back to the harbour and tell master all about it. But perhaps he won't know me either. Well, by Jupiter, I hope he doesn't! Then I'll shave my head and stick a freeman's cap on my noddle. [*He goes back the way he came.*]

MERCURY:

A good beginning. One inconvenient interloper
Chased from the door. Another hour or two
Gained for papa to fondle her ladyship
Uninterrupted. At least, I hope so. Now what happens?
The slave goes back and tells Amphitryo
He was refused admittance by a slave called Sosia.
Amphitryo doesn't believe him, obviously. 'Liar,'
He says, 'you never went near the house at all.'
That's it — I'll have them both and all the family
So muddled up they won't know where they are!
And then — when father's finished what he's doing
In there — we'll let them all into the secret.
    Jupiter of course will see that husband and wife

Kiss and forgive each other, and no harm done.
To begin with, naturally, Amphitryo
Will give his wife a devil of a talking-to
And call her all sorts of names. But in the end
Jupiter will sort it out and quell the riot.
    There's just one other thing –
I didn't tell you this before – Alcmena
Is going to be delivered of twin sons
Today. One is Amphitryo's child – nine months;
The other Jupiter's – he's only seven. Thus
One will be the elder – the other more highly connected.
I hope that's clear.
It was out of consideration for Alcmena
That Jupiter arranged to have both the children born
Together . . . to save her trouble . . . and avoid embarrass-
    ment.
Of course Amphitryo will have to know all about it,
As I said just now. But that won't matter so much.
The point is, Alcmena won't have to take the blame.
That's only fair. We don't expect you mortals
To suffer for our peccadilloes. . . .
Excuse me. . . . There's someone at the door. . . . It's them!
The vice-Amphitryo and his borrowed spouse.
    [*He retires to a distance.*
    From the house come JUPITER, *looking just as we imagine*
    Amphitryo will look, and ALCMENA.]
JUPITER: Good-bye, beloved. Look after yourself . . . and
    everything. You can't afford to take any risks now, it's
    near the time. I'm sorry I have to go away again, but it
    cannot be helped, I'm afraid. Take care of the little one.
ALCMENA: Is it so important for you to go back so soon?
JUPITER: Naturally I would much rather stay at home with
    you, beloved. But a commander cannot leave his men

to their own devices. Nothing goes right and far too many things go wrong.

MERCURY: Crafty old beggar! He's not my father for nothing. Watch how he handles her.

ALCMENA: Your wife isn't very important to you, it seems.

JUPITER: But you're the dearest woman in the world to me; isn't that enough for you? [*He embraces her again.*]

MERCURY: Steady on, old man. [*Glancing at the sky*] Somebody may be watching you up there. If *she* finds out what you're up to, you'll wish you were really Amphitryo.

ALCMENA: Words are not much comfort. You got here at midnight and now you're off again. You've hardly had time to warm the bed for me. Do you expect me to like that?

MERCURY: This is where I can do a bit of coaxing on my father's behalf, like a good lackey. [*Coming forward*] I'll take my oath, madam, there's not a mortal husband in the world that so passionately worships his own wife as my master passionately dotes on you.

JUPITER: Oh you're there, vagabond, are you? Who asked you to interfere? You just keep your mouth shut, or you'll get this stick across your back. . . .

ALCMENA: Gently, gently, please.

JUPITER: Another word out of you –

[MERCURY *is driven off.*]

MERCURY: That lackeying wasn't a great success.

JUPITER: You were saying, beloved . . . Please don't be angry with me. I oughtn't to be here at all, really. I managed to slip away from my troops, just to have a few moments with you, and to be the first to tell you of my exploits for our country. And I've told you, haven't I? The whole story. Doesn't that show you how much I love you?

MERCURY: I told you he'd got a way with him, didn't I?

JUPITER: Now I must nip back again before I'm missed. Or they'll be saying I put my wife before my duty.

ALCMENA: And leave your wife in t-t-tears?

JUPITER: Hush now, don't spoil your pretty eyes. I'll be back very soon.

ALCMENA: 'Soon' is much too long.

JUPITER: It's hateful to have to go away and leave you here.

ALCMENA: It is; especially when you go away the same night that you arrive.

JUPITER: Don't cling to me, beloved. I must go. I want to get out of the city before it's light. . . . Look – [*somewhere about him he has been carrying a small object wrapped up*] – I want to give you this . . . a token which was given to me for valour in the field. . . . It's King Pterelas's drinking bowl. . . . I killed him personally. It's for you, Alcmena.

ALCMENA [*pleased*]: Darling! Oh, how *kind* you always are! . . . Oh, isn't it *lovely*! A lovely present from a lovely man.

MERCURY [*prompting Jupiter*]: Now you should say: No, a lovely present for a lovely lady.

JUPITER: You again! Can't you keep out of my sight, pestilence!

ALCMENA: Please, Amphitryo: don't be angry with poor Sosia for trying to be nice to me.

JUPITER: Oh very well.

MERCURY [*aside*]: He's a monster when he's in love.

JUPITER [*to Alcmena*]: Is that all then?

ALCMENA: Only – love me, near or far, as I always love you. . . .
     [*Long embrace.*]

MERCURY: Dawn's coming up, sir. Time to go.

JUPITER: Get along, Sosia. I'll follow. . . . That's all, then?

ALCMENA [*sobbing*]: That's all. Come back soon.

JUPITER: I may do, sooner than you expect. Be brave, sweetheart. . . .

    [*They part at last:* ALCMENA *goes into the house.*]

Thanks, Night, for waiting for me. You can let Day take over now; and let it be a fine day for mankind, if you please. It'll have to be shorter than usual, I'm afraid, owing to the unusual length of the night. Carry on, Day.

    [*Dawn comes up with a swift radiance.*
    JUPITER *goes away.*]

               *

    [*Half an hour later.*
    AMPHITRYO *arrives from the harbour, with* SOSIA *and slaves carrying baggage.* SOSIA *is in no hurry.*]

AMPHITRYO: Where is that fellow? Come along.

SOSIA: I'm coming, sir, I'm coming.

AMPHITRYO: You're a fine rascal, you are.

SOSIA: Me, sir? Why, sir?

AMPHITRYO: Telling me a lot of things that never are and never were and never will be true.

SOSIA: You never can and never have and never will believe a person.

AMPHITRYO: What do you mean? I've a good mind to cut your damned tongue out.

SOSIA: Why not? I'm your property to do as you like with. In the meantime I'm telling you everything that happened here and you can't stop me.

AMPHITRYO: Idiot, do you mean to stand *here* and tell me you're *in there*?

SOSIA: That's right.

AMPHITRYO: God knows what will happen to you, and what I'm going to do with you.

SOSIA: Well it's for you to say. You're the owner.

AMPHITRYO: Are you making fun of your master, rope's-
end? Have you the face to tell me something no one has
ever seen on this earth and never will – one man in two
places at the same time?

SOSIA: I'm only telling you the plain facts.

AMPHITRYO: Jupiter strike you stiff!

SOSIA: I hope I haven't done you any harm, sir.

AMPHITRYO: Done me any harm? Telling me a cock-and-
bull story –

SOSIA: Oh I wouldn't do that, sir. I should deserve bad names
then. But I'm only telling you the honest truth.

AMPHITRYO: The man is obviously drunk.

SOSIA: If only I were.

AMPHITRYO: *If* – I say you *are*.

SOSIA: Am I?

AMPHITRYO: Where have you been drinking?

SOSIA: It must have been nowhere.

AMPHITRYO: I don't know what's the matter with the fellow.

SOSIA: I've told you ten times over. I'm in there, see;
in our house. And I'm out here, with you. Me, Sosia, in
there, out here. Don't you think that's plain enough, O
master?

AMPHITRYO: Oh go away.

SOSIA: Go away? Why?

AMPHITRYO: You're not safe to be about.

SOSIA: Why do you say that, master? I feel quite well, thank
you, I really do, master.

AMPHITRYO: Well, you won't feel so well when I've
finished with you, once we get home – if we ever do get
home. Come along, anyway. Telling me all that tale of
tomfoolery . . . coming here to make a jackass of me . . .
instead of carrying out your orders . . . inventing a lot of
nonsense the like of which no man ever heard of and

couldn't happen anyway. . . . Bag of bones! Your backside will learn what all those lies mean!

SOSIA: Oh sir! It's a poor look-out if an honest slave can't tell his master the honest truth without being whacked for lying.

AMPHITRYO: For goodness' sake, tell me – convince me – prove it to me – how can it be possible for you to be out here and in there at the same time? Go on, tell me.

SOSIA: Well, I am. I admit it's funny. I can't understand it myself, any more than you can.

AMPHITRYO: You can't?

SOSIA: No, I can't. I couldn't believe my own senses either, so help me God I couldn't; until the Sosia in there convinced me. He told me every blessed thing that happened in the battle; had it all pat. And he's got my looks, not only my name. Dead spit; as like as two drops of milk we are, I and . . . me in there. You know when you sent me on from the harbour, before daylight –

AMPHITRYO: Well?

SOSIA: I was standing in front of the house before I got here.

AMPHITRYO: Hell and damnation, man, don't talk rubbish. Are you mad?

SOSIA: Do you think so?

AMPHITRYO: Some devil has laid hands on him since I saw him last night.

SOSIA: That's right enough. Very heavy hands too.

AMPHITRYO: What? Who attacked you?

SOSIA: I did. I – Sosia – the one in there.

AMPHITRYO: Now wait a minute. Just answer my questions and nothing else. Who . . . is . . . this . . . Sosia?

SOSIA: Your slave – Sosia.

AMPHITRYO: I've never had more than *one* slave Sosia in my life – and that's one too many.

SOSIA: Ah well, that's where you're wrong, sir. I bet you anything you like, when you open that door you'll find another slave Sosia; son of my father Davus; same age as me; same face, same everything. Well that explains it, doesn't it? You've got twins!

AMPHITRYO: It's a most extraordinary thing. Did you see my wife?

SOSIA: I never got into the house at all.

AMPHITRYO: Who stopped you?

SOSIA: That Sosia I've been telling you about, the one who beat me.

AMPHITRYO: Which Sosia was that?

SOSIA: Well, me, I suppose. Oh, what's the use –

AMPHITRYO [trying a new tack]: Tell me; have you been asleep all this time?

SOSIA: Sleep? I never slept a wink.

AMPHITRYO: You may have dreamt you saw another Sosia.

SOSIA: I don't sleep on duty, sir. I was awake when I saw him; I'm awake as I look at you now; I'm awake while I'm telling you this; and I was awake when he gave me a beating . . . so was he.

AMPHITRYO: He, who?

SOSIA: Oh for love and kisses! . . . me, him, Sosia. Haven't I explained it to you? Don't you understand?

AMPHITRYO: Such a pack of nonsense, nobody could understand.

SOSIA: Oh you'll understand all right, as soon as you meet Sosia.

AMPHITRYO: Come on, then. We must get to the bottom of this. Have you got all the baggage from the ship?

SOSIA: I've seen to everything, sir.

AMPHITRYO: Let's hope everything you've seen doesn't turn out to be true.

[*They are about to move towards the house, when* ALCMENA *appears at the door; she doesn't see them.*]

ALCMENA:

For every pleasure in the path of life
How many pains we suffer! Such is our lot,
Poor mortals as we are. There is no joy
Without its sorrow, heaven has so decreed.
And still, the more the joy, the more the sorrow.
I know; now it comes home to me; I know;
A few brief hours of happiness with my husband –
One night – less than a night – dawn not yet come;
And he must go. And I am here alone,
Without the one whom most of all I love
In all the world. My joy at his return
Was great, but how much greater was the pain
Of parting from him. . . .

Still there is comfort –
This is the joy –
He has come home
A hero! Conqueror! Praised by all his people!

To let him go is not so hard, I see,
If he comes back with glory. I can be brave.
I can endure his going, I can endure it,
If this is my reward – to see my husband
Hailed victor, crowned with laurels, borne in triumph.
It is enough. There is no greater gift
Than valour. Valour is all. Valour protects
Our life, our liberty, our health, our wealth,
Our home, our kith and kin. Valour is all,
And he hath all that hath it!

AMPHITRYO: She loves me, by Jupiter. She loves me, bless

her; and I love her. She'll jump for joy to see me come home – especially after what I've achieved. Nobody thought we could do it, but we did. We beat them hollow – knocked them out in the first round, thanks to my inspiration and leadership. By Jove, she'll be glad to see me.

SOSIA: There's someone who'll be glad to see me too, I may say.

ALCMENA [*abruptly brought back from her dreaming*]: Is that my husband?

AMPHITRYO [*to Sosia*]: Follow me.

ALCMENA: What on earth has he come back for, after saying he couldn't stay a minute longer? Could he be trying to catch me out and make sure whether I really miss him? Well, it's his house; I suppose he can come back if he wants to.

SOSIA: Sir, I think we had better get back to the ship.

AMPHITRYO: Back to the ship? Why?

SOSIA: I don't think we're expected for breakfast here.

AMPHITRYO: What on earth are you talking about?

SOSIA: We're too late.

AMPHITRYO: Why too late?

SOSIA: The mistress looks as if she's had it. . . .

[AMPHITRYO *ignores this sally, but looks at* ALCMENA *with grave concern.*]

AMPHITRYO: She's near her time. Of course I knew she was pregnant when we went away.

SOSIA: Worse luck for me.

AMPHITRYO: Why for you?

SOSIA: I'm just back in time to bath the baby. It *is* nine months, I think you said.

AMPHITRYO: Well, don't be alarmed.

SOSIA [*with one of his unpredictable changes of mood*]: Alarmed?

I'm delighted. Let me get my hands on a bucket once more and I'll drain the well dry, never trust me again if I don't.

AMPHITRYO: Don't worry. We'll find someone else to do that. Come along. . . .

ALCMENA: I ought to go and meet him, I suppose.

[*At last they meet, and embrace.*]

AMPHITRYO: With joy Amphitryo greets the wife he has so long desired to see again, a wife without equal, in his eyes, among all the wives of Thebes, the wife whom all men of Thebes delight to honour for her virtue.

[ALCMENA *is dumbfounded.*]

Have you kept well? Are you glad to see me?

SOSIA: She'd be as glad to see a lost dog, by the look of her.

AMPHITRYO: You seem in splendid shape, my love. I am glad to find you in such excellent condition.

ALCMENA: Is this a joke, for heaven's sake? Why all this speechifying, as if you had just come home, instead of just parted from me?

AMPHITRYO: But I haven't seen you before today.

ALCMENA: Of course you have. Why deny it?

AMPHITRYO: I am not in the habit of speaking anything but the truth.

ALCMENA: It's a pity you've changed your habits. Don't you trust me? Why are you back so soon? Just now you said you had to go back to duty. What has happened? Something wrong with the omens? Or the weather?

AMPHITRYO: Just now? So soon? What *do* you mean?

ALCMENA: Oh *you* know. Just now. Not so long ago.

AMPHITRYO: I don't know what you're talking about. How long ago is just now?

ALCMENA: As if you didn't know. [*Playfully*] Well, then,

guess. After making me guess your riddles – saying you
have only just arrived, when you've only just gone.

AMPHITRYO: Has the woman gone mad?

SOSIA: Let her sleep it off.

AMPHITRYO: Or is she dreaming with her eyes open?

ALCMENA: My eyes are open all right. And I can tell you
what they saw. You – and him – this morning – just now.

AMPHITRYO: Where did you see us?

ALCMENA: Here, of course. In this house. Your house.

AMPHITRYO: Couldn't have done.

SOSIA: Hold hard, sir. Perhaps the ship sailed up the street
and brought us here while we were asleep.

AMPHITRYO: You don't believe the woman, do you?

SOSIA: Well, you know, you have to be careful. These
women in a trance, if you thwart them you're liable to
send them completely round the bend, and they'll tear
you to pieces. Humour them, and you may get off with a
black eye.

AMPHITRYO: I'll give her a taste of my humour, by Jupiter,
if this is how she welcomes me home.

SOSIA: You'll burn your fingers.

AMPHITRYO: Shut up . . . Alcmena, just tell me something.

ALCMENA: Yes, dear?

AMPHITRYO: Is this a foolish prank, or some kind of spite
against me?

ALCMENA: I can't think why you should wish to ask your
wife such a question. What's the matter with you?

AMPHITRYO: On other occasions you have always welcomed
me home as any faithful wife should. This time you seem
to be in a very different mood.

ALCMENA: But goodness gracious, didn't I welcome you
home last night, at this very door, and ask you how you
were, and take your hand, and kiss you?

SOSIA: Was this yesterday, madam?

ALCMENA: Of course it was; and you were there too.

SOSIA: Sir, I hoped your lady was about to be the mother of a son. But I'm afraid she's something else.

AMPHITRYO: Oh, what?

SOSIA: Mother of invention. She's off her head.

ALCMENA: I'm nothing of the sort. And, please God, I'll soon be a happy mother. What *you* deserve for your pains, you preposterous prognosticator, you'll very soon find out, and in full measure, if your master knows his business.

SOSIA [*aside*]: It's *her* pains he ought to be worrying about. . . . Give her a raw apple and let her chew on that.

AMPHITRYO: My dear, you say you saw me here yesterday?

ALCMENA: *Yes*, for the tenth time.

AMPHITRYO: In a dream, perhaps?

ALCMENA: No; wide awake; both of us.

AMPHITRYO: Oh, this is dreadful! . . . Sosia!

SOSIA: What's up, sir?

AMPHITRYO: My wife is really insane.

SOSIA: Just a touch of bile, sir. It always sends 'em off.

AMPHITRYO: When did you feel it coming on, wife?

ALCMENA: Heaven help us, I tell you I am perfectly sane and well.

AMPHITRYO: Then why in the world do you keep on saying you saw me yesterday? We only landed last night. I had dinner in the mess and spent the whole night quietly on board. I haven't set foot inside the house since the day I and my army embarked to fight the Teleboians – and beat them.

ALCMENA: Stuff and nonsense. You had dinner with me, and went to bed with me.

AMPHITRYO: What!!

ALCMENA: I am not in the habit of speaking anything but
the truth.

AMPHITRYO: As a general rule, perhaps. But this – no, this
cannot be true.

ALCMENA: At daybreak you went back to your men.

AMPHITRYO: I did?

SOSIA: That's just as she remembers it, sir; she's telling you
her dream, see? You know, madam, when you woke up
you ought to have said a prayer, with incense and a pinch
of salt, to Jupiter the Maker of Mysteries. . . .

ALCMENA: Go and boil your head.

SOSIA: . . . it'd be the best thing for you, really it would.

ALCMENA: Are you going to let him talk to me like that?

AMPHITRYO: Shut up, you. Now let's get this clear: I left
you this morning at dawn?

ALCMENA: Well, it must have been you; who else could have
told me all about the battle?

AMPHITRYO: You know all that too?

ALCMENA: Every word of it, all about how you took the
enormous city, and how you killed Pterelas with your own
fingers.

AMPHITRYO: *I* told you?

ALCMENA: *You* told me, on this very spot, and he [*Sosia*]
was here.

AMPHITRYO: Sosia, have you heard me tell that story in the
last twelve hours?

SOSIA: Where would I have heard you, sir?

AMPHITRYO: Ask her; she knows.

SOSIA: Not in my presence you haven't, I can swear to that.

ALCMENA: A remarkably loyal servant.

AMPHITRYO: Come here, Sosia; look me in the eye.

SOSIA: I'm looking.

AMPHITRYO: I want the honest truth; never mind what *I*

said. Did you or did you not hear me telling my wife what she says I told her?

SOSIA: Are you out of your mind too, for godsakes – asking me a question like that? Haven't I just now seen her for the first time, the same as yourself?

AMPHITRYO [to Alcmena]: You hear him?

ALCMENA: I've heard every lying word he has spoken.

AMPHITRYO: You won't believe him, then, or your husband?

ALCMENA: I can believe my own eyes better, and it all happened just as I say.

AMPHITRYO: Do you still say I came here last night?

ALCMENA: Do you still deny you went away this morning?

AMPHITRYO: Of course I deny it. I never came home till this minute.

ALCMENA: And you deny that you gave me that golden bowl this morning – the one you said was given you on the field of battle?

AMPHITRYO: God in heaven! I never gave it you, nor told you anything about it. I was going to give it you, as a matter of fact, and still intend to do so. Who the devil told you about it?

ALCMENA: You did, darling, and gave it to me with your own hands.

AMPHITRYO: Wait a minute, wait a minute, for the gods' sake. . . . Sosia, I am at a loss to understand how my wife could know that I had been presented with a golden bowl. Are you sure you didn't meet her some time ago and tell her about it?

SOSIA: I swear I never told her. I never saw her anywhere till I saw her here when you and I came –

AMPHITRYO: All right, all right . . . I don't know –

ALCMENA: Would you like to see the bowl?

AMPHITRYO: I would indeed.

ALCMENA: You shall. [*To a servant within*] Thessala ... will you bring out that bowl, please; the one my husband gave me this morning.

AMPHITRYO: Sosia ... come over here [*away from Alcmena*]. If she's got that bowl, it beats everything.

SOSIA: But it's impossible. I've got it still in its box, with your seal on it.

[*He produces the box out of the baggage.*]

AMPHITRYO: Is the seal intact?

SOSIA: See for yourself.

AMPHITRYO: Yes ... that's my seal all right.

SOSIA: You really ought to have her certified.

AMPHITRYO: Upon my word, I think I shall. She is undoubtedly possessed.

[*The maid brings out the bowl.*]

ALCMENA: Here it is. Now are you satisfied?

AMPHITRYO: Let me have a look at it.

ALCMENA: Yes, have a look at it, and deny your own act if you can. If that doesn't convince you, nothing will. Is it your bowl or isn't it?

AMPHITRYO: Jumping Jupiter! It is the bowl, not a doubt of it. I'm going crazy, Sosia!

SOSIA: Well blow me down – if the bowl isn't still in this box where it ought to be, your wife is the world's greatest female illusionist.

AMPHITRYO: Open the box. Go on, open it.

SOSIA: But – why, it's ridiculous – the seal's not broken, everything is as it should be. Tell you what, sir – you've got a twin Amphitryo, I've got a twin Sosia, and if the bowl's got a twin bowl we're all seeing double.

AMPHITRYO: Open it and see.

SOSIA: Kindly inspect this seal, sir; I don't want any of the blame.

AMPHITRYO: That's all right; open it; the woman will have us all stark staring mad.

ALCMENA: Where do you think it could have come from, if you didn't give it me?

AMPHITRYO: That is what I mean to find out.

[SOSIA *opens the box, which is empty.*]

SOSIA: Ow!! Jupiter!

AMPHITRYO: Well?

SOSIA: It's gone!

AMPHITRYO: What!!

SOSIA: The box is empty.

AMPHITRYO: If that bowl's not here, you're a dead man.

ALCMENA: But it *is* here.

AMPHITRYO: Then who gave it you? Alcmena, look at me and tell me who gave it you?

ALCMENA: The person I am looking at gave it to me.

SOSIA: There you are, you see. Trying to blame it all on me, as usual. It's obvious you nipped up here last night by a back way, nipped the bowl out and gave it to her, sealed up the box again, and nipped back to the ship.

AMPHITRYO: Gods above!... are you on the crazy woman's side now?... [*To Alcmena again*] We came here yesterday, did we?

ALCMENA: You came here yesterday. You greeted me out here. I greeted you. I kissed you.

SOSIA: Far too much kissing for my liking.

AMPHITRYO: Go on.

ALCMENA: You had a bath.

AMPHITRYO: I had a bath. What then?

ALCMENA: You sat down to dinner.

SOSIA: Now we're coming to it. Ask her what next.

AMPHITRYO: You keep quiet.... Go on, what next?

ALCMENA: We had dinner. Both of us. On the couch. Together.

AMPHITRYO: On the same couch?

ALCMENA: On the same couch.

SOSIA: Very unwise.

AMPHITRYO: *Will* you let her finish her story? We had dinner. Then what did we do?

ALCMENA: You said you were ready for bed. The table was removed. We went to bed.

AMPHITRYO: Where did you sleep?

ALCMENA: Well . . . in our room . . . in our bed.

AMPHITRYO: Ruin! Ruin!

SOSIA: Oh sir . . .

AMPHITRYO: This is a mortal blow!

ALCMENA: What is, if you please?

AMPHITRYO: Don't speak to me.

SOSIA: Sir . . .

AMPHITRYO: This is the end. In my absence she has been vilely ravished.

ALCMENA: My good man, what *are* you talking about?

AMPHITRYO: Your good man am I? I am no man for you . . . I am no man for any –

SOSIA: Not a man? Oh dear, that's bad.

ALCMENA: What wrong have I done to be spoken to like this?

AMPHITRYO: What have you done? You have *told* me what you've done, and you ask me what wrong?

ALCMENA: I don't see anything wrong in spending the night with my husband.

AMPHITRYO: With your husband! The brazen shameless impudence! If you have no respect for your own modesty you might have some for mine.

ALCMENA: You cannot convict me of unfaithfulness,

however hard you try. Such a thing has never been known in my family.

AMPHITRYO: Gods above! Sosia, you know me, I think?

SOSIA: Well, pretty well.

AMPHITRYO: Did I dine on board yesterday?

ALCMENA: Oh, I can produce witnesses too.

SOSIA: It's a mystery to me, sir; unless there's some other Amphitryo perhaps, to stand in for you and do your job when you're away. That duplicate Sosia was surprising enough; if there's a duplicate Amphitryo, it beats the lot.

AMPHITRYO: It's witchcraft, that's what it is.

ALCMENA: By the kingdom of Jupiter Almighty and by Juno our Mother whom I should most fear and adore, I swear no other mortal man but you has touched my body to my dishonour.

AMPHITRYO: If it could be true!

ALCMENA: It is true. But what help is that, if you will not believe it?

AMPHITRYO: A woman will swear anything.

ALCMENA: An innocent woman is not afraid to speak out boldly for herself.

AMPHITRYO: Too boldly.

ALCMENA: Why should not innocence be bold?

AMPHITRYO [sneering]: Innocent by your own account.

ALCMENA: And what is my dowry? Not that treasure which the world calls dowry. What is it if not honour and purity and temperance, fear of the gods, love of my parents, the happiness of my family, and the will to love and obey you, to be good to all good friends and helpful to all honest men.

SOSIA: There's a picture of a perfect wife – if you can believe it.

AMPHITRYO: She has almost bewitched me into doubting whether I know my own name.

SOSIA: Your name's Amphitryo all right. But mind someone doesn't borrow it off you. There's been a lot of borrow-
ing and lending since we came home from abroad.

AMPHITRYO: Well, madam, I shall certainly not let this
matter go without thorough investigation.

ALCMENA: I shall be obliged to you.

AMPHITRYO: Tell me this. Suppose I bring your cousin
Naucrates up from the docks? He was with me on the
voyage. If he says your story is all nonsense, what will you
deserve then? Is there any reason why I shouldn't divorce
you?

ALCMENA: None whatever, if I have done wrong.

AMPHITRYO: Good. Sosia, get these fellows in with the
baggage. I shall be back shortly, and bringing Naucrates
with me. [*He goes.*]

[SOSIA *sends the slaves into the house.*]

SOSIA: Now we're alone, my lady, just tell me one thing, on
the level. Have I got a double in there named Sosia?

ALCMENA: You and your master are a double. Get out of my
sight.

SOSIA: Very good, my lady. [*He goes into the house.*]

ALCMENA: O merciful gods! It is incredible that my husband
should make such a monstrous charge against me without
the slightest reason. I must wait for my cousin Naucrates.
He will tell me the explanation, if there is one. [*She goes
into the house.*]

*

[*An hour later.*
JUPITER *returns to the house.*]

JUPITER:
Now which Amphitryo am I? . . . That's right,
I am the one whose servant Sosia

Is also Mercury when necessary.
I'm also Jupiter, when I feel like it.
I live up there in the attics. Down on the ground
I turn into Amphitryo, clothes and all.
This time I'm here entirely for your benefit;
Otherwise the play would come to a sudden end.
I have also come to help Alcmena out;
Of course she's innocent, but Amphitryo
Insists on trouncing her for infidelity.
It's all my fault. I should never forgive myself
If the innocent party had to take the blame.
So I'm going to be Amphitryo again
And cause as much confusion as I can
In the family circle. But in the end, you'll see,
I'll have the mystery cleared up all right.
Then there's Alcmena's lying-in to see to.
I want to make sure her husband's child and mine
Turn up together, with the minimum of inconvenience.
Mercury has orders to be on immediate call,
In case I need him. . . . Ah, here she comes.

[ALCMENA *comes from the house.*]

ALCMENA: I cannot stand this house a minute longer. To be
accused by my husband of such vile, disgraceful, filthy
conduct! Insisting that what never happened did happen,
and declaring I did something I never did and could never
think of doing! If he imagines I can laugh that off, he's
mistaken. I certainly can't, and don't intend to. I'm not
going to sit down under such wicked and unjust insinua-
tions. Either he apologizes or I've finished with him. He'll
have to swear that he withdraws all the accusations he has
made against his innocent wife.

JUPITER [*aside*]: Quite right. I shall certainly have to see that
he does; otherwise I shall not be able to enjoy her delightful

company any more. It would be too bad if *his* righteous
indignation against his wife fell on *my* innocent head just
because *my* little affair has upset *his* virtuous propriety.

ALCMENA: A man who can make such foul charges. . . . Oh,
here he is.

JUPITER: May I speak to you, Alcmena? Don't turn away.

ALCMENA: I don't exactly enjoy looking at my worst
enemy.

JUPITER: Enemy? Oh, come now.

ALCMENA: That is what I said, and mean. But I suppose you
won't believe anything I say now?

JUPITER: You don't mean it; you're upset, naturally –

ALCMENA: Don't touch me! If you were in your right mind,
I shouldn't have thought you would want to exchange a
word, in jest or earnest, with your wife after calling her a
whore to her face, unless you're a bigger fool than you
look.

JUPITER: What I *said* doesn't make you . . . what I said;
and I don't really think you are. Now I have come back to
apologize. I was terribly upset when I heard how badly you
had taken it. Why in the world did I say it, then? Well, I'll
tell you. *Of course* I could never think you capable of being
unfaithful to me. I was just making an experiment . . .
to see what you *would* do if I *had* said such a thing . . . how
you would react under such a . . . just a joke really. Everything I said just now was supposed to be taken in a humor-
ous spirit. . . . Well, let's ask Sosia, shall we?

ALCMENA: I thought you said you were going to bring
Naucrates here to swear you had not been here before?

JUPITER: Ah well, that was part of the joke, not meant to be
taken seriously.

ALCMENA: It was serious enough to me.

JUPITER [*seizing her hand*]: Alcmena, by this hand, I implore you, I beseech you, pardon me, forgive me, do not be angry with me.

ALCMENA: I am not angry. I have shown that my virtue has nothing to fear from your accusations. I have never done anything shameful and I don't want to hear any more of your shameful language. Good-bye. Keep what is yours, and give me what is mine. And kindly let my servants go with me.

JUPITER: You are out of your mind!

ALCMENA: Or if need be, I will go alone, and my honour shall be my only companion.

JUPITER: Wait. To convince you, I will give you my solemn oath – the most solemn oath you could ask for. I swear I believe my wife is guiltless. If I swear falsely, may the wrath of Jupiter Almighty fall upon Amphitryo!

ALCMENA [*a gasp, a pause, and she is convinced*]: Oh no, his blessing, his blessing!

JUPITER: So be it; for I was not forsworn. . . .
    [*They embrace in reconciliation.*]
    Not angry any more?

ALCMENA: No.

JUPITER: That's right. You know, things often happen like this – to people. One minute they've got their heart's desire, the next minute – disaster. Parted by a quarrel, and again rejoined in reconciliation. But you know, when quarrels of this sort do occur, the reconciliation makes love twice as strong as it was before.

ALCMENA: You should really have thought twice before saying what you did; but ... if you can be as kind to me as you were cruel ... I can bear it.

JUPITER: When I was on service I vowed thanksgiving for a safe return home. Tell them to make ready the sacred vessels, and I will pay my dues.

ALCMENA: I will see to it.

JUPITER [*to someone within*]: Send Sosia out here. . . . I'll get
   him to invite Blepharo, my pilot, to lunch with us. [*Aside*]
   He won't find any lunch, as a matter of fact, only me turning Amphitryo out neck and crop!

ALCMENA: What is he plotting now, I wonder?

   [SOSIA *comes out.*]

   Sosia is here.

SOSIA: You wanted me, sir. What's the orders?

JUPITER: Yes, I want you.

SOSIA: Oh *sir*; have you and the mistress made it up, sir? Oh
   I *am* glad, sir, it's a pleasure, sir, it really is, to see you both
   happy again; well, it's only a good servant's place, isn't it,
   to take his tone from his masters, be sad when they're sad
   and happy when they're happy; do tell me, sir, are you two
   friends again?

JUPITER: Now that's enough; you know quite well I was
   only joking all the time.

SOSIA: *Were* you? And me thinking it was all in solemn
   earnest!

JUPITER: The whole matter has been cleared up; peace has
   been declared.

SOSIA: Well, that's fine.

JUPITER: I am just going to pay my thank-offerings in the
   house chapel.

SOSIA: Yes, I should do that if I were you, sir.

JUPITER: I want you to present my compliments to Captain
   Blepharo and ask him to come over to lunch with us, *after*
   the service. Be as quick as you can.

SOSIA: I'll be back before you think I'm there, sir. [*He goes.*]

ALCMENA: Is there anything else, or shall I go and get things
   ready?

JUPITER: Oh do, yes, please . . . see to everything.

ALCMENA [*still a bit suspicious of his preoccupation*]: You will
    come, won't you? ... any time you like. ... I'll have
    everything ready.

JUPITER: That's right, my love ... my good little wife. ...
    [ALCMENA *goes in.*]
    They both think I'm Amphitryo! Mistress and servant,
    both fooled completely! ... Sosia! the immortal Sosia,
    come here! Or rather, don't come; you can hear what I
    say wherever you are. When Amphitryo comes back, I
    want you to keep him away from the house; think of some-
    thing, anything you like. Bamboozle him somehow, while
    I am occupied with my temporary wife. Do the best you
    can for me. I'll depend on you. Now I've got to go and
    sacrifice to myself. [*He goes into the house.*]
    [*After a pause,* MERCURY *arrives, as if in a great hurry and
    excitement.*]

MERCURY: Out of the way, out of the way, everybody ...
    excuse me, please ... let me pass, will you ... urgent
    business ... don't stop me. ...
    Well, I suppose a god can order people about if a slave
    can; you know – those slaves in a comedy, who rush in to
    announce that the ship has just come in or the angry old
    man is on his way. I'm here on Jupiter's orders and business,
    so I can surely expect people to get out of my way and let
    me pass.
    Yes, my father Jupiter calls me and I follow, and I am ever
    obedient to his word. Even as it behoveth a good son to
    serve his father, even so serve I my heavenly father; for
    instance, when he feeleth like a little love affair, I am his
    go-between, aider and abettor, adviser and congratulator.
    Nothing pleases me more than to give him exactly what he
    wants. After all, he knows what he's about. He knows what
    he wants, and if he wants it he has a perfect right to have it.

So has any man – within reason of course. At the present moment he wants to fool Amphitryo; so I shall make it my business to see that he is well and truly fooled; as you shall see, ladies and gentlemen.

This is what I am going to do. I'm going to put a garland on my head and pretend I'm drunk. Then I'm going to climb out on the roof up there; that'll be a good place from which to shout at him as soon as he arrives and divert his attention; he won't know whether he's drunk or sober. His servant Sosia will get the blame for it, because his master will swear black and blue it was him. Well, that's not my business, is it? I am under my father's orders, and him only must I serve.

Here comes Amphitryo. I'll lead him a dance. . . . You will watch, won't you? . . . I'll pop inside and get myself up like a tosspot. Then I'll be up on that roof . . . keeping him at bay. . . . [*He goes into the house.*]

[AMPHITRYO *comes along the street, tired and in ill humour.*]

AMPHITRYO: Couldn't find Naucrates anywhere. Not on the ship. Not at home. Nobody seems to have seen him. I've crawled from street to street, been into every gymnasium, beauty parlour, arcade, market, forum, sports ground; tried all the surgeries and barbers' shops; and every blasted temple in the town. I'm sick to death of it. I don't know where he is. I'm going home now, to ask my wife a few more questions. I'm determined to find out who this fornicator is. I'll get at the truth if it kills me. [*He tries the door.*] Locked. Well, that's a nice thing. Just what I should expect too. [*He hammers at the door.*] Open this door! Hey, is anyone in? Will somebody open this door?

[MERCURY *appears on the roof, as foretold.*]

MERCURY: Hullo-o-o? Who's there?

AMPHITRYO: I am.

MERCURY: Iam? Who's Iam?

AMPHITRYO: It's me, I say. Open this door.

MERCURY: Ooh, I say ... you mustn't go knocking doors down like that. . . . Jupiter and all those gods will be ever so angry with you.

AMPHITRYO [*peering up at him*]: What's going on there?

MERCURY: It's the way you're going on that you will be sorry for, for the rest of your life.

AMPHITRYO: You're Sosia, aren't you?

MERCURY: Oh yes. Did you think I had forgotten myself again? Do you want anything?

AMPHITRYO: Do I *want* anything? What the –

MERCURY: That's what I'm asking you. You've almost bashed the doors off their hinges, you silly man. This isn't a public building, you know; we have to buy our own doors. Don't look at me like that, you owl. What do you want? Who are you, anyway?

AMPHITRYO: Who *am* I, cat-o-nine-tails! ... Perishing pitchforks, who *am* I? I'll tan your hide for this.

MERCURY: You must have been a very extravagant young man.

AMPHITRYO: What the hell –

MERCURY: Because you're now a poor old beggar asking for *harms*.

AMPHITRYO: You'll be gibbering on a gibbet very soon, you swab.

MERCURY [*waving a goblet*]: Allow me to pour you a libation, sir. . . .

AMPHITRYO [*looking up*]: What's that?

MERCURY: To your very bad health! [*He flings the dregs in his face.*]

*AMPHITRYO: Gods and goddesses strike you dead, you

*see page 225

impudent monkey! Come down from there this minute
and let me into my house.

MERCURY: I'll come down if you'll stay there. I don't know
that I can let you into the house. My master doesn't care for
strangers calling without an appointment.

AMPHITRYO: I'll give you an appointment with a gallows
as soon as I can lay my hands on you.

[MERCURY *disappears from the roof.*]

Upon my word, I don't know what's come over the
fellow. He must have been drinking with the servants to
celebrate his return home. I was a fool to let him out of my
sight.

[MERCURY *comes out of the house.*]

Now then, what have you got to say for yourself?

MERCURY: First tell me what *you* have got to say for *yourself*;
then I'll see if *my* master can receive you.

AMPHITRYO: Your master? Have you taken leave of your
senses? Who do you think your master is?

MERCURY: Amphitryo is my master.

AMPHITRYO: I should hope so. And now your master has
come home and demands admission to his own house.

MERCURY: Of course I know he has come home; he came
home last night; and he is in his own house at present.

AMPHITRYO: Is he indeed? Then kindly tell your master
that a friend of his is outside and would like to speak to
him.

MERCURY: Very good, sir. [*He goes into the house.*]

AMPHITRYO: This will be the scoundrel who has been
seducing my wife. And he is actually in the house with
her now! Now I shall catch him red-handed, and if
I don't tear the hide off his back, may Jupiter strike me
dead.

[MERCURY *returns.*]

MERCURY: I'm sorry, sir; my master Amphitryo is engaged, and says if you will call again in three or four days' time he will be glad to grant you all you desire.

AMPHITRYO [*mystified and enraged, but deciding to play it coolly*]: Is my wife at home?

MERCURY: How should I know where your wife is, when I don't know who you are or where you live?

AMPHITRYO [*patiently*]: Is your master's wife at home?

MERCURY: Oh yes, sir, she is at home; with my master.

AMPHITRYO: Gods above, you have destroyed me utterly! I am lost and ruined! This is the end of all I ever lived for! Where, oh where shall I turn for help?

MERCURY: The man is insane. He's calling for help. A doctor, where's a doctor? Help! [*He calls at the house door.*]
    [ALCMENA *comes out.*]

ALCMENA: What is the meaning of all this noise? Sosia, what do you want? What is happening? [*Seeing Amphitryo*] My husband! Why have you left the house again? You were preparing to sacrifice to Jupiter for our happy reunion.

MERCURY [*now deciding to play safe with Alcmena at any rate*]: Yes, sir; that would be best indeed, to sacrifice to Jupiter –

AMPHITRYO: I'll sacrifice you to a gallows with the greatest of pleasure.

ALCMENA: What is the matter, Amphitryo? What has poor Sosia done now? Surely you have forgiven him for his foolish talk?

AMPHITRYO: I have forgiven nobody; and I am still waiting to hear you express contrition for your vile and deceitful conduct.

ALCMENA: But you said it was all a joke.

AMPHITRYO: A joke? To be shut out of my own house and assaulted by a drunken tosspot, while my wife entertains her paramour with lascivious embraces under my own roof?

ALCMENA: You must be mad.

MERCURY: That's what I thought, madam. Shall I run for a doctor? Or pour a pot of water over his head?

AMPHITRYO: Get out of my sight, or I'll pour a pan of red-hot coals over your head.

ALCMENA: Alas, he is surely out of his wits. Come in, and we'll send for the doctor immediately.

[*She is trying to coax him gently in, when* BLEPHARO *arrives from the harbour.*]

BLEPHARO: Ah ... so the happy couple are reunited again. Greetings to you, Alcmena, and congratulations on your brave husband's safe return from his victorious campaign. Hullo, Sosia, you got back quicker than I did, it seems?

MERCURY: I came on winged feet, sir.

BLEPHARO: I wish I had, by Jove. I've walked the whole way from the harbour. Now I've a good appetite for that lunch you promised me, Amphitryo.

AMPHITRYO: What lunch? When did I promise you a lunch?

BLEPHARO: Your servant Sosia found me at the harbour and brought me your kind invitation.

AMPHITRYO: My invitation? Have you been playing more tricks, rascal? When did I send you to invite Captain Blepharo to lunch?

BLEPHARO: Of course, if I'm in the way... [*He turns to go.*] ... But who is this?

[*It is* SOSIA, *returning slowly and tired.*]

SOSIA: Oh Captain Blepharo, so here you are. I'm glad I've found you at last. I've been searching for you all over the town. If I'd known you were coming up here, I could have saved my poor feet.

AMPHITRYO: Gods above! What is the meaning of this? Two Sosias, before my very eyes! Am I possessed with a devil? [*Looking from one to the other, but finally addressing Sosia*] Who are . . . who are you?

MERCURY: He's my twin brother, sir. We have been parted since we were babies, so it's no wonder if he doesn't recognize me. Greetings, brother Sosia. [*He crosses to Sosia and by threatening gestures bids him keep his mouth shut.*]

AMPHITRYO: You may be brothers, for all I know; it's certain you're a couple of insolent rogues. Now then, Blepharo, I don't know what brought you here, but as you are here you can be a witness to the dispute between me and my wife.

BLEPHARO: Can there be a dispute between so gallant a husband and so virtuous a wife?

AMPHITRYO: Virtuous, is she? Judge for yourself. I come home after my victorious campaign and arrive at my house early this morning, to learn from her own lips that she has spent the night, in this house, in my bed, with a paramour, a licentious adulterer. She then, in answer to my questions, changes her tune and denies what she had just confessed. I leave the house for an hour, hoping to find a friend to witness that I had never been at home last night or seen her till this morning; and this time I find the door locked against me, no one to answer my summons but that impudent drunken lout, who, not to mention pouring a flagon of wine over my head, informs me that his master is in there with my wife. And here she is, again denying her flagrantly immoral conduct and expecting me to rejoin her in the house as if nothing had happened. Now tell me what you think of that.

BLEPHARO: Upon my word, I don't know what to think. This is either a terrible judgement visited upon you by Jupiter for some impiety which you have, no doubt unwittingly, committed; or someone is playing a cruel trick on you both. Is it the truth, Alcmena, that your husband tells me? I cannot believe that you would either be knowingly unfaithful to your husband or seek to cover your shame with a lie.

ALCMENA: It is he that is lying, as he knows quite well. He was with me last night; he returned to the house this morning, to accuse me of shameful conduct in his absence; then, having admitted that he was wrong and having obtained my forgiveness, he left the house again without my knowledge, and now returns to repeat the accusations which he had previously withdrawn. If that is not the whole and undoubted truth, accuse me of what infamy you will.

AMPHITRYO: Then who is the man you are entertaining in my house at this very moment?

ALCMENA: As Jupiter is my witness, no man but you has entered this house since you left it to go to your wars. Must I repeat it a thousand times?

AMPHITRYO: But you said – [to Mercury or Sosia] – you – one of you – didn't you say your master was in the house while I was standing out here? Didn't you try to prevent me from getting in? Didn't you forbid me, with threats and insults, to knock at the door? Explain the meaning of that, if you can. Can you explain it, Blepharo?

BLEPHARO: Such a farrago of prevarications and cross-purposes – I doubt whether Jupiter himself could explain it.

[JUPITER himself appears at the door, still in the exact image of Amphitryo.]

JUPITER: Alcmena, my love, why have you left the house to wrangle with these strangers outside our door? What man is this? Are you not ashamed, sir, to lay siege to a peaceful house and trouble a lady – who is in no condition to withstand your assaults – with violent and unmannerly abuse?

ALCMENA [swooning]: Two husbands before my eyes! ! . . .

two Amphitryos! . . . Jupiter preserve me! . . . Let me die!

JUPITER: Look to her, you.

[MERCURY *and* SOSIA *assist her into the house.*]

BLEPHARO: This passes all wonders. Is this some masquerade, or a trick with mirrors?

AMPHITRYO: Now do you believe me, Blepharo? Now do you see for yourself the shameless intruder who has dared to borrow my house, my bed, my wife, my very clothes, to pass himself off as her lawful husband?

BLEPHARO: I doubt if I can believe my own eyes ever again.

JUPITER: Believe them, Blepharo, rather than this lying scoundrel's preposterous pretensions. He is no more Amphitryo than I am Jupiter. You know me; I am Amphitryo, and these hands shall prove it, by haling this ruffian by the neck to a punishment from which nothing but the mercy of Jupiter will be able to save him.

AMPHITRYO: You keep your hands off me, whoever you are. Blepharo, you are not going to believe this impostor, are you?

BLEPHARO: If I knew which was the impostor –

JUPITER: You see, your own friend won't own you.

AMPHITRYO: A fine sort of friend, if he doesn't know which of us is me. [*To the audience*] Doesn't anyone here know me? Am not I Amphitryo, and is not this the vile and shameless seducer who has stolen my wife in my own house? Have not I caught him in the very act?

JUPITER: It is you who should be ashamed to show your face in public or expect honest citizens to believe such an outrageous falsehood.

AMPHITRYO: You hear him, friends? You hear, Blepharo, what infamous effrontery the mountebank is capable of? Can't you say something?

BLEPHARO: I'm off. I've business to attend to. You must sort it out for yourselves. I've certainly never seen a more extra-ordinary mix-up in all my life.

AMPHITRYO: No, don't go, my dear fellow. Stay and back me up.

BLEPHARO: It's no use asking me to back you up. How do I know which of the two I want to back up? Good-bye. [*He goes.*]

JUPITER: I shall go in. Alcmena needs me.

[*He pops into the house,* AMPHITRYO *not noticing.*]

AMPHITRYO: Oh gods, whatever shall I do? Deserted by every friend and counsellor. I'll have my revenge on that twister anyway, whoever he is. I shall go straight to the king and tell him the whole story. I'll get that fellow punished for sending my whole family off their heads – that conjuring Thessalian. . . . Where is he? Where has he got to? Gods above, I believe he's gone into the house again, to my wife . . . Ah! ! !

Lives there a man in Thebes more cursed than I?
What shall I do, disowned, mocked, made a mug of,
By all mankind? By force, I am resolved,
Into that house I'll enter. Whomsoever
I find within, be't servant, man, or maid,
Or wife, or paramour, or my own father,
Or my own father's father, there and then
I'll hew them into pieces. This I'll do,
For thus I am resolved. Let all the gods,
And Jupiter himself, do what they may,
I *will* go in. . . .

[*He won't, for a stroke of lightning fells him on the threshold.*]

*

[*Five minutes later.*
BROMIA, *the nurse, rushes out of the house in panic.*]

BROMIA: Oh, oh, oh! This is my last minute alive, for all that I can see or do; if death isn't staring me in the face I don't know what is, I've not a crumb of hope to cling to, the sky's a-falling, the sea's coming up to drown me, the earth wants to swallow me up, whatever shall I do, whatever's happening, the house is bewitched, oh dear I do feel bad, where's some water? I'm all to pieces, I feel like dying, oh my head does ache, I can't hear, and my eyes are all funny, I don't think anyone's ever suffered more than I do at this minute. [*A little more coherently*] It was the mistress. What she's gone through this day I couldn't tell you. She felt her pains coming, and was saying her prayers; then crash, bang, thunder and lightning; ever so sudden it was, all in a minute, crashing and banging of thunder. We were all standing there and we all fell flat on our faces. Flat, where we stood. Then we heard a loud voice from somewhere or other; 'Alcmena,' it said, 'fear not, help is at hand. The regent of the skies is here with comfort for thee and thine. Rise, all ye that have fallen in terror of my voice.' I had fallen, so I got to my feet. The house was all lit up, I thought there must be a fire somewhere. Then Alcmena called for me. I was in a terrible fright, but I remembered my duty to the mistress, and ran to see what she wanted. And what do you think? She had given birth to twin boys – and not one of us knew when it happened, so we'd got nothing ready... Eh!! [*She sees Amphitryo on the ground.*] ... Whatever's that? Who's that poor old man on the ground? Just outside our door? Has Jupiter struck him down too? Godsakes, I believe he has. The poor old man looks as dead as a corpse. I must go and see who it is ... Oh!! It's Amphitryo, my master Amphitryo. .... Master ... are you all right?

AMPHITRYO: I'm done for.

BROMIA: Can you get up?

AMPHITRYO: Let me die.

BROMIA: Give me your hand.

AMPHITRYO: Who are you?

BROMIA: It's Bromia, sir.

AMPHITRYO: I've had a terrible shock . . . a bolt from Jupiter . . . it's like returning from the dead. What are you doing out here?

BROMIA: We've had a terrible shock in the house too, sir. Your house is a house of miracles today. The things I've seen! Oh dear, I think I'm going to faint again.

AMPHITRYO: Hold on; just tell me this: are you sure I am your master Amphitryo?

BROMIA: Well of course I'm sure.

AMPHITRYO: You're the only sane person in the house.

BROMIA: Oh no, sir, they're all right, nobody's mad.

AMPHITRYO: My wife has driven me mad with her wicked conduct.

BROMIA: Oh no, sir, you can't say that. She's a good and honest woman, that I can tell you, ay and prove it this minute from what I've seen and know. For one thing – your wife is now the mother of twin sons.

AMPHITRYO: You don't say? Twins?

BROMIA: That's right.

AMPHITRYO: The gods are good to me.

BROMIA: And that's not all. Wait till I tell you how good the gods have been to you and your wife.

AMPHITRYO: Tell me everything.

BROMIA: As soon as her labour began and the pains were in her womb, she prayed for the gods' help, as any mother does, with her head covered and hands washed. Suddenly there was a tremendous clap of thunder. My, we thought your house was falling down, it was all filled with light, like shining gold it was.

AMPHITRYO: Yes, well, never mind the imaginary details. Come to the point, and set my mind at rest. What happened then?

BROMIA: Well, with all this going on, none of us heard a cry or a groan from the mistress. And lo and behold, there she was with her two babies, and never felt a thing.

AMPHITRYO: I am very glad. Whatever she may have done to me.

BROMIA: Never mind that, sir. Listen to what I'm telling you. She told us to bath the babies, and we got to work. And my goodness, the one I was washing, he was that big and strong it was more than we could do to swaddle him.

AMPHITRYO: Astounding. If it's true, there's no question but that some divine hand was supporting her.

BROMIA: And that's not all. I've more wonders to tell you yet. We got him into his cradle at last, and the next minute two great crested snakes came slipping down from the roof into the water-pond. There they were, rearing up their heads –

AMPHITRYO: What a terrible thing; was – ?

BROMIA: Keep calm, sir. The snakes had a good look round at all of us; then they spied the babies and made straight for the cradles. I was terrified for the children, and for myself too, but I seized the cradles and tried to drag them this way and that, and the snakes coming at us closer and closer. Then one of the babies, that bigger one, as soon as he saw the snakes he jumps out of the cradle like lightning and goes for them and snatches hold of them one in each hand.

AMPHITRYO: Amazing. It must have been a ghastly sight. It makes me shiver to hear of it. How did it end?

BROMIA: He killed them both. At the same time we heard your wife's name called loudly –

AMPHITRYO: Who called her?

BROMIA: The Almighty King Jupiter. And do you know what he said? He said he had slept with Alcmena unbeknown; the child that had strangled the snakes was his child; the other was your child.

AMPHITRYO: Well, well ... So I am to share my happiness with Jupiter. ... I am content to do so. Go in, please, Bromia, and tell them to prepare a sacrifice, so that I may make my peace with the Almighty with generous offerings.

[BROMIA *goes in.*]

As for what is next to be done, I think I will send for Teiresias and ask his advice. I shall have to tell him the whole story....

[*His rumination is interrupted by another clap of thunder.*]

God, what is that? Another thunder peal. Have mercy on me, gods....

[JUPITER *appears in his divinity.*]

JUPITER: Have no fear, Amphitryo. I am with you and with your house. Nothing can harm you.

Think not of soothsayers and seers, they cannot help you. I can reveal to you the future and explain the past, better than they, for I am Jupiter.

It is the truth, I employed your wife Alcmena and made her pregnant with my child. As you did, before you went away to war.

These children are now born in twin birth – and the one that was begotten by me will live to make you famous for ever by his deeds.

Be happy once more in the love of your Alcmena. She was not to blame. She could not resist my power.

Now I go back to heaven.

[*He vanishes.*]

AMPHITRYO: I will obey; and I pray that your words may be fulfilled. Now to my wife . . . and Teiresias? . . . no . . . we don't need old Teiresias.

Spectators, applaud – and loudly, for great Jove's sake.

EXIT

A description of another volume in the Penguin Classics,
together with a list of the most
recent titles, appears in
the following pages

THE RISE AND FALL OF ATHENS

Plutarch

Writing at the turn of the first century A.D., Plutarch intentionally blended two cultures in his parallel lives of Greek and Roman heroes. The nine biographies chosen for this modern translation by Ian Scott-Kilvert illustrate the rise and fall of Athens from the legendary days of Theseus, the city's founder, to the age of Pericles and the razing of its walls by Lysander. The volume forms a companion to Plutarch's *Fall of the Roman Republic* in the Penguin Classics.

However unreliable in places, Plutarch's readable accounts have necessarily been a prime source of much historical knowledge.

THE PENGUIN CLASSICS

THE MOST RECENT VOLUMES

*For a complete list of books available please write to Penguin Books
whose address can be found on the back of the title page*